UNMASK

Let Go of Who You're "Supposed" to Be &
Unleash Your True Leader

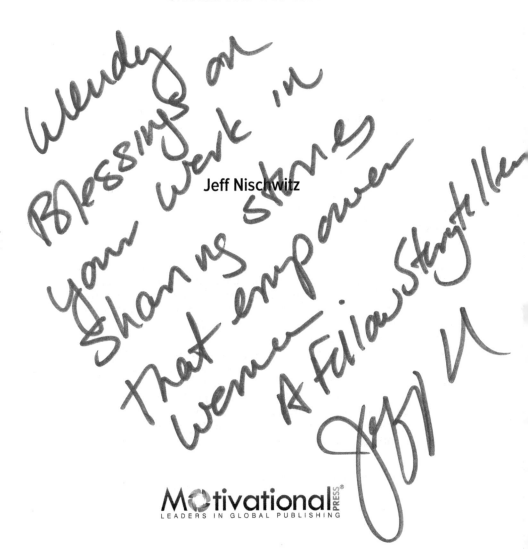

Jeff Nischwitz

MOtivationalPRESS®
LEADERS IN GLOBAL PUBLISHING

Published by Motivational Press, Inc.
7777 N Wickham Rd, # 12-247
Melbourne, FL 32940
www.MotivationalPress.com

Manufactured in the United States of America.

ISBN: 978-1-62865-135-5

Praise for *Unmask*

"It is so refreshing knowing the author of *Unmask* actually LIVES the message of this important book. Jeff Nischwitz not only introduces the world to Livingship, but he puts us all on a journey to living, leading and loving differently."

- *Tommy Spaulding,* New York Times Bestselling author of
It's Not Just Who You Know

"*Unmask: Let Go of Who You're 'Supposed' to Be & Unleash Your True Leader* is such a good book you are going to think you robbed a bank! Make a deposit for your career and read this book."

- *Jeffrey Hayzlett,* Primetime TV Show Host
Bestselling Author & Sometime Cowboy

"*Unmask* illustrates persuasively that who you spend time with and what you choose impacts the results you get in life."

- *Nido Qubein,* Entrepreneur, Author, American Success Story

"Nischwitz's book is a road map of key learning points to move you forward in your life and career. Jeff's message will help you shift your thinking, transform your language and be a truth teller to yourself. With his authenticity, true stories and compelling questions, Jeff will lovingly and truthfully guide you to Unleash the best of who you are."

- *Elizabeth Jeffries,* Keynote Speaker, Executive Coach & Author of
*The Heart of Leadership: How to Inspire, Encourage, and Motivate People
to Follow You*

"*Unmask* is a book for any person who wants to go from being a good leader to great leader. Jeff Nischwitz nails all the key components to being a leader that can take a group and organization to places they couldn't have gone otherwise."

- John R. DiJulius III
Author of The Customer Service Revolution

"Jeff is a special human being. *Unmask* is filled with powerful insights that are both valuable and thought provoking. I encourage you to join Jeff on this amazing journey."

- *Toni Newman,* Business Growth Expert, The Innovation Advantage

"Jeff is not only an amazing speaker but a person who 'walks the talk.' His passion and love of life come though in his words whether they are on paper or in one of his dynamic presentations. From our first encounter Jeff impressed me with his love of life and his boundless energy. You can't go wrong by reading his insights and experiences that he so eloquently shares......."

- *Hal Becker,* Author and Sales/Customer Service Strategist

"In a conversational and narrative style, Jeff illuminates a rich landscape of ways for leaders to lead from inside out. He demonstrates how conscious leaders draw on their own inner transformation invoked by new distinctions and questions. The book is as practical as it is profound in challenging all of us to find our relational power."

- *Jack Ricchiuto,* Writer and 15-time Author
including the recently released *Making Sense Of Time*

"Jeff Nischwitz seamlessly blends personal and professional examples in a timely and relevant way, and in a way that reflects a realistic understanding of today's workplace, where many people spend more time than at home. Anyone can benefit from Jeff's book, a manager trying to improve performance on a team, an employee trying to shine in a competitive environment, or someone who just wants to explore how the stories they are telling themselves are limiting their potential. Jeff opens a door and invites you to walk through; on the other side is your opportunity to improve your life, your relationships and, most important, the relationship you have with yourself. I think everyone should walk through."

   - Bethany Friedlander, Chief Operating Officer, VIP Restoration, Inc.

"Jeff Nischwitz is a man on a mission, empowering his readers to simultaneously transform their inextricably linked personal and professional lives. He speaks from first-hand experience, as he first blazed the trail of transformation in his own life. In *Unmask*, Nischwitz distills what he himself learned to provide us with a guide to successfully transform ourselves into the authentic leaders we are each meant to be. The answers lie within, and Nischwitz is the guide to understanding how we can each find and implement the next steps on our personal and professional journeys."

   - David J. Akers, President & CEO, Collaborent Group

"This book *Unmask* will be a game-changer in your life. Not many people truly lead by example but Jeff Nischwitz does! His humility in opening his stories of transformation allows individuals to begin to put down their masks and tap into their authentic selves. *Unmask* will inspire you, challenge you and help put you on the path where personal transformation can occur. It's time to take the leap of faith alongside this man of integrity and honor and start peeling back the layers to the true you!"

   - Jennifer Chernisky, President, Jennasis and Associates | Jennasis Speaks

"Jeff Nischwitz's book *Unmask* is a brilliant body of work that will help you to unleash your true authentic leader … not only in your business, but in your life as well!"

> *- Joe Contrera,* President ALIVE @ WORK ® LLC,
> Author of *LIGHT 'EM UP: How to Ignite the Fire in Your Sales Team in Just 21 Days* and *I Could Love No One Until I Loved Me*
> (A grown up book written for the kid in you)

"*Unmask* delivers! Consistent with his personal brand, *Unmask* is riveting and impactful with a quiet intensity that has the ability to change your life … if only you let it. You may be hesitant to receive Jeff's authentic message for changing your life and leadership, but Jeff daringly AND caringly challenges you to let go of your old ways of being in order to unleash your true leader. Be BOLD and dare to discover your greatest leadership and livingship potential."

> *- Stacy Ward-Braxton,* Chief Engagement & Learning Officer,
> The Significance Group

"If you never met Jeff, you are missing the model of soulful leadership and listening. Through *Unmask*, you can let go of what does not serve you and embrace a new way to be more present in every relationship in your life."

> *- Glenn Gordon,* Master Facilitator, Speaker & Coach

"Jeff's honesty and transparency in sharing his journey through his own personal stories is priceless. If you sense your life is unbalanced but don't know why … you need this book. If you feel lost, scared or hurt … you need this book. If you are suffering … you need this book. Take it from someone that has been infected by Jeff Nischwitz … *Unmask* will be a game changer in your life."

> *- Melanie Jatsek,* CEO of Bust Your Diet

"Jeff Nischwitz sharing ideas on leadership is a natural fit. Jeff's journey of 'unmasking' himself led to insights that changed the way he lived his life at home, at work and within himself. As he changed, his entire world changed. And as he shared these principles with others, Jeff witnessed similar dramatic transformation, time and time again. In *Unmask*, Jeff now shares with all of us this powerful path of inner discovery and self-insight. A journey to bring out your natural leader. Jeff offers more than just thought-provoking visionary discussions or theoretical concepts. These concepts are practical. They work."

 - *Tom Mannion,* Managing Partner, Mannion & Gray Co., L.P.A.

"I have watched Jeff travel on his own personal journey of self-discovery, awareness and self-accountability, which has led to some very hard but rewarding choices. This is only possible because EVERY DAY Jeff makes a conscious choice to be authentic with himself. At HIS core, Jeff is a unique, caring being that helps others become the same. In doing so, lives are enriched and new connections are made—making this world a little smaller one conversation at a time. Jeff's book *Unmask* is a peek into Jeff's journey and a guide for you on your leadership and life journey."

 - *Darlene Goldbach,* Strategic Thinker and Professional Banker

"Your leadership impact is determined by who you choose to be as a person. *Unmask* will help you get clear on what type of leader you want to become and provide you with a road map to help you get there."

 - *Ron Finklestein,* International Business Coach & Author of
 Make a Difference: From Being Successful to Being Significant

"I love this book and everything Jeff Nischwitz and The Nischwitz Group espouses. I highly encourage anyone interested in fully waking up and living their own magical journey to the fullest to read and re-read *Unmask*."

 - *Brian Porter,* Sales and Brand Evangelist

"Jeff Nischwitz is one of my favorite people in the business community. In 31 years in the legal business, I rarely have met anyone with Jeff's knack for understanding human nature and cutting through peoples' 'stories.' When it comes to helping people get the most from themselves, Jeff just 'gets it,' and *Unmask* is another way to experience Jeff's insights on leadership and life."

- H.L. Stephenson III, Business Development Partner,
Ward and Smith, P.A.

"Knowing the heart and perspective that Jeff has poured into *Unmask* helps me unequivocally recommend reading it. Jeff's background gives him a unique perspective, and his focus on telling true stories is powerful. Happy reading!"

- Craig Mathews, Chief Thinkologist, Big Think Innovation, Inc.

"*Unmask* ... and find your true authentic self could not be a more poignant direction for the leader of any organization. In *Unmask*, Jeff lays the foundation for becoming your authentic self and "unmasks" the mistaken beliefs that are blocking your way to becoming truly *remarkable*, both personally and as a leader. As a successful entrepreneur, author, and leader of people and organizations, I cannot recommend a more powerful investment of your time than to read *Unmask*."

- Robert A. Schepens, CEO Champion Personnel System 2.0 &
Author of *The Great Workplace 2.0*

GRATITUDE

At the risk of being cliché, this book has certainly been a journey, and in many ways it was an unexpected journey and an unanticipated road. I started this book because I had a story inside me that needed to be told about my personal journey from broken to better to brilliant. It has been a challenging and sometimes painful process, but the outcomes have been well worth the effort, discomfort and fear. While I have much ongoing work to do inside myself, I consider myself a transformed man—a man who purposefully left behind the pretending nice guy to become an authentic good man. I believe we are meant to write about that which we know intimately, and I know so well what it means to pretend and wear masks in life—to be one person in one context and a completely different person in another context. My life was a masquerade party (although I was mostly unaware of it), and it left in its wake a failed marriage, wounded people, financial devastation, broken relationships and a lost me.

I thought that this book was about my journey, but I did not anticipate that it would also be part of my journey. I knew that sharing my story would help others have their own awakening experiences and that the tools that I have learned and used for myself on this journey would help others achieve personal and professional transformation. What I did not see coming was the healing, clarity and insight that writing this book has provided to me. It has proven to be a blessed gift to me and for me, and this is the source of the deep gratitude I feel for the book-writing experience.

I am also grateful for the many people who have supported me on my life journey and through this book creating process. I was blessed to walk this road over the past several years alongside an amazing woman, Jennifer Chernisky, who believed in me, challenged me and taught me about faith, hope and dreams. Jennifer also gifted me with her time and insights in reviewing this book and its messages. Thank you for believing in me, Jennifer, and for seeing even more of me than I saw for myself. I am a better man because of you and this book will touch more lives because of you.

The following people also invested their valuable time to read and review the book, providing their perspectives, thoughts and insights (and even challenges) to help me make this book the best that it can be: Ron Finklestein, Brian Porter, Melanie Jatsek, Glenn Gordon, Robert Schepens and Jennifer Cabic. I am especially grateful to Bethany Friedlander, who took a deep dive into the book, its stories and its messages to help make it even more impactful. I am indeed blessed by many people who care about me, believe in me and motivate me to keep going, to go deep and to go big.

I must also express my deep gratitude to David Akers, a dear friend and my coach, who not only reviewed the book and provided feedback, but who has also supported, guided and challenged me over the past three years. I will never forget the insightful questions that David has offered to me to help me see what I cannot see, to know what I was afraid to know and to create what I did not believe was possible. Thank you, David, for believing in me and for seeing the giant in me!

They say that writing a book is like giving birth, and in that spirit I am so grateful for Mindy Gibbins-Klein of The Book Midwife. When I met Mindy in the summer of 2013, I was introduced to her book-writing workshop, which I attended in the fall of 2013. Mindy delivered on all of her promises and exceeded my expectations. She shared her wisdom, and her process helped me to create what you are about to experience. Thank you, Mindy and Book Midwife!

As for the many people who generously offered their endorsements for *Unmask*, I have only three things to say: Thank you; I am humbled; I am honored.

Special thanks also to Justin Sachs and Motivational Press for believing in and agreeing to publish *Unmask*. I am grateful to be sharing this publication experience with Motivational Press and Justin.

Finally, I am deeply grateful for the amazing effort, time and love that Ben Barnhart invested in this book. Ben was my editor and he did so much more than edit. He made this book better. He challenged my thoughts and ideas. He asked great questions. Most important, he cared. As I read Ben's many notes and comments, it was clear that he was engaged with the book, not just editing the book. It was also clear that Ben experienced the book and shared that experience with me in his comments and with you through his thoughtful edits. Thank you, Ben for making *Unmask* the best that it could be.

Lastly, I dedicate this book and express my thanks to the two people who had the biggest impact on my own personal journey and healing, but probably without knowing—my two sons, Eric and Kyle. For most of their lives, I was not present for them (at least not the way I wanted to be), and I caused them both a great deal of pain through my choices. Since my personal awakening four years ago, I have been committed to be the best person, man and father that I can be. My hope was and is that they see the father and man I am today—a caring, honest, loving and transformed man—and will be able to see me in a new and different way. It turns out—much to my surprise and joy—that they saw more of the good man in me over the years than even I saw. I still have work to do on myself and with my life, but I am honored to know that Eric and Kyle "get me" in significant ways. For this reason, I dedicate this book to them and to the possibilities that every person has to wake up, unmask, and choose to live a conscious and authentic life. My hope and prayer is that Eric and Kyle will be among the people who experience this book and fully unleash their *livingship*.

CONTENTS

WAKE UP CALL

"Remember, all the answers you need are inside
you; you only have to become quiet enough to
hear them."

Debbie Ford

In a world filled with business talk, strategic think and tactics speak, leaders are inundated with different perspectives and theories on what it means to lead and ways to lead. From the beginning of modern business theory, leadership has been at the forefront of debates, books, training and business education.

Likewise, our personal lives are filled with self-help books, reality television shows, personal development workshops and spiritual growth resources, all proclaiming ways to be happier and healthier. I recently read that the self-improvement industry is a $12 billion industry. But with the billions of dollars spent every year on self-improvement, do people really change? In reality, the majority of self-help books are never even read. Apparently, people believe that merely buying the books will change their lives.

Call me judgmental, but people seem more willing to talk about changing than they are actually willing to change. One business owner and client recently told me this: "I feel better talking about how I am off course, but maybe talking about it makes me feel better so I don't actually have to change things or myself." We also carve up our world into business and personal. It seems like we have to choose—we can work on our businesses, strategies and leadership <u>OR</u> we can work on improving ourselves. There are several problems with this approach:

1. With our very full schedules, it is difficult enough to work on and invest in one thing (business or personal development), so working on both business and personal seems overwhelming;

2. It suggests that we either have improvement opportunities at work OR at home, ignoring the likelihood that we have these opportunities in both realms; and

3. It implies that there are two different you's—the work you and the personal you.

All these ways of thinking ignore the reality that there is only one you, and that one you shows up at work, in relationships and in the rest of your life. The reality of this unified self is why I assert:

> We mistakenly believe that you bring your business
> into your life, but the opposite is true. You bring your
> life into your business, and your business will never be
> better than your life.

This book came into existence based upon this truth—that there is only one you, the leader of your business (or career) and your life. The person you are in your professional life is the same person that you are in your relationships and personal life. I decided to write this book to share my own experiences of personal and professional success, failure, discovery, awakening and transformation. It was a personal journey, a business journey, a relationship journey and a spiritual journey, all rolled into one life—my life.

This book is not for everyone. It is certainly not for someone who wants to tweak his or her business model or management skills. The ideas and perspectives I share involve profound shifts in the way you see and experience the world, as well as fundamental shifts in how you think, intuit, communicate, listen and interact with other people. This book is most definitely about shifts, mostly within yourself, and the shifted outcomes that you will create as you activate your internal shifts. At its core, this book is about choices and living a life of self-leadership with full ownership, responsibility and accountability for your choices. It is not the easy road, but it is the transformational road for any of you who are willing to put away what you thought was true, put down your old stories and strap on the armor of the new conscious warrior. It is now time to begin, and as predicted, it begins with a fundamental choice.

Time for Your Pill

In the movie *The Matrix* (1999), Keanu Reeves (Neo) struggles to differentiate between true reality and a simulated reality called "the Matrix." As Neo becomes more self-aware and questions what he thought was real, he is guided by Morpheus (played by Laurence Fishburne). Morpheus invites Neo to trust what he is feeling and ultimately gives him a choice—take the blue pill (stay asleep) or take the red pill (wake up and live in the truth).

> *Morpheus:* I imagine that right now you're feeling a bit like Alice. Tumbling down the rabbit hole?
>
> Neo: You could say that.
>
> ….
>
> *Morpheus:* Let me tell you why you're here. You're here because you know something. What you know, you can't explain. But you feel it. You've felt it your entire life; that there's something wrong with the world. You don't know what it is, but it's there. Like a splinter in your mind —driving you mad. It is this feeling

that has brought you to me. Do you know what I'm talking about?

Neo: The Matrix?

Morpheus: Do you want to know what it is?

Neo: Yes.

Morpheus: The Matrix is everywhere; it is all around us. Even now, in this very room. You can see it when you look out your window, or when you turn on your television. You can feel it when you go to work, or when you go to church or when you pay your taxes. It is the world that has been pulled over your eyes to blind you from the truth.

Neo: What truth?

Morpheus: That you are a slave, Neo. Like everyone else, you were born into bondage, born inside a prison that you cannot smell, taste, or touch. A prison for your mind. Unfortunately, no one can be told what the Matrix is. You have to see it for yourself. This is your last chance. After this, there is no turning back.

Morpheus: You take the blue pill and the story ends. You wake in your bed and believe whatever you want to believe. [A red pill is shown in his other hand.] You take the red pill and you stay in Wonderland and I show you how deep the rabbit-

hole goes. Remember—all I am offering
is the truth, nothing more.

(Neo takes the red pill and swallows it with a glass of
water.)

As we all know, Neo chooses to wake up and live in the truth, which continues to unfold before him. Morpheus was speaking to Neo about the difference between what is true and what is false (or simulated). I am not claiming to know the truth of the world, but I am suggesting that you have a choice either to accept everything as true or to question everything and decide what is and will be true for you. That is the choice I offer you in this book.

And such is your life—you have the opportunity to choose to wake up, challenge your own stories and connect to your authentic story. You also have the choice to stay asleep and to live and lead as you have before. If you want to choose the blue pill, then put down this book, stop reading and get back to your life as it already is and as you already are. If you want to choose the red pill and to begin to question everything about you as a person and as a leader, then turn the page and let us begin the journey together—into the rabbit hole of your life. But know this—the world we live in today in business and relationships *is not working*. People are lost, businesses are just getting by and relationships are crumbling, and we need a change for the different and better. Conscious leadership is part of that positive change, impacting you as a leader in your personal life as well as in your business, career, organization and community.

Unmask

The path to becoming your own conscious leader will be different from the path of others, but every path shares several core elements. One of these is the vital role that questions—mostly inside questions— will play in your journey of self-discovery, self-awareness and self-truth.

In that spirit, we begin with inside questions for you to explore about yourself, your journey to date and your internal commitments. Critically, you must be willing to tell yourself the truth and to seek others who will help you see your own truth. This is the way of the conscious leader.

Your leadership, personally and professionally, is not the outcome of your skills, intellect and training. Your leadership is the outcome of who you are as a person, the choices you make, the self-accountability you embrace, your intuition, your humanity and the degree to which you choose to be authentic and vulnerable in all of your relationships and communication—*plus* skills, training and intellect. In essence, you must unmask the old you and choose to lead and live from a place of authenticity and vulnerability, all supporting your personal commitment to be the person you choose to be.

Essentials of Conscious Livingship™

You may be the owner of or the main leader in your business. You may be a team leader in your organization. You may be leading a cause, group or initiative in your non-profit organization or in the community. You are certainly leading and guiding your career.

You may be leading a group of young people in your church or on the athletic fields. You may be leading students in some learning environment.

You may be leading the way with your family. You may be leading conversations and inquiries. You may be sharing leadership within your personal relationships.

Without question, every one of you is leading your life—whether you know it or not and whether you are leading consciously or unconsciously.

With all of these different leadership opportunities, claimed and unclaimed, it can be difficult to determine where to look for leadership guidance, insight and tactics. Is it in business books? Is it in personal development books? Is it in spiritual books? Is it in comic books? The truth is that leadership is neither business nor personal. Each one of you has always been a leader in your life through the choices you have made, the questions you have asked, the decisions you have executed (or failed to execute) and the person you have chosen to be.

The essence of leadership in business and in the rest of your life is a matter of self-leadership, because the person you choose to be and how you choose to show up in your life will determine your outcomes in your business, career, relationships, community, and family. This new way of thinking about leadership through self-awareness, self-mastery and self-reflection will create your future in all of these areas, and the aging concept of "leadership" cannot cover all that this evokes and requires. Enter *LIVINGSHIP*—a new way of living, being, thinking, modeling and leading in every part of your life.

In this book and through these stories—my own and those of others—you will experience what it means to embrace *livingship* as a way of being, influencing and achieving. The concept of conscious leadership is not new, but the integration of business leadership and self-leadership *is* new, and many of the ideas, strategies and shifts in this book represent new and different ways to think, be and act. Livingship is the encapsulation and representation of this integration, and it will serve you in every aspect, element and endeavor in your life. This integration also requires that you put aside the false you, the separate you, the business versus the personal you, and the inside stories that have comforted and hidden you for many years. In short, you must unmask yourself in order to unleash your authentic and conscious leader.

The process and mindset of separating business and personal is easy and, frankly, anyone can do it. Most of us do. In contrast, embracing, living and modeling *livingship* takes personal courage, requires internal awareness and honesty, and necessitates fundamental shifts in how you

- Blocking Stories – The stories you develop (often unconsciously) to protect you, which are often filled with some truth, but keep you stuck or off course.

Each of these types of stories plays a very different role in your life, and understanding these stories is at the heart of your path to conscious livingship on the road to your *authentic story.*

The stories of your life are just that—the stories about your life and life experiences, including the stories about your journey. These include your memories and the events that are the fabric of your life. These Event Stories are a core part of who you are as a person and have helped to mold and shape you. Event Stories often impact you and your future in ways known and unknown because they serve as the source of Belief Stories.

Cultural Stories are those stories that become accepted as true simply because they have been with us for a long time and because we have never questioned them. These are often seemingly harmless stories, but they will impact your life because you live your life according to them. Common examples include *don't jump in puddles, color in the lines, money doesn't grow on trees, life is hard, men don't cry, you can't have your cake and eat it too*, etc. Think about the Cultural Stories that you grew up with and which may be playing a significant role in your decisions, choices and outcomes.

Belief Stories are the main focus of this book because they are the stories that keep you where you are, prevent you from changing and justify your present position. Belief Stories are just that—stories that reflect and support what you believe to be true about business, life, relationships and yourself. These stories—especially the stories you believe to be true about yourself—are often self-limiting and keep you from becoming who you were meant to be as a person and as a leader. Examples of Belief Stories are *I'm not good enough, I'm not smart enough, I'm not worthy enough, I don't deserve*, etc.

Created Stories are often similar to Belief Stories, but they typically do not have any factual information to support them. These are the stories that you create based upon situations or events, and sometimes Created Stories are also Belief Stories. One example of a Created Story that you will read about in the book is about Barbara, whose father died in a plane crash when she was a little girl. This tragic event led Barbara to create this story: My father would rather die in a plane crash than be my father. While the story does not make sense or seem to follow logically from the event, it was nonetheless a story that Barbara created which had a significant impact in her life.

Blocking Stories are also created (again, largely unconsciously) by you to justify or support what you are doing (or not doing), where you are (or where you are not) and your decisions or choices. Rationalizations are a classic type of Blocking Story, and an entire chapter is dedicated to bringing to the surface and facing these stories so that you can debunk them and begin to live without them.

Finally, we come to your *authentic story*. This is not a story you have, but rather the story you are seeking to uncover, unleash and re-write for yourself and your life. Your personal journey of self-reflection and self-discovery is the path you walk to lead you to your authentic story. My personal journey has been to discover and unleash my authentic story of who I am, who I am meant to be and who I choose to be. Your authentic story will be the outcome of all of the inside work and truth-telling that you have done and that you will do, including the shifts you choose as a result of experiencing this book.

These are the stories of your life, and they are the essence of this book, especially Cultural, Belief, Created and Blocking Stories that form you, define you and in most cases limit you. This book is an invitation for you to confront your many stories, to reflect on them and the ways that they are impacting your life, and to make conscious choices about which stories you will keep and which stories you will put down on your journey to your authentic story. It is time to construct and embrace your authentic story.

If you are ready to unmask yourself and step into this new model of livingship in your business, your career, your relationships and the rest of your life, then let us begin together on a journey toward becoming yourself and your conscious leader.

CHAPTER 1: WIDE AWAKE AND LEADING (THE AWAKE LEADER)

"We must learn to reawaken and keep ourselves awake, not by mechanical aid, but by an infinite expectation of the dawn."

Henry David Thoreau

In a famous scene in the movie *Field of Dreams (1989)*, Ray Kinsella's (Kevin Costner) brother-in-law Mark (Timothy Busfield) finally sees the ballplayers after Ray's daughter is saved from choking by one of the "ghost" players. After this emotional and frightening experience, Mark says, "When did these ballplayers get here?" If you asked Ray Kinsella, his wife, his daughter, or Terrence Mann (the movie characters), they had seen the players from the beginning, while Mark had seen only an empty baseball field. Mark was blinded by his old stories of what was true and real, so he could not see the players—the miracle. Yet when he experienced the near death of Ray's daughter, Mark had a new and different experience—he woke up and saw things that he had never seen before.

Waking up in your life is much the same. You have a view of your world and your life, whether it is created on purpose, by accident or by default. When you wake up, everything changes. Your awakened self sees the truth of yourself and your life (or at least parts thereof). The only remaining question is whether your awakening will stick and you will choose to stay awake and live on purpose.

Too often and usually without knowing it, we are asleep in our lives. We see things and ourselves the way we want to see them, not as they actually are. We create a dream world—a false reality—that allows us to

of other lawyers joined me to start a new law firm, and I spent the next five years leading and building that firm into something that was fun, that was successful, and that I was proud of. I had now (and again) achieved virtually every form of success that anyone could imagine: The firm was a success and had a great reputation; we delivered high-quality, valuable services for our clients; I was leading the firm and the team; I was making good money; and, most surprisingly for the profession, I had a great quality of life. I did not work the same crazy hours that most lawyers did, and many other lawyers wanted to know how I had done it. In their view, I had it all—but there was one big thing missing. I was not happy. I loved managing, growing and building the firm, but I did not love the practice of law. I did not want to be a lawyer; I just wanted to lead a law firm. It was time to change again—to move on to what I was convinced would be yet another business and financial success.

Boy, was I wrong about that.

What I had missed for my entire career to date was that there were giant holes in my personal "success" and satisfaction. My marriage was not working, and rather than work on it I had chosen not to be there, to hide and run away from it, not knowing that was what I was doing. I can only identify and own this truth now in hindsight, because at the time I thought I was doing what I needed to do. I spent lots of time working, and if I was not working I was networking, and I was doing what I wanted to do (e.g. hanging out with friends, playing sports, etc.). I had MY life the way I wanted it, but I was already hopelessly lost—and I had no idea. Only when I later woke up was I able to explore my past life and see so clearly where I was lost and off course, but that awakening came much later. At this point in my life, I was still very much asleep at the wheel.

The next several years should have been my awakening, but sadly they were not. Perhaps if I had allowed myself to wake up, I could have turned and righted the ship faster and without so much pain and heartache, but

I didn't have the lightning bolt moment and stayed asleep. After leaving not only the law firm that I founded but the career that I had chosen as a teenager (after 17 years), I purchased a coaching franchise and began what I expected would be another success. I was going to help business owners improve their businesses by sharing with them what I had learned in building my own business—and I was going to make lots of money doing it. Three years later, the business had failed, but I did not admit that failure for many years. Instead, when talking about my coaching business, I told Blocking Stories: The franchisor had not delivered on its promises (true), the business model and processes were not what the franchisor had represented (largely true), and the economy was terrible (true). In all of these stories, however, I left out a key player in the failure—me.

Taking Responsibility for Your Life

It was not until a speech that I gave in September of 2009 that I for the first time took responsibility for the failure of that business. All of the foregoing stories were true (or mostly true), but the biggest truth was that I was not ready to make that business succeed, and I did not do what needed to be done to create that success. My ego got in the way, and I took the attitude that people would flock to me because I am amazing at what I do. Instead of asking what I needed to do to create success (and doing it), I asked questions like "Why wouldn't someone hire me?" Instead of doing all of the little things that create big results, I waited for the phone to ring. I networked and met lots of people, but I never did the things I needed to do to build the business. I was lost, and I did not know it.

With 20/20 hindsight, I now see that I was creating my own self-fulfilling destiny of a man who was not good enough and not worthy of success. Perhaps I was lucky in the practice of law because it was a profession where I could be successful (mostly) by being good at what

I did and because I had enough momentum from my large firm career to continue having some success with the new firm. In any event, three years later I was broken, battered and broke, so I picked up some familiar Cultural Stories: *you have to take care of your family, you have to be conservative and secure, you have to play it safe*—and so I did.

For the next several years, I had a job and worked for other people. I did what everyone told me to do and what culture seemed to reward—safe decisions. I was working to dig myself and my family out of the financial crater that we were living in, but it was never enough. I did my job well and created some success, but I was never all in. I was living a life that was not my own. It was my rationalized life—my safe life—but it was not my life. Yet the moment of awakening or push to waking up never came. I stand today a transformed man who has woken up and who lives purposefully and with awareness (growing every day), yet I cannot tell you why I did it or what motivated me to do it. I can point to key turning points such as my deepening connection to God and to things beyond myself. I can point to a transformational Mankind Project (www.mkp.org) retreat that I attended in May of 2010, but I cannot tell you what motivated me to attend.

I can point to the moment when I was starting to pursue my life's passion of speaking and coaching, but only on the side while I had a full-time job. I remember driving around in January of 2009 and asking this question of God: "Can I move into the life that I am meant to live when I am still living the life that I believe that I have to live [my steady job and income]?" I felt this need to take off with my speaking and coaching business, but I was tethered to my existing job. A couple of weeks later, I got the answer when I was laid off. I remember when I heard the words, and my first thought was *there is the answer to my question.* I guess you could say it was a sign of sorts, but it certainly was not earth-shattering. Perhaps some of us just wake up gradually and over time, without any great fanfare or notoriety. I actually believe a slow awakening experience is true for most of us, and it all begins with telling yourself the truth about yourself.

Who Do You See in the Mirror?

When you look in the mirror every morning, you ask yourself (consciously or unconsciously) one question: *Am I where I want to be?* But when you answer, do you tell the truth? Do you know the truth? For when you are asleep in your life, it is difficult or impossible to know what is true. So many years of telling "stories" and creating deeply ingrained false truths makes it difficult even to recognize the real truth. Too many of us falsely answer this mirror question either through affirmations (that we do not really believe) or by falling back on the ultimate safety net of mediocrity. You tell yourself that you are "doing okay," "getting by," "surviving," "managing" or "could be worse." These settling statements allow you to stay where you are in our life, for the moment that you acknowledge that you are off track or not where (or who) you want to be, you *must take action to change things.* It is difficult to impossible to look in the mirror every day, see a person and a life that are not what you desire them to be, and do nothing. Change happens when you take different actions, but changes rarely happen unless and until you wake up and choose to seek your own truth.

> When you look in the mirror every morning, you ask yourself (consciously or unconsciously) one question: *Am I where I want to be?*

Lost in Translation

I remember well a conversation with a couple one evening a few years ago. We will call them Bob and Amy.[1] They were both in their early fifties,

---

[1] Unless otherwise indicated or where a first and last name are included, fictitious names are used in this book for privacy and confidentiality reasons.

had been together for a long time, and had been living together for several years. I was introduced by a friend who described me as a motivational speaker. When they asked me what I spoke about, I told them about my business and personal speaking, which focused on enhancing relationships and helping people get out of the rut of mediocrity to live the life that they were meant to live. They both responded with the same question: "Why would anyone need that?"

They went on to tell me how amazing their relationship was and how all of their friends had great relationships, jobs and lives. I told them that I was thrilled for them because they were the first people I had ever met to say that they and most of the people they knew were really happy. I left that conversation wondering if what they had told me was actually true. I wondered in part because I so rarely hear such positive and affirming perspectives and in part because their response sounded almost defensive—as if claiming a marvelous relationship and life was what they needed to believe and they were feeling the need to push back against what they perceived as an attack on their false reality.

I love meeting people who are awake, aware and abundant in all parts of their lives, and I can usually tell when what they share feels true or feels like just a story. Many of you are unconsciously asleep, so what you share with yourself in the mirror and with others is the "truth" as you have seen and experienced it. Yet I look into many eyes, whether in an audience or sitting across the table from me, where I see fear, sadness and longing—*longing for that part of them that is hiding, wounded, hidden or completely unknown to them.* My personal mission is to share my own awakening experience and transformation with others to help awaken people to themselves and to help guide them through their own personal transformation.

I have been told that I listen differently from most people and that I hear things that are never spoken—what I call full soul listening and the Bible calls discernment. This different listening has allowed me to help people confront their stories. It has jokingly been said that if you are having a conversation with Jeff, bring tissues and be prepared for the tears. While I never intrude or inject, I hear and see people's sadness and longing, and, armed with the courage to ask authentic questions, I have been blessed to see people begin to awaken. As you touch and experience that which is hidden and holding you back or begin to experience the truth of your life, it is in these moments that the door of awakening appears—yet each one of you must step through that door into your new awakening and awareness.

Back to our "happy" couple. Later that evening, Bob and Amy were embroiled in a nasty argument, which led to Bob yelling into Amy's face and occasionally grabbing her arm. While this disagreement was not "my" argument, I could not let this situation continue because of the physical elements of the conflict and because this was certainly not the place (in public) for this discussion. I stepped between them, and Bob tried to engage with me verbally and physically, leaning into my face, poking me in the chest, etc. I chose to remain calm (and hopefully calming) in the midst of the angry words and energy. Things were not good that evening between Bob and Amy, but alcohol was involved and I reasoned that perhaps this disconnection was a rare one amidst a healthy, loving and thriving relationship. I hoped for the best, but something told me that the depth of this argument did not bode well for the future. Sadly, this was true.

Love Is a Battlefield

Several weeks later, Amy reached out to me and asked to get together. When we met, Amy shared with me that shortly after that evening Bob had severely beaten her and sent her to the hospital, that she now had a restraining order and that felony charges were being brought against him.

Amy said Bob had never physically assaulted her before, that she had not seen this abuse coming and that she was dismayed that someone she loved and who said that he loved her had attacked. Amy was confused and looking for answers. She was blaming herself and asking what she had done to bring on this physical assault. Surely, she said, she must have done something to cause Bob to assault her physically. While I wondered if there really had been no warning signs and pondered the source of Amy's need to blame herself, I just listened without judgment, accusations or observations. I simply shared that Bob's actions were his own and that she should not blame herself for the attack.

How could this happen? How could the virtually perfect couple with a great relationship and a marvelous life together suddenly come undone? The only answer that makes any sense is that they were not perfect and that their relationship was not so marvelous. Even if they had embraced a false reality that their lives were great, they were either consciously or unconsciously living their lives according to this skewed view of reality. Over the next several months, I got together with Amy several times, and each time I listened as she struggled to find the answers to how and why a man who said he loved her could assault her. Did Bob really love Amy? We can argue this question forever, but I choose to believe that this is not love. Perhaps it is the best some people can do with love, but loving someone does not include physically assaulting them.

I do not know what drove Bob to unleash his anger, rage and violence on Amy. Most likely he has his own personal wounds, hurts and stories that form who he is. I cannot know what is inside another human being, but Bob's actions suggest a man who was (prior to the attack) carrying around something or many things that ultimately drove him to physically assault the woman he said he loved. It may be that he grew up in a family, a neighborhood or a community where physical violence was the norm or accepted, but that is not for me to know or say. What is clear is that both

Bob and Amy were asleep and comfortable in their lives and that sadly they both had a wake-up call. Time will tell whether Bob or Amy wake up as a result of these events and whether they choose to think, believe and live differently. As horrific as these events were (especially for Amy), the hidden silver lining is the opportunity to wake up, reassess their lives and change their future paths. I have also learned that you often do not get a defining moment to motivate you to change, which we will explore more in my story below.

Lost

If you think you are already awake, remember that you may not be able to discern your own state of unconsciousness accurately. It is easy to be lost without knowing it, so you must be diligent to look deep inside yourself and make an honest assessment of yourself and your life. It also helps to have a support network (e.g., truth-speaking friends, family or business relationships) that will help you see that which you may not be able (or willing) to see for yourself. After all, they call them "blind spots" for a reason.

I recently talked with someone who was struggling with his business. He contacted me to talk about his business challenges, but the conversation quickly shifted to an inside look. This man (we will call him Adam) was 50 years old and had started his own business 18 months prior to our talk. Throughout his career consisting of several sales jobs (typically staying at least 10 years at each), he had been successful. He hit his goals, he achieved objectives, he won awards and contests, and he was highly regarded by his employer. In his personal life, he had a long-standing marriage, and he and his wife had raised several children into adulthood. Adam was confident, got things done, and had thrived professionally in every job he had ever held. As a business owner, though, Adam was struggling and on the verge of failure.

All of the things he had done so well as an employee, Adam was not doing as a business owner. He told me that he knew what things he needed to do but found that he was rarely doing them enough or well enough. When I asked him what was holding him back, he said that he did not know. When I asked him if he was afraid of anything, he said he had some fear of failing, but he could not understand why that fear would keep him from doing the things that would make him successful. When I asked if he might be afraid of succeeding, he initially did not understand the question. He asked, "Why would I be afraid of succeeding?" However, after I shared a bit of my own personal journey and my perceived lack of worthiness that led me to believe that I did not deserve to have success, happiness or love, Adam began to tell a new truth to himself—likely for the first time in his life.

Adam told me that he felt that he had been faking success his whole life. While he always presented himself as confident with his friends and at work, inside he had always doubted himself and felt he was alone, did not belong and was not good enough. He told me that he had never told his wife these truths. Ultimately, he said that he felt he had been wearing a mask for his entire life and that only now was his true self emerging—a true self that did not believe he was worthy, that thought he could not succeed and who appeared to be self-sabotaging his business and his life. Adam was unmasking himself and his leadership.

> While he always presented himself as confident with his friends and at work, inside he had always doubted himself and felt he was alone, did not belong and was not good enough.

Our Deepest Fear

Adam then told me that it did not make sense: If he did not feel good enough, then why wouldn't he do the things he needed to do to succeed and thereby prove himself good enough? While this perspective makes some sense, we love to be right. As a result, you may actually fail (despite your best intentions) to do what you know you need to do to be successful and thereby create the outcome (failure) that you say you do not want. When you fail, your beliefs about yourself (that you are not good enough or worthy) become true, and thus the Belief Stories you accept about yourself become true when you fail. This self-fulfilling prophecy is the essence of a fear of success or self-sabotage.

After a long conversation, Adam asked me this question: "How could I be successful and on course my entire life and suddenly wake up at the age of 50 and be lost … because I do feel lost?" I did not hesitate to give this answer: "My guess is that you have been lost for a long time, but you are finally waking up and realizing that you are lost." That is the nature of waking up—it is like waking up from a dream and realizing that it was just a dream. When you wake up in life, you realize that in many ways your life has been a dream, but typically not what you thought or believed it was.

Choosing to Stay Awake

When you have an awakening moment, it may slip away from you. Your old stories may be so ingrained or your wounds so painful that you consciously go back to sleep. We are all masters at rationalization, so you may rationalize the moment away and chalk it up to an aberrational event or experience. We crave rationalizations so much that they become a daily part of our self-communication. Think about it—you live with and hide behind rationalizations (sometimes called excuses) virtually every day of your life.

Consider some of these all too common rationalizations or "stories" that we use (or hear) every day:

- "I hate my job, but I can't make a change because of the economy."
- "I wish I could change the situation, but it's not a good time in my life."

- "I'll do it [whatever change we talk about] someday."
- "I would like to move/change jobs, but it is not that bad."
- "I need to be realistic about things."
- "I wish I could [insert the change], but I have to be realistic."

People tell me that they are just being realistic, but where is the line between a rationalization and being realistic? The only difference is your perspective, and your perspective is the result of your stories and the degree to which you tell yourself the truth. If you are unconscious and asleep, then you may not be able to tell the truth or distinguish between rationalizations and "being realistic."

When you have an awakening moment, it is decision time: Will you choose to actively work to stay awake (and it will take work and it is a choice), or will you choose to go back to sleep and settle for the old life, the old stories and the old outcomes? Waking up is a choice, and similarly, staying awake is a choice.

Stop Settling

One of the reasons that it takes work to stay awake is that we live in a culture today that is designed for settling, for staying the same and for staying asleep. Most of the people that I meet are in some state of being asleep, and they have a long litany of reasons to avoid risks, to stay the same and not to change—to stay asleep. Think about the day-to-day conversations that you have with people. When people talk about their businesses and especially about their lives, their answers usually sound like this: "I'm okay." "I'm getting by." "I'm surviving." "I'm pretty good." In today's American culture, getting by has become the top rung of the ladder. We have so lowered the standard that mediocrity is viewed as a success. With so many people ready to tell you to stay the same and to avoid risks—to tell you what is not working versus what can work—it takes effort to resist this old message and dare to step into a new message and life of opportunities, expectations and even dreams.

"Why would I ever want to go back to sleep after waking up?" you might ask. In addition to the obvious reasons (whatever caused you to go to sleep in the first place), there is a "cost" associated with living your life awake and aware. The cost is that you have to give up certain ways of being and thinking when you are awake—or at least cannot stay in those places or ways of being very long. One of the first things you have to throw away is blaming and making excuses. When you wake up and are aware, you receive the gift of having full control, ownership, and responsibility for your life and every part thereof, including your career, your relationships, your happiness, your fulfillment, etc.

I love and am blessed by having this real control over my path and my life—not control over the outcomes, but over how I experience every part of life. Still, this accountability for my life cannot co-exist with blame and excuses. No longer can I blame others, situations, or things outside of my control for my experience of life. When I am awake, I have the unique ability to create change in my life, and I must make those changes. I cannot rely on others or hope that things will change for the better; I must create better in my life.

I have to admit that taking personal responsibility for my choices, changes and outcomes is sometimes painful or frustrating. There are times when it would be easier to make excuses or to start pointing the finger of blame, but I am aware of this behavior (most of the time), and I choose to live and lead awake. This choice virtually requires me to step back quickly into a state of life accountability, rather than blame and excuse making. In a culture where excuses and blame are often the norm, you have to fight against that flow, but you can do so because your new awareness allows you to see and tell the truth as you never have before. Once you become aware, you must put down the "they" of blame and excuses and pick up the "I" to be fully accountable for your own life." In doing so, you will create your own positive momentum toward deeper self-awareness, new levels of awakening and the peace of mind that comes from living your life awake, aware and on purpose. As Mel Gibson offers in *Braveheart* (1995), "Every man dies, not every man *really* lives." Waking up and living life aware is the essence of really living.

Do Not Wait

I will talk more about my personal journey, awakening, and growing awareness in the following chapters, but for now let me leave you with this crystal clarity from my own experiences. DO NOT WAIT—until you are at the edge of the cliff, until you have crossed over from okay to depressed, until your most important relationships are in shambles, until you have determined that your life is not worth living—because you may already be there and not know it. Waking up is the first chapter of this book because it could not be placed anywhere else. Unless and until we wake up—even begin to wake up—we cannot begin to transform our lives and leadership.

You can make changes (just as I did), but the changes will be superficial and will not have the positive impact you desire them to have. Think about it—if you are making decisions and choices while you are asleep in your life, how good or impactful can you expect them to be? While sleep is good for our bodies, minds, and spirits, living life asleep does not add value to it. Yes, it seems easier, but is it? Yes, at times it might allow you to ignore or bury your pain and sadness, but only when you are awake can you face and move past the pain and sadness. While facing your fears and

> Unless and until we wake up—even begin to wake up—we cannot begin to transform our lives and leadership.

"stories" may seem daunting and frightening, I invite you to shift your perspective and instead see that in facing them you are able to move through and past them. While you may not be healed overnight, ignoring that which is holding you back is just that—ignoring—and it does not allow you to move forward. If you are asleep, you will naturally stay in that state, and your life will continue to be limited to that which an asleep person can possibly experience or achieve (which at best is mediocrity in all areas of your life).

Can you truly love deeply when you are asleep and playing it safe? Can you live fully for yourself, others and the community when you are focused on protecting yourself? Can you experience joy and passion when you are burying your sadness and doubts? Can you lead and create the impact you desire when you are asleep? There is a high price to pay for living your life asleep, and while there may be some potential short-term costs to waking up (discomfort and fully experiencing that which you have been hiding from), an awakened life is a passionate, joyful and loving life. I encourage you not to wait for someone else to push you into your awakening or to wait for that lightning moment, but to instead move swiftly, purposefully, and courageously into the life that you were meant to live and the person that you were meant to be. It can only begin when you *Wake Up!*

CHAPTER 2: MIRROR, MIRROR (THE AWARE LEADER)

"What is necessary to change a person is to change his
awareness of himself."

Abraham Maslow

The good news is that waking up is a beautiful gift to yourself, your business, your community and the world. The bad news is that it is only the beginning. While you can continue to wake up in deeper and more meaningful ways, your personal awakening thrusts you into the realm of personal awareness, which requires continual sharpening the rest of your life. Conscious leaders embrace the journey from awakening to awareness and then leap into the exploration of personal awareness, knowing that their leadership (in business and life) will be most impacted by their awareness. Awareness is the lynchpin to everything. As a result, every chapter in this book will hinge upon the depth of your awareness and your willingness to continually push beyond your personal comfort zone to further sharpen your awareness. What follows are core ingredients that combine to create a level of personal awareness that allows you as a leader not only to engage and inspire others, but also to support others in their own awareness and personal acceleration.

Self-Reflection and Assessment

In the prior chapter, you were introduced to the concept of *the mirror*, but unlike a mirror that we use to examine ourselves physically, this much more important mirror is the place where you examine yourself emotionally, psychologically, mentally and spiritually. This mirror is also the place where you ask yourself deeper and more difficult questions about where you are, who you are and where you are going. This mirror is also your opportunity to tell yourself the truth about everything. If you think this mirror and looking into yourself can be scary, then you are getting it. I would be lying if I told you that this depth of self-reflection and assessment is easy or not laced with any fear.

Many of you are not familiar with this type of mirror for a couple of simple reasons. First, it can be frightening to really face yourself. Second, few of you have had people in your life that model this type of inner assessment and truth-telling. Without having seen it before, you do not know how to do it or even that there would be value in doing it. You live in a culture where superficial living and wearing masks are sadly the norm, and looking in this mirror requires you to step outside everything you have seen, heard and experienced in your life.

Third, most of you were taught that the best way to assess yourself is through the eyes of others and by what they and culture think is correct, true or appropriate. By always looking outside of yourself, you let your confidence and leadership be determined by others, and you gear your actions toward meeting their expectations. Those expectations are often off-course and based upon the stories that others have come to accept in their lives. The truth is that if you compare yourself to the bar of others, you will most certainly come to the end of your life having played significantly smaller than your potential.

Finally, few of us have the courage to connect with people who can and will provide us with valuable outside perspectives to help us see what we cannot see for ourselves (our blind spots). While many of you have advisers, mentors and friends, you often surround yourself with people who either tell you what you want to hear or who are not themselves self-aware enough to give you the deeper perspectives and truths that you need to sharpen your awareness blade.

Inside Questions Everywhere

One of the most critical tools of the conscious and self-reflective leader is the willingness to go inside continually for answers, no matter what the circumstance, situation or perceived cause. Conscious leaders embrace internal questions that they repeatedly ask of themselves when things go well, when things go poorly and when things are unclear, including the following:

1. In what way could I have done things differently?

2. In what ways could I have *been* different?

3. What can I learn about *myself* from this situation?

4. What were the internal drivers (emotions, stories, perspectives, attitudes, beliefs, etc.) that fueled or supported my decisions, choices or actions?

Armed with this internal truth-telling and often going to deeper layers than the first, second or even third answer, the umbrella question that conscious leaders ask is, *were my decisions, drivers, choices and actions in alignment with who I am choosing to be as a person and as a leader?* Conscious leaders not only rely on their own self-reflection and assessment, but they also proactively seek out and encourage direct and honest feedback from others. They ask for feedback *and they really mean it.* Talk about a new way of being as a leader!

Too often, leaders focus their questions outwardly and toward others. They learn to use questions to help others become better in their roles, positions and personal effectiveness, but they do not as frequently turn the questions on themselves. The unconscious leader is satisfied with outwardly directed questions because those let the leader off the hook and allow him or her to blame others for circumstances and outcomes. The unconscious leader who does ask internal questions often asks the wrong questions. For example, a typical inside question of an unconscious leader is, "How did I do?" which is nothing more than a quick and superficial check-in. It is the rare and conscious leader who has a compelling desire to grow as a person, not just as a leader. The conscious leader recognizes that his or her personal growth will be the greatest driver of leadership growth.

The following is an example of a conscious leader's approach to a communication disconnect. An organizational leader and one of his managers had experienced a significant miscommunication—one that had a negative impact on the business. It was not a catastrophic impact, but it was one that they did not want to repeat in the future. When the leader and manager convened to discuss the miscommunication, the manager quickly took full responsibility for it. Notably, this was not a situation where the manager was "falling on her sword" and taking the blame. The manager truly believed that her own poor communication had caused the problem. In this situation, the unconscious (but perhaps good) leader would typically support and encourage the manager for taking responsibility and help (perhaps as a mentor) to make that manager better in the future. That approach exemplifies today's model of a good leader.

In this case, however, the conscious leader did all of the above **and** took the additional and self-reflective step of asking the manager, "What could I have done differently (or do differently in the future) to avoid or minimize the miscommunication?" The manager insisted that she was responsible for the miscommunication, but the conscious leader knew that communication is a two-way process and wanted to ensure that the solution for the future was not solely dependent on the manager changing her communication or behavior. This "both/and" thinking allows conscious leaders to create an environment where responsibility and solutions are co-owned, knowing that having more people committed to heightened awareness, corrections and solutions will enhance the likelihood,

> When faced with outcomes that were neither intended nor desired, conscious leaders insist on going within themselves for answers, change opportunities and personal growth, even if the circumstances suggest that such self-assessment is unnecessary.

sustainability and predictability of the change. This mindset also models self-reflection and collaborative assessment for the manager and others, as well as a level of personal responsibility and accountability that is rare in many leaders. When faced with outcomes that were neither intended nor desired, conscious leaders insist on going within themselves for answers, change opportunities and personal growth, *even if the circumstances suggest that such self-assessment is unnecessary.*

Life Is a Choice

In a culture that has grown far too accepting of and comfortable with pointing fingers, blaming circumstances and relying on outside events to determine our outcomes, conscious leaders are a rare voice of personal empowerment in embracing (rather than avoiding) the power of choice. Conscious leaders understand and believe that choices are at the heart of change, innovation and consistent execution. They also know that choices define leaders and leadership in bigger and different ways than ever before. Conscious leaders understand that in the end they do not control the outcomes, but they control everything up to the edge of the outcomes, including most significantly their choices. In the search for impact opportunities, conscious leaders recognize that the power of choices (and taking full ownership of and responsibility for choices) is one of the few true ways to drive results, engage your team and make the right things happen. Conscious leaders constantly look within to find opportunities for change and impact, and choices are the most significant of these opportunities.

Let us get those objections out of the way right up front. I have heard them all, and they can be simplified into one single whale of an objection—I often do not have choices in my life because there are things that just happen to me and situations where I do not have control. Sound familiar? Ready to jump on board with that "story?" You certainly will have lots of company on that train (I call it the blame train), but in doing so—in accepting this perspective—you give up the most powerful tool you have in guiding and creating your life: the power of choice. We will talk later about why it is so easy and seductive to give up the power of choice and believe that we are at the whim of the world and all its circumstances, but what is important right now is to dive head-on into the proposition that life is all about choices. In short, you are not only the sum and substance of the stories that you have chosen to believe are true, but you are also defined by your choices. Achieving the extraordinary is the outcome when people own, take responsibility for and embrace their choices and the power of those choices.

Realistic Is Relative

In my version of the story and my interpretation of the power of choices, you all have gifts that you are meant to use and share in the world. Choosing to ignore them or not use them, especially without great consideration and reflection on the choices that you have, is one of the greatest tragedies—not only for the person but for the world. Imagine being given a Ferrari to drive and then choosing to drive it only 35 miles an hour around the neighborhood. Likewise, imagine the waste of asking a thoroughbred horse to pull a plow or a cart. Even more relevant, imagine all that this world misses out on when people choose to settle in their lives—to leave their greatest gifts in storage while they live the lives that someone told them they needed to live.

I know. Here it comes: "But Jeff, you are not being realistic. Sometimes there are realities that prevent us from doing or being what we want to do or be." Well, here comes my response: bull shit. Yes, you heard and read me right. It may not be easy, it may not make sense and it may be risky, but no one is required to do anything in his or her life. You have been given the gift of choice, and where you go and what you do with your life is most directly impacted (sorry folks—no guarantees) by the choices that you make—even more than by your circumstances. As Debbie Ford affirms, "Choice might just be our most precious gift." *The Right Questions: Ten Essential Questions to Guide You to An Extraordinary Life* (Harper San Francisco 2003) at 2. Yes, some of these choices are hard. Yes, some of these choices are risky and scary. Yes, some of these choices have potential consequences that are catastrophic (perhaps financially, but rarely physically). Yet they are still choices because the fact that something is hard, risky or scary (which are all merely perceptions) does not cause something to cease to be a choice.

In early 2009, I was in a job where I did well, but it did not utilize my gifts and did not feed my soul. I was working for someone else, when my spirit was straining at the bit to be set free to go back to having my own business. But the decision to choose an entrepreneurial path again was very risky, especially financially. I had succeeded in my first business (my law firm), but when I left law to go into my first coaching business, it (and I) had failed, sending me back to work for someone else. My own story at the time was that I "had to" (my words and belief at the time) go to work for someone else because I had financial obligations and a family to support and the prior business failure had left me financially devastated. Add to that the fact that I was separated and heading toward a divorce that was putting even greater financial strain on me and increasing my financial obligations. It was definitely time to play it safe ... or so I thought.

To feed my passions, I had started doing some speaking and coaching on the side, which gave me a chance to fuel the most important part of me. It was not enough, and I found myself constantly wanting to pursue my dream, but I was tethered to my realistic life and the choice that I had made to have a "safe and secure" job. As we all know, "safe and secure" changed dramatically in the mid-2000's, with hundreds of thousands of people finding themselves losing that safety and security through no apparent fault of their own. While there was ample evidence for this lesson that many of our parents (and certainly grandparents) had given us—get a secure job, work for that company for 40 years and retire with a pension—the world had changed, but many people had not changed themselves or their choices with it.

I wanted to fly on my own, but I felt the "need" for a secure job and income source. I was stuck not by circumstances, but by the life I was *choosing* to live. When my employer laid me off, I had my answer. It was time to fly.

It Is Always the Right Time for the Right Thing

It has not been easy, and there have been many challenges and setbacks, personally, professionally and financially, but I have always kept going and living my choices to the fullest. I distinctly remember attending a cocktail gathering for an area job-seekers group where I had spoken about how to network and build relationships that matter. I was approached by Bob late in the evening, and when he asked me how I was doing, I said "I'm great." Bob said that he did not hear that very much around the job seekers group, and I told him that this absence of positive attitudes was unfortunate because attitude might be the most important factor in if and when someone gets their next job (and how well that job fits their desires and dreams). In response, Bob chided me a bit, saying that my perspective was different because I had a job, to which I said, "I don't have a job. I lost my job six weeks ago." Now Bob was confused and intrigued.

Bob asked me what I was doing, and when I told him that I had started a business to pursue my passions in speaking and coaching, he said

"Are you crazy? Why would you start a business in the middle of the worst recession since the Depression?" I told him that I thought there were lots of opportunities. The following is a short version of the brief conversation that followed:

Bob: "Well, you must have a book of clients that came with you."

Jeff: "Actually, I don't have any clients. I also don't have any cash flow. I know what a sales pipeline is, but I don't even have a pipeline yet, but I'm working on it."

Bob: "Well, you must have had a good financial foundation to start this business."

Jeff: "Actually, I don't have any financial foundation. With some prior financial issues and a pending divorce, there is no financial net. In fact, this is the worst time financially in my entire life for me to start this business. Every day, I wake up and look over my shoulder and the bridge is burning. My feet aren't on fire, but it's not a forest fire in the distance, and I can feel the heat. I get up every day and start running."

Bob: "Then with all of this, how are you great?"

Jeff: "I decided that when I got up this morning. It's a choice."

Bob: "I just can't believe you chose to start a business now—in these economic times."

Jeff: "The way I see it, it's not a question of whether it's the right time, but whether it's the right

thing because I believe that it's always the
right time for the right thing."

And I have been running (and often flying) ever since, soaring on the
wings of my choices, my passions and my gifts. One thing I have learned
about taking risks and jumping off the cliff—the main difference between
falling (imagine me flailing my arms and screaming) and soaring (imagine
my arms outstretched like an eagle) is attitude.

Risky Business?

Was my choice risky? Of course, but risk is relative not only to the
risk-taker, but to how we perceive our other choices. Risk itself is a *story*.
Thousands of people thought they had taken the low-risk path with a safe
and secure job, only to find out that their job and income was neither safe
nor secure. So much for that *story* about risk. Was my choice easy? Who
knows? It certainly was difficult at times, but which is harder—pursuing
my dreams or living a life and working in a job that I did not love (that I
believed that I "had to do")? It is amazing to find out what we are capable
of when we are all in and fully committed to a path and pursuit that we
are passionate about. The ancient Vikings knew something about being
all in. When they invaded the enemy's shores, the first thing they did was
burn the boats so that there was no means of escape. Talk about being
motivated. While I did not burn the boats (I did not have a fleet to burn),
I was all in with my choices.

In many ways, I do not know how I did it. Several years into the
business, I hired a coach, and when he reviewed my business financials, he
was astounded because he discovered that in the first year of my business
my *total revenue* (before any expenses) was almost exactly the amount
that I paid that same year to support my soon-to-be ex-wife and family.
"How," he asked, "did you survive? You had an apartment, a car and
maintained a living with no apparent means to do so." He asked if I had

run up a large amount of credit card debt, which was not the case because I did not have the credit card balances available to do so. I told him that I owed a few dollars to Uncle Sam, but it was all being paid off. My coach equated it to

> This is precisely the mindset that conscious leaders nurture and model—always looking for the choices that they can make in terms of how they think, what they believe and what they do to create desired change.

the loaves and the fishes story from the Bible—a modern day miracle—but all I knew is that I just did it. Perhaps there is something magical about Nike's "Just do it" directive. I made my choices and I just did it, and the "what" I was doing was my passion and the "why" behind my choices was my life's mission. This is precisely the mindset that conscious leaders nurture and model—always looking for the choices that they can make in terms of how they think, what they believe and what they do to create desired change.

For conscious leaders who embrace the power of choice in taking full responsibility and accountability for their lives and their choices, another core element is the firm belief that there is no "can't," only choices—even on the smallest scale. I used to believe (and say) that I could not do something because "I had to work," but this position is not true. I may have work to do, but I choose to do work or to do something else. No matter what the situation, even facing a client or governmental deadline, I still make choices about my actions and activities. Some choices may objectively be bad choices (for example, choosing not to file my taxes on time), but they are still choices. I choose where I invest my time, including the choice to invest it in myself. Therefore, I no longer tell people that I "can't" do something because I am busy. I tell them that I am choosing to do something else (even stay home). By embracing choice as my daily reality, I am taking control and accountability for my life. In contrast, the moment you allow yourself to believe that you must do something or that you cannot do something, you have given away the power to create or inspire change. Conscious leaders are not willing to give up this power, and they embrace choice as the means to retain impact and change opportunities.

This choice (to own your choices and not rely on "can't" as an excuse) is not always easy, and it is certainly a new way of communicating that some people are not used to hearing. Imagine the first time I told my girlfriend that I was choosing to work instead of spending time with her. She immediately noted (correctly) that I was making my work a priority over her, and that is the truth. In owning my choices, I am telling the truth. When we choose one activity over another, we are saying that the thing that we choose is more important to us in that moment. While the initial discomfort with the truth of choice can be a challenge, once you begin to live it you see the power that comes to everyone involved. Both sides of the relationship (personal, social or business) are speaking their truth to each other, which deepens the relationship.

Conscious leaders make clear decisions and clearly communicate those decisions. And it feels good. It feels good to say that you are honoring yourself by taking care of yourself. It feels good to say that you are choosing to honor a commitment rather than do something else. It feels good to say that you are choosing to focus on your business at a particular time rather than distracting yourself with some other activity. When you say these two words—*I Choose*—you are stepping into your own personal power and taking what may be never-imagined control of your life and your decisions. While you never have ultimate control over the outcomes in your life, the power of choice (over the power of "can't") is the only ultimate control that you can have or ever have had. Conscious leaders crave the power of choice, both personally and professionally.

considering all of the choices that lead to the undesirable outcomes (big or small). Why is blaming so seductive? Simple—because it lets you off the hook. It lets you avoid personal responsibility for anything that happens in your life that is not how you envisioned it or which is inconsistent with a promise or commitment that you made. Indeed, blaming (and playing the victim) is enticing because it allows you to claim that most things *are not your fault*. In short, many people choose *blaming* over *choosing* because it appears to be easier.

As crazy as it sometimes sounds, many people would rather say that they are stuck in a place, job, situation or relationship ("I don't have a choice") than take responsibility for where they are in their lives. This abdication of choice is not only crazy, but it totally emasculates any power you had to change your situation since when you are in a place because you have to be (you do not have a *choice*), then the only thing that will or can change your situation is a change in your fortunes or circumstances. Who really wants to be that aimless, adrift and out of control? Apparently, millions of people.

Still, I have discovered one reason for this abundance of seemingly irrational behavior: being helpless and without (perceived) choices to change our circumstances allows us to stay stuck and avoid the real or imagined risks associated with working to change our circumstances. We are afraid (for many reasons) to work to create change, and as a result, staying stuck is less frightening than taking the risks associated with pursuing change through our choices.

Imagine a person who is feeling stuck in a job that does not suit them or, worse, subjects them to abuse and harassment almost daily. They may want to change their situation (or say that they want to change it), but if they accept responsibility for their situation, then they can no longer hide behind their own walls or old stories. In accepting responsibility, you lose the ability to blame and play the victim, and for some people the devil you know (being unhappy or even miserable) is better than taking the risk of trying to change and possibly failing in that attempt. There are no guarantees about change or results in your life—sometimes things do not work out the way you hope, expect or dream, and when that happens many people want to be able to say that it was not their fault. It is faulty (or at least iffy) logic, but it feels safe to many people, and many times people *choose* safety over change. Once again, choice shows up as a reality in all of your decisions, including a failure or refusal to decide. In truth, choices are what make you who you are, and you always have the choice to do what is right—even when it is hard, scary and uncertain.

The Gift of Choice

Choice is a gift that you have and receive every day, but the gift exists only when it is claimed and utilized. The potential to make a choice is not a choice and, while failing to make a choice is often a choice, it is not the type of choice that empowers us. In fact, default choices—those that occur because we failed to make a choice because it was too hard, too complicated or too risky—are really the result of ignoring or not claiming the gift of choice. Despite all of the seductive reasons to *choose* not to choose—easy excuses, avoiding responsibility, being able to blame others and circumstances—the gift of choice is precious because it gives you one of the few options to have any control over your life, your results and your outcomes. As Tommy Newberry said in *Success Is Not An Accident* (Tyndale House Publishers 2007), "You are rich with choice, and your choices reveal who you really are." This truth is at the heart of everything that you will experience throughout the rest of this book.

Are you enduring your life or living your life? Are you full of options (choices), or are you stuck and just holding on? Are you making decisions and choices in pursuit of your dreams, or are you at the whim of circumstances and hoping for the best? Are you designing and deciding your future, or are you hoping for a lucky break? Will you choose or be left with few if any choices because you failed to choose when you had the opportunity? In the song "Freewill" by the band *Rush*, we find great wisdom in this lyric:

"If you choose not to decide, you still have made a choice."

This perspective is precisely the mindset of conscious leaders.

Conscious leaders are also aware of the impact (often negative or limiting) of not making conscious choices (i.e. procrastinating, waiting for someone else to decide, etc.). Long ago I heard this proposition:

We often fail to recognize that not making a decision is still a decision … and it's almost always the wrong one.

When you fail to make a decision or a choice and wait for circumstances or someone else to make the choice for you, you are giving up your ability to have real influence on or over the outcomes. This form of deferral disempowers leaders, teams and organizations, often without the leader even realizing that the power of choice is being given away. That is a core difference between conscious and unconscious leaders. Unaware leaders do not realize when they are deferring or giving up the power of choice, whether directly (going to the blame mode) or indirectly by letting decision opportunities slip through their fingers. In contrast, aware leaders protect, preserve and hang onto every choice opportunity, which includes making sure that *they* make decisions rather than give away those choice opportunities.

Awareness Is a Commitment

While the tools and skills outlined above must be practiced and honed, the underlying foundation is a heightened level of awareness by anyone seeking to lead—leadership being the desire to create positive change and impact for a person, a team or an organization. This leap into awareness is mostly about a decision—a commitment to the desired outcomes and improvements in communication, effectiveness and execution. With this commitment to awareness, any person can and will find ways to slow life down and be able to observe themselves and others at a different and deeper level, and thereby fundamentally change the way they think, communicate, act and choose. Welcome the awareness revolution and the conscious leaders that it will breed. Are you ready to commit to this new way of leading?

CHAPTER 3: UNMASKED (THE AUTHENTIC LEADER)

"Authenticity is the alignment of head, mouth, heart, and feet–
thinking, saying, feeling, and doing the same thing–consistently.
This builds trust, and followers love leaders they can trust."

Lance Secretan

If you have not already guessed or figured it out, these core and foundational elements of a conscious leader all build upon each other. In many ways, they depend on the others and often naturally flow from the others. This layering of elements is certainly true for the authentic nature of conscious leaders, since it is difficult to imagine an awake and aware person not also being authentic. While authenticity is not an absolute or a constant occurrence, conscious leaders are purposefully committed to living and being authentic, both personally and professionally. This commitment in turn is exemplified when a leader uses authenticity as a benchmark against which to assess and ultimately make decisions. In other words, a conscious leader will ask himself or herself this question when making decisions: "*In what ways can I be authentic in my actions, communication, deliberations and decisions?*" Alternatively, the question could be phrased "*What does authenticity look like in this situation?*" This intentional integration of values or ways of being into a person's thoughts, strategies, tactics and actions is a clear indicator of a conscious leader.

There are three pillars of authenticity that will accelerate any leader into a new level of effectiveness and influence:

1. Conscious leaders are open and transparent;

2. Conscious leaders are courageously vulnerable;

3. Conscious leaders walk the talk.

These three pillars are well summarized in these words of wisdom from Ralph Waldo Emerson: "Your actions speak so loudly, I cannot hear what you are saying." Conscious leaders are not only willing to be judged by their actions, but they invite heightened scrutiny of themselves and their actions based upon their commitment to transparency and personal alignment (i.e. what they do is consistent with what they say and believe).

The Masquerade Ball Is Over

Do you ever feel exhausted? Do other people tell you that they are or feel the same way? There is a very good reason for this exhausted state of our culture, and it is not because we are all busy. The cause of this exhaustion is simply that many of us wear masks every day—and they are heavy. It is physically, emotionally and mentally exhausting to put on and wear a mask every day—*and the more we are faking it, the heavier the mask is.* These masks are the resting place or storage locker for all of the ways that we fake it, cover up or pretend in our personal and professional lives. Sadly, we have accepted an old story that leaders are stoic, unemotional and detached, and we continue to perpetuate the fallacy that leadership strength equates to *putting on a good face* or *never letting anyone see you sweat.* These fallacies have created a generation of "strong" leaders who have been unable to accomplish their often-stated goal of engaging and inspiring a committed team. The reason for this failure is simple—leaders that pretend and wear masks prevent team members from connecting with them, and it is these missing connections (i.e. missing trust and relationships) that keep teams from zealously charging into execution and impact.

Sadly and to our great disadvantage, generations of potential leaders have been handed (and then accepted) a leadership message and model that says that strong and tough is *the way* to lead. This model is reinforced every day and in many ways in the workplace, at home, at school and in the media, but the model has been blindly accepted without questioning whether it is working or will work. The verdict is in: it does not work, and it is not the way to engage a committed team (what Seth Godin would call a tribe of raving fans).

Some time ago, I was working with a business owner who had been going through some difficult times in her personal life. Her father had just passed away after a long last illness (which had taken her regularly away from the business and certainly distracted her), and she told me that she was struggling with the emotions surrounding her father's death. Perfectly natural response, right? Just what you would expect any reasonable person to experience, right? Yet this business owner believed that she could not show her emotions at work or even let her team members know that she was experiencing any of the emotions she felt about her father's death. Talk about a giant mask—she was pretending that the death of her father did not impact her.

Just imagine what her team members might conclude or assume based upon this persona of always being in control by asking this question: *What kind of person does not experience emotions after a father's death?* The list is long and not terribly kind—uncaring, cold, stoic, disinterested, mean, unloving, etc. This situation exemplifies one of the big issues with wearing a mask—people will judge you and make assumptions about you no matter what. Do you want to be judged for who you really are (your authentic self) OR based upon who you pretend to be? Either way, people will be watching and making judgments and assessments, and you have the choice to decide what they are basing those judgments and assessments on—your real self or your fake self. Remember, the person you pretend to be is just as likely to be negatively judged, and often these judgments are far more detrimental to you as a leader than judgments based upon your authentic emotions and self.

Back to our business owner. When I suggested that she should be more open to letting her team members see her emotions, she pushed back, saying that it would not help her as a leader to be "bawling her eyes out in front of her team." Note what happened—I invited her to be more authentic as a leader, but she took it to the far extreme to a form of emotional behavior that would not be helpful or productive in any business environment. Like many leaders, she was confusing authenticity with a breakdown. I was not suggesting that she should come into the office and blubber in front of her team, but she imagined that extreme in order to justify her denying or covering up her emotions. Which would you rather see in a leader— someone who seems never to be bothered by anything OR someone who acknowledges having feelings, emotions and states of mind like other people?

More importantly, which type of person do you trust more—the person that always *seems* to be in control OR the person that *shows up* authentic and human (imperfections and all)?

> Remember, the person you pretend to be is just as likely to be negatively judged, and often these judgments are far more detrimental to you as a leader than judgments based upon your authentic emotions and self.

That is the core of it after all—TRUST! Leaders (like you) cannot—I repeat, CANNOT—lead without being trusted by those who are following them. Still, many leaders fail to consider or commit to the types of critical thinking, behavior and actions that create, build and nurture trust. These foundational ways of building trust include authenticity, integrity, alignment (actions matching words) and transparency. Conversely, absence of these foundations or acting in ways that are in direct opposition to them sends a loud and clear message: *You cannot trust me.* Today's ever-present inauthentic leader essentially communicates to those he or she seeks to lead the following message: *I am not willing to let you know me, understand me or support me, but I want you to trust me.*

Too often, leaders jump right into leadership and the actions that they believe embody leadership without ever asking a couple of basic questions:

1. What do I need to do in order to earn the right to be followed?
2. What do I need to do in order to earn my followers' (or potential followers') trust?
3. Who do I need to be (inside out) in order to be trusted and therefore followed as a leader?
4. Who will I commit to being in order to be trusted and followed?

Yes, these questions seem obvious (almost ridiculously so), yet so many leaders still believe that leadership is about setting a course, giving orders and watching others execute those orders. Leaders today often assume trust and expect followership, yet never take personal responsibility either for their leadership decisions and actions *or* for consciously choosing who and how they will be as a leader in order to earn trust, nurture relationships and be worthy of being followed. These questions and conscious choices are at the heart of what it means to be a conscious leader, whether of an organization, a team or your own life. Our business and personal worlds are in chaos, and we do not need a superhero—we need more conscious leaders. Will YOU be one of these conscious leaders that will choose to be different, lead differently and create differently?

As an authentic leader myself, I cannot pretend that I have always lived and led in this conscious way. Like many inauthentic leaders, I was off-course as a leader and did not even know it. People looked up to me (in my business, in my community, in my network and in my family), but I was a fake. Not only was I wearing many diverse and manipulating masks, but I had no awareness that I was doing it. I was doing what everyone else did, and I had created success in my business and other ventures. I had also established a wide network of relationships that many people envied in their quantity and quality. I was the person that others talked about even when I was not there. They said things like, "Do you know Jeff Nischwitz?" They saw me at events and told other people, "You have to meet Jeff Nischwitz. He knows everyone." People sought me out for meetings and interactions, wanting to be a part of my tribe and perhaps to benefit from my energy and connections.

I attracted people into my life and circle merely by showing up. It was like the bright light that attracts bugs to the zapper, except that I was not designed to hurt the people that sought me out. I certainly did not seek to let them down on any intentional or conscious level, but it was all a sham. It was mask upon mask upon mask. My entire life was one grand masquerade party, where I was the full-of-life host and everyone wanted to be a part of the party. Well, not quite everyone. There were people who saw through my many masks, and when they chose not to follow, I dismissed them as people who were jealous and who simply did not get it. My ego was out of control, yet it masked a wounded man who was surviving through internal conflict and pain, and I felt I could not let anyone else see those truths about me. If I let them see me, they would know who I really was (imperfect and human), and ultimately they could (and in my story would) reject me.

Like most changes we make in our lives, my transition from inauthentic to authentic was not in an instant and did not come like a bolt of lightning; however, I remember a seminal moment of awareness that happened about five years ago. I had the opportunity to attend a book tour event featuring Keith Ferrazzi, who was on the road to promote his second book, *Who's Got Your Back* (2009). Keith was describing an event in his life that happened when his first book, *Never Eat Alone* (2005), was launched. A friend of his hosted a mega party at Keith's home in California, and a couple of hundred people were there to celebrate with Keith in this tremendous accomplishment. He had achieved great things in business success, authorship, notoriety and

not about denial, but rather about choosing to be calm and courageous in the midst of chaos and fear.

Reframing Courage

One of the best ways to experience the difference between a conscious and unconscious leader is to examine the concept of courage and what it means for a leader (or any person) to be courageous. Here are some of the most common definitions of courage:

- Mental or moral strength to persevere, and withstand danger, fear or difficulty (Merriam Webster)

- The state or quality of mind or spirit that enables one to face danger, fear or vicissitudes with self-possession, confidence and resolution (American Heritage)

- The ability to do something that frightens one (Oxford)

Isn't that interesting! All of these common definitions focus on facing something, doing something or persevering despite something that invokes fear or hesitation. Courage is decidedly NOT about avoiding or being without fear or uncertainty, yet it seems our cultural belief (especially for leaders) is that courage means never experiencing fear. This is simply off-course thinking and believing. Frankly, when I hear anyone claim to be fearless, my natural response is to call that person a liar. Everyone is afraid of something or experiences internal hesitations, yet unconscious leaders believe that leadership requires denial of these very real feelings and thoughts. Conscious leaders, however, acknowledge their fears and questions, yet confidently and decisively take action and lead others *through* the difficult or challenging times, thereby demonstrating courage through their authenticity.

People today are seeking leaders that they can get to know, leaders they can see for who they are and leaders who are self-confident enough to fully show themselves to others. Consider this dichotomy—the old way of leadership involved pretending as if nothing bothers you (believing that this shows self-confidence), yet we all know from our own life and business experiences that when we pretend that nothing bothers us or "gets in," we are actually modeling a *lack* of confidence. We lack enough self-confidence to be ourselves. In contrast, the new way of being as a conscious leader embraces the reality that true self-confidence (even if imperfect) is demonstrated when a person (even one modeling leadership) is willing to acknowledge that things do get tough, that things bother them and that they have doubts and hesitations. The myth that stoicism equates to confidence and thus leadership is thankfully dying in our culture, leaving open the door for conscious leaders to step up into a more collaborative and cooperative leadership role and experience—an experience that empowers everyone to be more, to achieve more, and to be themselves, even in the midst of chaos and uncertainty.

Conscious Leaders Are Courageously Vulnerable

Yes, I did it. I brought the dreaded "V" word into the business conversation, and it is about time because our world and our businesses need a whole lot more vulnerability. In many ways, vulnerability is slowly and quietly becoming the new strategic weapon for business leaders. It is also at the heart of the gap that exists in our personal lives and relationships. The challenge has been and continues to be that vulnerability is treated like a dirty word both in business and personal interactions. It is something to be avoided at all costs—at least it has been—but the shift is happening because people and leaders are beginning to understand that the old way of being (closed off and covering up) is not working. It is not serving us as leaders, it is not serving us in our relationships, and it is not serving us in our families. Now is the time for you to throw off the masks and embrace your authentic and vulnerable self for all to see, experience *and trust.*

Conscious leaders are courageously vulnerable because they have learned that the path to whatever you want, whether it is in your business or in your personal life, will be relationships. People talk about wanting to have a great team, an engaged team, a committed, passionate team. That is going to come from relationships, and the missing link in relationships is trust. We have a trust crisis. We do not trust ourselves, we do not trust the people close to us and we definitely do not trust the people we work with. Yes, you trust that they are not going to cheat you or blatantly lie to you about something important. But will they tell you the truth? Probably not, because we do not have authentic relationships that allow (or ever invite) direct and honest feedback. We do not want to hear criticism because it is just that—critical. Rather than being benign information, most so-called constructive criticism is a pile of judgments—judgments about what you did, how you did it, how you failed or got it wrong, and often about who you are as a person. No wonder we do not like getting constructive criticism.

Sadly, our culture continues to hang on to the misguided notion that being authentic and vulnerable is a sign of weakness. In contrast, I invite you to shift your perspective on vulnerability dramatically. As I like to say, *vulnerability is courage in action*, and putting it in action is critical in order to change the cultural myth that vulnerability is a weakness. The best and perhaps only way to create this shift is by modeling vulnerability. You cannot merely talk about it or espouse it—you have to be able to take off your mask and let people know who you truly are. Only in this way can you show people that it is safe for them to be vulnerable.

I have often seen this dynamic in my own interactions with people. Consistent with the Cultural Story that vulnerability equals weakness (which needs to be debunked), I am often told people do not want to take their conversations and relationships to this deeper level—that people "do not want to go there." To this I say: "Wrong." My personal experience is that men and women are starving for a place—a safe place—where they can be themselves, take off their masks and lower their shields. You, as a conscious and courageous leader, can create this safe, inviting and vulnerable space where others have permission to open up and expose their authentic selves. As a friend of mine and fellow speaker, Glenna Salsbury, said, "When you tell your truth you free others to tell and live their truth." This type of thinking is the essence and outcome of being courageously vulnerable, both in your business and your personal life.

Well known TedX speaker, researcher and author Brené Brown has studied and written extensively on the topic of vulnerability, and she famously stated that "vulnerability is our most accurate measurement of courage." Not strength. Not ability to persevere. Not ability to act as if nothing gets to us. Vulnerability is not just courageous—it is the *measurement of courage.* It is the evidence of our courage. The trouble with courage is that we cannot truly define it or even know where to go looking for it. Rather, courage is the visible outcome when you are afraid and do it anyway, when you are uncertain but are decisive anyway, and when you are hesitant and leap anyway. Imagine yourself being in a moment of uncertainty or fear and saying to yourself, "Come on, let's get that courage up." Where would you look for it? Where do you think you would find it? Certainly, there are questions you would ask yourself to get through or past the fear, and you might also seek the support of others to help you, but in the end, courage is the label we put on ourselves or others *after* we have done it anyway.

In contrast, being vulnerable is easier to identify in terms of what it is, what it looks like and what we need to do (or not do) in order to demonstrate vulnerability. In fact, the easiest way to know when we are being or moving towards vulnerability is to listen to the fear inside us. We fear vulnerability because there is an old Cultural Story that says being vulnerable is the equivalent of being weak. We also fear

> Yes, vulnerability may be safe—but at the cost of your authentic self, at the cost of trust, at the cost of relationships, and ultimately at the cost of failing in leadership, both personally and professionally.

vulnerability because it exposes us to judgments from others and to the ultimate fear for many of us—rejection. Moreover, this is a potentially painful rejection because it would be based upon who we really are. If we are wearing our masks, then the judgments we receive are of who we are *pretending to be*. At least that is safer than being flayed open and judged as our most vulnerable self. Yes, vulnerability may be safe—but at the cost of your authentic self, at the cost of trust, at the cost of relationships, and ultimately at the cost of failing in leadership, both personally and professionally.

Conscious leaders are willing to show up vulnerable, let people know who they really are, allow the connections to happen, and let those relationships flow from all that trust that is created when we let people know who we really are. Talk about engagement—you want a committed team? Show up as who you are. Let them understand that you have the same fears they do. Let them understand that you go through the same uncertainty that they do. Vulnerability may be the linchpin to all of it, and it is definitely one of the key attributes of a conscious leader.

The interesting (or even ironic) thing about vulnerability is that it is one of the things that we simultaneously deeply crave and actively seek to avoid. Think about it. If you ask people if they want to be more vulnerable, their honest and heart-felt response would likely be that they would love to be more vulnerable. Wearing masks is exhausting them, and they long to show themselves to the world, so they desire the opportunity to be vulnerable. Still, these same people will simultaneously say that they do NOT want to be more vulnerable because being vulnerable exposes them to judgments and rejections that they *believe* do not exist if they wear masks and hide their true self. The courage to be vulnerable is essentially a commitment to being judged and even rejected based upon who you are, rather than based upon your masked persona. This is the choice that you as a conscious leader can make every day when you choose to be authentic and courageously expose your true self in daily acts of vulnerability. Conscious leaders risk judgments and rejection in order to create, build and nurture trust and resulting relationships, all of which are the basis for effectiveness, satisfaction and impact.

How critical is this shift from unconscious and misguided inauthenticity to conscious and vulnerable authenticity? It is at the heart of conscious leadership, which in turn is the foundation of getting more of the right things done right and of creating transformational impact in lives, families, communities, teams and organizations. Brené Brown offers this:

> "Vulnerability is not weakness. And that myth is profoundly dangerous."

Consider the depth of this statement—vulnerability as a weakness is not just mistaken or off course, but it is a "profoundly dangerous" myth! So long as we cling to old beliefs about what it means to be a leader and remain closed off in a culture of mask-wearers, *NOTHING* will change. Staying the same is too easy, but it is not working. Our businesses, our families and our communities are starving for leadership—authentic and courageously vulnerable leaders (even if simply leading our own lives)— that will change things for the better. We are at a tipping point and a precipice both in business and in life, and we need conscious leaders to change things. As long as we are stuck on the old belief that vulnerability is a sign of weakness, then we will remain closed off. We will remain in a crisis of distrust; we will remain lost without meaningful and mutual relationships; and we WILL stay stuck in a way of doing business, working in teams and living our lives that IS NOT WORKING.

I long ago heard it said that we change only when things are so bad that we decide that we have no other choice—that we change only when the pain of staying the same is so great that we would rather explore the uncharted waters of new ways of thinking and doing than stay stuck in the painful place of our current reality and ways of being and doing. Now is the time for conscious leaders to step up—for YOU to step into your own conscious leader—in order to change things for the better at work, at home, with your family, in your communities—and most definitely from there to the rest of the world.

Conscious Leaders Crave Direct and Honest Feedback

Feedback is the realm where conscious leaders soar out of the darkness of vague comments and general input and into the light of personal and professional growth and acceleration, all on the wings of vulnerability. Conscious leaders invite and embrace direct and honest feedback all the time and receive it with genuine gratitude, knowing that without feedback they cannot change.

In a world where the norm is to avoid feedback and everything that comes with it (the judgments and true criticisms), conscious leaders genuinely and continually seek to know themselves better (for better or worse), so they invite and crave feedback. They seek feedback for the same reasons as others—it is the best way to improve—but conscious leaders desire outside feedback because more than others, they understand the reality that they have blind spots (things about themselves and their leadership that they *cannot see for themselves*). Thus, conscious leaders know that outside feedback is the only way to see the way that others see them, their decisions, their actions and their leadership.

While conscious leaders are adept at introspection and embrace looking into their own mirror for insights, clarity and self-truth telling, they also understand the nature of blind spots: the things about themselves that they cannot see except through outside feedback. Other people can see what you cannot see about yourself, but that knowledge and perspective is irrelevant unless and until it is communicated to you (as feedback). Sadly, we live in a social and business culture where feedback is considered to be negative, and the primary concern is about not hurting anyone's feelings. We have dedicated hundreds of thousands of hours of research, millions of dollars worth of consulting and untold numbers of pages in books to learning how to give feedback, provide constructive criticism and engage in honest conversations. It seems as though most of our efforts have been directed at learning how to give feedback so that people do not take it personally or become defensive (we will talk more about this issue later in this book), but we have largely missed the boat and are looking for solutions in the wrong place.

Yes, conscious leaders can play a vital role in enhancing the process of delivering honest communication and feedback. As we will discuss in Chapter 11, the use of questions to deliver feedback is one of the conscious leader's best tools in facilitating understanding, providing support and changing behaviors and performance. Feedback, however, is one of the many areas where leadership requires a paradigm shift in order to develop conscious leadership traits in a wide range of people (e.g. your entire team), including a different perspective on giving and receiving feedback.

Imagine a work place, a community and even a world where people *wanted* direct feedback and craved this information as a way to improve themselves, their relationships and their impact. When people understand what they can get from a different way of being, many people will want to experience it and live it for what it gives them in their businesses and their lives. What we are discussing is not just about leadership skills for people in positions of authority. It is a matter of livingship skills for all people.

Rather than trying to pretty it up, clean it up or nice it up, conscious leaders embrace direct feedback because it is the only way to get better and change who you are, how you communicate, how you live and how you lead. Without direct feedback, you will only be as good as you can discern that you need to be, which is ultra-limiting. Learning from and relying primarily on your own insights and perspectives is the typical way that leaders function, but conscious leaders go deeper, learn more, change more and create more because they seek out, invite and appreciate honest feedback from others.

Admittedly, there are many people who say that they want feedback. They ask their teams to give them feedback, but they never or rarely receive it. When they do not get input or feedback, unconscious leaders reach one of two conclusions: 1. I'm good; or 2. My team members (or partners or friends) are not willing to share it, so shame on them for not sharing. If they are not willing to share, then there is no reason or nothing for me to change.

> Without direct feedback, you will only be as good as you can discern that you need to be, which is ultra-limiting.

Excuse me?

What about a third option: your team members, partners or friends do not *trust you* and do not believe you when you say that you want direct and honest feedback. They have heard that before from others and probably from you, yet they experienced something other than openness and receptivity when they shared. Likely, many of their prior experiences with providing feedback, whether downstream to people that report to them, to peers or partners on their same organizational level, and especially upstream to managers, is that the receivers of the feedback were defensive, did not listen and certainly did not change. Admittedly, feedback does not always mean that the receiver will change, but the person sharing the feedback should have a reasonable expectation that he or she will be heard and not attacked for it. Most people have a long history of unpleasant experiences in providing feedback (usually genuinely designed to provide support and help), and it will take some time for them to be willing to be vulnerable in this area themselves.

This is where it is so critical for you as a conscious leader to model openness, receptivity and gratitude when you receive feedback, no matter how critical it might feel or sound. Even if they perceive that the person sharing the feedback is being judgmental, harsh or even personally offensive, conscious leaders are willing to receive the feedback, assess it (independent of the person providing it and even independent of the judgments that accompany it) and integrate it into their ways of being, thinking and leading going forward. Not everything should be changed, but conscious leaders genuinely embrace the feedback (no matter the source or the context) and use the parts that fit to create new ways of leading and doing in the future. A genuine desire to receive and a true sense of gratitude when you do receive feedback are critical elements of all conscious leaders. And you demonstrate your gratitude not only by hearing the feedback, but by answering any form of feedback with the magic words: *Thank You!* Even if they vehemently disagree with the feedback, conscious leaders are grateful to have it because at least they learn what the other person thinks and feels. This is invaluable information for any leader, especially in terms of managing relationships, teams, people and outcomes.

The Authenticity Imperative

On the road to conscious leadership, you will certainly encounter obstacles, challenges and setbacks, as well as confusing messages from other people and leaders that you respect. They will fling old thinking and clichés at you, all designed to keep you leading as it has been modeled for them.

- Never let them see you sweat.
- The key to leadership is a good poker face.

- Leaders must master the art of spin, especially to avoid looking bad when things go wrong.
- Leaders must always remain cool, calm, collected and in control.

No wonder so many people are looking for someone real to follow. No wonder so many organizations have a leadership hole with no one able to fill it. No wonder so many teams are disengaged, ineffective, lost or simply mediocre. Leadership can be and often is messy, filled with stumbles, falls and even crashes. If it were simple and easy to be successful, then everyone would achieve it.

People are tired of following pretenders and are looking for women and men who are willing to be themselves, no matter what the circumstances. It is easy for a leader to seem authentic when things are going well or right (often to accept the credit or perhaps to deflect the credit). Too often we confuse a leader's deflection of credit as a sign of their authenticity and willingness to share the glory, but this is often an act of misdirection (even if done unconsciously). Many leaders have learned that deflecting praise (at least publicly) is a way to appear to be humble and a team player, yet behind closed doors and when people are not looking, they model deflection of responsibility and false confidence (the "I've got this" mask). Fundamentally, conscious leaders are willing to let people see who they are, admit their mistakes, and acknowledge that they do not always have everything under control.

CHAPTER 4: LIVING INTEGRITY (THE SELF-ACCOUNTABLE LEADER)

"Continuously lying to yourself is just as fatal as suicide; only slower. Take ownership of your life, be accountable to you."

Noel DeJesus

Business books and consultants all emphasize the importance of accountability, yet it is an often misunderstood and misinterpreted concept that must be clarified for the sake of leadership and organizations. This same sense of urgency applies to your own personal self-leadership, which has the most impact on what you do, how you do it and what you create. One of the most fundamental misconceptions about accountability is that it relates to getting people to do things. In other words, you tell people what they need to do or should do and, *if/when they don't do it*, then you hold them accountable by delivering consequences. While consequences (of some form) may sometimes change behavior, the best way to sustainably change behavior and be effective in execution is to model and support others in being self-accountable *even (and especially) when no one is watching.*

There are several critical elements to integrating accountability in business and culture. First, it is critical to clarify what it means to be accountable and debunk the ways that we create easy outs from accountability. Second, we must deepen our understanding of the elements of accountability—clear commitments, personal responsibility and ownership of those commitments—and the ways in which conscious leaders model personal accountability and integrity. Indeed, our failure (or unwillingness) to equate lack of accountability with lack of integrity is one of the primary causes for our existing accountability crisis. When you embrace the reality that being out of accountability means that you are out of integrity, and therefore understand that choosing to honor your commitments (and thus be accountable) is the primary means for you to be in integrity, you will find the motivation you need to do whatever it takes to stay in integrity. Another positive outcome is that you will be more focused and intentional in making commitments, assessing your priorities and being clear about what it means to do whatever it takes.

Imagine the impact in our businesses, communities and lives if we created a culture of accountability, integrity and personal responsibility. Talk about a game-changing shift in thinking and doing! This is precisely why self-accountability is such a core trait (and indeed a commitment itself) for conscious leaders. Before we take the deeper dive into accountability, one foundational premise must be addressed: Accountability is ALWAYS a matter of self-accountability, not accountability to others. Lack of awareness and understanding about this fundamental truth is the most critical obstacle to becoming more accountable and creating greater accountability in your organization, team and personal life.

Yes, we often use the phrase that others will "hold us accountable," but the reality is that we are accountable to ourselves based upon the commitments that we make to others. I may make a commitment to someone else, but I am accountable to myself. It is my personal integrity that is on the line when I make commitments. While other people may deem me to be lacking in integrity when I fail to honor commitments that I make, it is MY integrity that is at issue. Therefore, accountability is always a matter of self-accountability. While other people can support me in being accountable, if I am relying on other people to help me stay in accountability (if they are doing it for me or taking on the responsibility to remind me), then I am not truly and fully committing, and I am not accountable.

For this reason, I and other conscious leaders speak in terms of asking for support with our commitments rather than abdicating the commitments and the accountability. Think about a common example of abdicating your personal accountability. You have made a commitment, but you ask someone else to remind you to do it. This certainly helps to make sure that you get it done and done on time because even if you forget, someone else is helping you to remember; however, who in this case is accountable? You made the commitment, but you are relying on someone else to remind you to do it. You have essentially asked another person to make a commitment to you so that you can honor your commitment. I am NOT suggesting that you should be on your own in honoring your stated commitments, and you absolutely can and should seek out support from others, but the key question is whether you are getting support or giving up responsibility for your own commitments.

If self-accountability is the opposite of blaming others, then what happens when you ask someone to help you stay in accountability with your commitments? The answer is that you have created a situation where you can now blame someone else for your own failure to honor the commitment. This is the differentiator between accountable, conscious leaders and unaccountable, unconscious leaders.

Similarly, if you actually need someone else to hold you accountable, then you are not really self-accountable. In my coaching work, part of my role is to provide accountability. The clients that I work with make commitments to engage in certain specific activities over a certain time period. The next time I meet or talk with them, I check in to see if they have honored their commitments. Many of my coaching clients admit, in the beginning, that they do the activities primarily because they do not want to admit to me that they did not do what they committed to do. In other words, my holding them accountable motivates them to do what they said they would do.

Do you see the problem with this model and thus the problem with any model that ultimately depends on people holding other people accountable? You guessed it—what happens when I am no longer there to hold them accountable? The answer: They go back to the same behavior of not doing the things that they know they need to do and should do. While teams and organizations can create short-term accountability, if people have to hold other people accountable for long (or even unlimited) periods of time, this creates a heavy investment of time and manpower in order to achieve what should be achievable without this investment—people doing what they said they would do and honoring their commitments. Holding others accountable also does not provide lasting results and is subject to failure at any time, especially when the person doing the "holding" is not there to prevent the failure.

> One reason that organizations do not do well with accountability is because they are attempting to create an accountability culture based upon holding others accountable rather than based upon personal integrity and self-accountability.

One reason that organizations do not do well with accountability is because they are attempting to create an accountability culture based upon *holding others accountable* rather than based upon personal integrity and self-accountability. Instead of relying on other people to hold you accountable or help you remember to do what you said you would do, try seeking support from others in being self-accountable (the conscious leader way).

Here is an example of the difference between getting help (abdicating) and getting support in a situation where you have agreed to complete a written report by 5:00 p.m. one week from today. Now let's consider two different approaches:

Abdicating Accountability: "Can **you** touch base with me on Thursday

| | to make sure that I'm on track to have the report done by Monday at 5:00? |
| Support for Self-Accountability: | "Can *I* touch base with you on Thursday to check in on my progress towards having the report done by Monday at 5:00 p.m.? |

See the difference? Both involve getting help with your commitment, but the first sets you up to blame someone else (even if unconsciously), while the second gives you support to stay in personal integrity by honoring your commitment. This is the way of the conscious leader.

Are you prepared to do whatever it takes to honor your commitments? Are you prepared to be self-accountable in your life and as a leader? Follow me and we will find out what it takes to claim and live this new way of leading.

Conscious Leaders Walk the Talk

One fundamental attribute of conscious leaders is that they walk the talk. Unlike leaders who talk a good game but walk a different one, conscious leaders make decisions, take action and show up in ways consistent with what they say they believe. The lack of congruence between a leader's words, beliefs and actions is at the heart of most of the disconnections and dysfunctions in organizations today. I often work with teams and organizations where the leader says that his or her team needs, for example, to be more accountable, yet when I meet with the team members, they are quick to tell me that the lack of accountability begins and ends with the leader. Why would a team change when their leaders are not modeling that which is being asked of the team? Answer: They won't. The team might pretend to go along with the change for a period of time, but they know that eventually things will go back to the way they were because the leader is not truly committed to any changes (because those changes would require the leader to change).

The Accountability Crisis

We are experiencing an accountability crisis, and it is taking a heavy toll on individuals, families, relationships, communities, teams and organizations. Sadly, a promise no longer seems to mean much to most people. We make promises, we fail to honor them, and it does not mean a thing. We do not care that we are not honoring promises and failing to do what we said we would do. To our individual and collective detriment, we say one thing and do another. We make promises, and we fail without even giving our commitment the effort it requires.

In 2013, I participated in a leadership program called *Whatever It Takes* (or W.I.T.), the premise of which is simple: Make clear and action-oriented commitments *to yourself*, work with a small group to support you in your personal accountability, and do *whatever it takes* to honor your commitments. In other words, it was an exercise in taking my commitments seriously so that I would not so easily let them slip. The W.I.T. program gave me a whole new understanding of what it means to make a commitment and what it means to be self-accountable with *no excuses*.

I made commitments in three key areas of my life, including exercise. Like so many people, I know that exercise and healthy eating are important ways for me to take care of myself and help me to be fully present and engaged in all aspects of my life. My health is the most important part of my life, since without that health and the energy I need, I cannot achieve the impact I want for my business and my life. Despite "knowing" the importance of exercise, I was not doing it and had not exercised much in the past couple of years. One thing I liked about the W.I.T. program was that it was activities-focused, rather than objectives-focused. In other words, while my physical goal included losing weight, my W.I.T. commitment was to a certain amount of aerobic exercise every week (30 minutes of aerobic exercise—walking, running, biking or rowing—at least three times every week). Notice how specific my commitment was, with no room for fuzziness, gray areas or waffling. In fact, I measured my exercise time using a stopwatch to avoid the slippery outcome of saying that I exercised for "about" 30 minutes. Conscious leaders understand and embrace the importance of this level of commitment clarity.

I was on target with all of my commitments through the first four weeks, but in week 5 I ran into a significant obstacle to my exercise commitment–pneumonia. While I could have continued to exercise with the pneumonia, I made a good choice not to exercise that week. Here is the interesting and critical point: I had a *really good reason* to justify not honoring my exercise commitments for that week. In fact, my W.I.T. group suggested that having pneumonia was a good enough reason to be able to say that I actually did meet my commitments, even though I chose not to exercise all week. I disagree, and conscious leaders would certainly disagree. Yes, I had a really good reason not to exercise, but the reality is that I still did not honor my clear commitment. That is the thing about accountability—it is black and white. If you make (as you must) clear commitments, then you either did it or you did not do it. There is no sort of, kind of or mostly, and there certainly is no place for "I had a good reason" that I did not honor my commitment. This black-and-white perspective is how conscious leaders view accountability–clear, concise and like the blade of a well-honed knife—in this case, the sharp edge of leadership.

Make no mistake; the clarity of a commitment does not mean that I will *always* honor the commitment. There are times that I consciously and knowingly choose not to honor a commitment or I seek to modify a commitment. The key is that when I make changes with my commitments I do so thoughtfully, purposefully and fully aware that I am not honoring my commitment (rather than telling myself a story or not even giving it a thought). We are all faced with conflicting commitments; however, if I am more intentional in making my commitments I will necessarily be more thoughtful to avoid conflicting commitments.

For example, recently I had a telephone conference scheduled with a business associate. We had agreed to the date and time for the call, and I respect his time and know that in scheduling time to talk to me he was likely choosing not to use that time for some other call or meeting. I am, therefore, very hesitant to cancel any scheduled call or meeting. However, when the time for the call came I was engaged in deep and important conversation with my son—a conversation that dealt with a significant issue in his life. In that moment, I thoughtfully and consciously chose to reschedule my call in order to remain fully present with my son. I did fail to honor my scheduled call commitment, but I did so in full awareness that I was doing precisely that—not honoring a commitment—and understanding that there might be consequences from that decision (even if unintended). I am not suggesting that you will never fail to honor a commitment, but if you are clear that you are making a commitment you will more consistently keep them *and* you will only abandon or adjust them thoughtfully and consciously.

Interestingly, several people that I talked with about not honoring my commitment due to my pneumonia (and my *choice* not to exercise) suggested that this was a unique situation because I did not have choices to examine. In their view, the pneumonia was an outside circumstance beyond my choices. I disagreed. My opportunity to grow in awareness and accountability was to examine the choices I made leading up to that week—choices that contributed to me getting pneumonia. I chose not to get enough sleep; I chose not to eat well; I chose to push myself to the point of getting ill. These are choices, and they led to me contracting pneumonia, which in turn impacted my ability (or inability) to honor my commitments. As we discussed in Chapter 2, choices are at the heart of our lives, our outcomes and our leadership.

Unfortunately, this type of what I consider razor's edge accountability is often lacking in our businesses, with our teams and in our personal lives. It would be good for all of us if a promise really meant something, but promises today often lack any real commitment, and people are all too often willing to *fail* to honor those promises. In my work with hundreds of teams, one theme is consistent—100 percent have listed lack of accountability as one of their top three challenges, and 80 percent of the time lack of accountability is listed as the number one improvement opportunity for the team and the organization. Number One! This evidence all further supports the reality that we have a significant accountability crisis in our culture and in our business world. Yet notably, accountability is something that you have direct control over because you have the opportunity to be personally accountable for your commitments.

In addition, you have the opportunity to help others be self-accountable. What I have found in my work with organizations is that the challenge is not that accountability does not work (i.e.

> Unfortunately, this type of what I consider razor's edge accountability is often lacking in our businesses, with our teams and in our personal lives.

that the organization practices holding team members accountable, but they do not comply). Rather, the organization, its team members and its leaders (it always starts at the top) are doing a poor job of "holding" others accountable (or failing to do so completely), often stating that they do not know how to do it and that they cannot hold someone else accountable that does not report to them. This belief is a fallacy, which we will cover in detail in Chapter 11. For now it is enough to know that we are failing at accountability, and the key to changing this reality is for leaders—conscious leaders—to commit to and model self-accountability at a whole new level of personal integrity.

Think about how easily you say "yes" to a request. Did you think about it before you said "yes" and thereby made a promise? Did you ask any or all of these vital questions before you said "yes"?

- Do I have time available to honor this promise?
- What other priorities do I have that might impact or be impacted by this promise?
- Am I prepared to do whatever it takes to honor this promise?
- What other thing or things am I saying "no" to in order to say "yes" to this thing?

And the big question that overlays all such promises is this:

Am I willing to put my personal integrity on the line to make this promise?

Most of us make promises without asking any of these questions, and thus we make unconscious promises without setting clear intentions to honor them. By definition, conscious leaders think through these and similar questions so that they (and the person to whom they are making the commitment) are clear about the commitment and the accountability.

Welcome Integrity

One differentiating trait of conscious leaders is that they understand the impact words have on behaviors, and one example of this understanding relates to the theme of *integrity* within accountability. Our culture today is one where promises are often viewed as nothing more than words—that a "yes" does not equate to a promise. I would hope and expect that any promise would be treated as important by the person making it and that the person receiving it could count on it, yet that does not seem to be the case. Think about how often and how easily people (including you) agree to a demand, a request or a suggestion. Consider the following examples of exchanges that happen every day both in the workplace and at home:

> Question: Can you get this report to me by tomorrow?
>
> Answer: Yes.
>
> Question: Can you call the client today and check in with her?
>
> Answer: Sure.
>
> Question: I need a draft of this to me by Friday morning.
>
> Answer: No problem.
>
> Question: Do you have 15 minutes to talk about the issues with the customer?
>
> Answer: Sure.
>
> Question: Can you get the garage cleaned out this weekend?
>
> Answer: Certainly.

Yes, these seem like fairly clear questions (setting of needs and expectations) with equally clear answers; however, they have come to mean much less than a commitment, and that is one reason that our accountability has become so loose or slippery (more on the topic of slippery below).

Here is where "integrity" comes in. The great thing about integrity is that it is something that people desire to be known for, something that other people want to see in a leader and something that we can control, mostly by becoming more purposeful about commitments, the meaning of integrity and the desire (demonstrated in actions) to be a person of integrity. Think about it–do you know anyone who wakes up in the morning and plans to be out of integrity during the day? Do you know anyone who has a daily goal to be out of integrity? Of course not. I have found that most people want to be people of integrity, and even people who appear to be willing not to honor promises will change how they think and their behaviors (by honoring their promises) when they see the promises as commitments and they understand that not honoring commitments sets them up as lacking integrity. The problem is that culturally we let people (and ourselves) off the hook all the time when it comes to promises.

While it may be only a matter of a word (integrity), its impact is much bigger; it is transformational when it comes to accountability. If you treated every promise you make as a commitment (and ideally you used the word *commitment*), then you would do so knowing and understanding that if you fail to honor that commitment, then you are out of integrity. That is a big difference, and it impacts how often and in what ways you honor your commitments. It also impacts the degree of effort you will invest to assure that you honor your commitments. If you knew that not honoring your commitment would create the reality of being out of integrity, how hard would you work to make sure you did what you said you would do? This is the way of conscious leaders, and conscious leaders also take the extra step of incorporating that word ("integrity") when they fail to honor a commitment. Here is an example of how a conscious leader would take ownership and responsibility when they fail to meet a commitment: "I am out of integrity. I committed to get this report to you by 5:00 p.m. on Friday, and I was late in getting the report to you."

While it may be difficult to fully tell the truth on yourself, this clear, intentional language of ownership changes everything for a self-accountable leader. It also proves itself as a powerful self-motivator to encourage people to be clear and purposeful in their commitments, do whatever it takes to honor those commitments, and avoid being out of personal integrity.

Conscious leaders understand that leadership includes giving people a reason to think and act in ways that further the mission and vision of the team or the organization. Even better than a leader giving a reason is when this reason comes from within the person. This is precisely the dynamic that is created when the reality of the relationship between commitments and integrity is injected into conversations and the accountability process. When personal integrity is at stake, two things change: 1. People take their commitments more seriously in advance (knowing that their integrity is at risk if they fail to honor their commitments); and 2. People are even more dedicated to the execution of their commitments in order to preserve their personal integrity.

Clear Commitments

Just as the injection of the word *integrity* enhances the engagement of the person making the promise, making the word *commitment* a part of your accountability process further deepens that engagement. While it would be terrific if all our promises carried the same weight with us as our commitments, that is simply not the case. We swiftly and unconsciously agree to do things or not do things without considering any of the implications of those promises. Everything changes, though, when we focus on *commitments* rather than on mere promises.

There are several key components of commitments:

- Use the term "commitment" with respect to your promises.

- Be clear in terms of exactly what you are committing to do (or not do).

- Be clear in terms of when or by when (timing) you will do what you are committing to do.

> Just as the injection of the word integrity enhances the engagement of the person making the promise, making the word commitment a part of your accountability process further deepens that engagement.

Without this level of clarity, there can be no accountability. When we proceed with mere generalizations or vague promises, it is impossible to hold ourselves accountable and even more challenging to hold others accountable. This is why conscious leaders are invested in clarity of commitments.

I was recently invited to join the board of an organization that I am already involved with. It was a great honor to be invited, but I had lots of questions before I gave my answer. I needed to know what they expected of me, as well as knowing everything that is involved in being a board member. Without this information I could not make an informed decision about whether I was willing to make the commitment. Part of my intentional process of decision making about commitments is that I typically do not make commitment decisions in the moment. When I make decisions in the moment, I tend to make unconscious decisions without considering my other priorities and commitments (short term and long term). This often results in unintended consequences such as conflicting or excessive commitments without enough time to honor them all. I also made it clear to them that I needed a couple of days to consider their invitation (and my response) because if I made the commitment, I would be fully engaged and committed. In my words, I would be IN! This whole process is part of being more intentional and conscious about my commitments.

When I work with teams and leaders, I often find that they are loose with their promises, unconscious with their commitments and unclear with setting expectations. When I ask people if they have set (required) or given (offered) clear expectations, objectives and commitments, they often tell me that they have not been clear. For example, a typical question I ask the parties to a supposed promise/commitment is, "What exactly was the agreement?" I am sure that you can guess what some typical answers are:

- What agreement?
- What do you mean by the agreement?

- I'm not exactly sure.

- In general it is ....

- My understanding was ....

Essentially, there was no clear agreement, no clear expectations and insufficient details and clarity to allow for any accountability, self or otherwise.

This is yet another example of a simple shift in accountability that can yield big rewards for everyone involved—understanding that when we make promises and commitments, we are entering into agreements. I know this is probably a new concept to most of you, but the absence of this understanding is an impediment to effective accountability for all. When you enter into agreements, you take them seriously. You think about what you are agreeing to, and you think about the consequences of your agreements. For more significant agreements, you may also seek outside input. Yet we often give little thought to the things that we are promising to do (or not do) and to how those agreements impact other agreements that we have already made. Are you getting the picture? Are you starting to get a feel for how elevating our reactive promises to thoughtful agreements can change the likelihood of having those agreements honored and thereby keep us and others in more consistent and predictable accountability?

Think about the impact in your business, with your team or in your life if you knew that you would consistently do what you said you were going to do. Imagine the impact if everyone on your team or in your organization could reasonably expect that every person's promises/commitments would be honored. Much of our personal and organizational ineffectiveness is the outcome of lack of clarity in commitments and our inability to rely on each other honoring our various commitments. Every time someone fails to do what he or she committed to, there is a likely snowball effect (short-term and long-term), the degree of which depends on the significance of the failure to meet expectations and how long it takes to get the commitment met:

- Execution is delayed (time that cannot be recovered).
- Team members lose faith in each other.
- Team members learn that they cannot trust each other.
- Team members fail to support people that have already let them or the team down.
- Projects lose momentum, stall or even fail.
- Organizational objectives are delayed, miss opportunity windows or fail.

On top of the foregoing, every delay in execution has a cost, and these additional costs can doom initiatives, projects and teams. The costs of ineffective execution (which also represents a failure of accountability) are not just incremental, but they compound and build upon each other. Too many leaders believe that the missing link in their organization is execution, but in most cases the true missing link is accountability. The opportunity to create a culture of accountability is why it is imperative to have more conscious leaders to change the face of teams, organizations and their execution.

In summary, the following are key ways to further wake yourself up as a leader, to enhance your personal and organizational accountability, accelerate your personal and organizational effectiveness and deliver consistent and predictable outcomes:

- Integrate personal integrity and self-accountability into your organization.
- Insist on clear expectations and commitments, by you and to you.
- Consistently think in terms of making commitments, not just promises.

- Treat your promises and those of others as agreements.

These are hallmark traits and practices of conscious leaders and their organizations.

Slippery On Purpose

What is the answer most often given when people do not do what they said they would do (when they fail to honor a promise)? No, it is not to hold people accountable. It is not to support them in changing their behavior to honor promises in the future. It is not to help them understand the impact of their failure to honor their promise. Sadly, the most often given answer is, "Don't worry about it" or "That's okay." We let other people off the hook all the time because we struggle to know how to hold them accountable. We also struggle to hold people that do not report to us accountable (I will debunk this obstacle—holding people accountable that do not report to you— in Chapter 11). Unconscious leaders also do this with themselves— let themselves off the hook—while conscious leaders treat every promise as a commitment (intentionally using the word *commitment*) and hold themselves accountable with a razor sharp edge.

After asking thousands of people this question—Why would I not hold others accountable?—I found the resounding answer to be, "It allows me to be unaccountable." Yes, we often fail to hold others accountable and let them off the hook from their own commitments because we do not want to be held accountable (now or in the future). While the thought of letting others off the hook to justify my own lack of accountability may initially be confusing, it is highly logical and rational—and almost always done at an unconscious level. If I make it "okay" for you to miss a deadline or fail to honor a commitment, then (logically) it will be "okay" for me to do the same in the future. We

> We often seek to avoid accountability to such a degree that we will not hold others accountable in order to create an environment where we do not have to be accountable.

often seek to avoid accountability to such a degree that we will not hold others accountable in order to create an environment where we do not have to be accountable.

This practice of letting others off the hook believing that it will give you a free pass from your own commitments in the future is called a *covert contract*. The "contract" is that *I won't hold you accountable if you won't hold me accountable*. It is covert because it is not conscious or thoughtful and the "parties" to the contract are not really negotiating it or even having a conversation about it—it just plays out. Unless and until you admit the drivers of your own behavior (even unconscious drivers), then you cannot change the behaviors. Only when you become more and more conscious of the drivers and thoughts that support your actions can you begin the process of shifting your thinking and owning your drivers, thereby allowing changes in your actions and behaviors. Understanding and owning the thoughts that drive your actions is the path of conscious leaders.

If you doubt this current and prevalent way of being, think about your reaction when someone asks you to make a clear and time-sensitive commitment. Clarity causes resistance in us for two reasons. First, there is now a definitive time deadline for you to complete the task or project, and most of us do not like this definiteness. Second, this clarity of commitment now makes you subject to being held accountable, and most of us do not want to be subject to accountability. Think back to the last time someone asked you for more clarity about a commitment. My guess is that your response to a request for clarity—when you were asked to make a clear and accountable commitment—was that you got a little hesitant and uncomfortable (or even resistant). If you are leaning towards being more conscious, this is the point where you might ask for time to think about it before you make the clear commitment. This is what conscious leaders do—they do not make accountable commitments unless or until they have been able to consider their existing priorities and commitments so that they can make the new commitment in integrity and with the full and *knowing* intention to honor the commitment. In contrast, the majority of our population today will simply agree, thereby making a loose promise without enough thought to have fully committed and thereby be clearly accountable.

At the beginning of this section, I used the term "slippery," and this is the most prevalent means that we use to avoid making commitments and thereby avoid being accountable. Simply put, slippery is what we are when we do things (or do not do things), sometimes consciously but most often unconsciously, that allow us to avoid being accountable. Most often, this involves making vague, loose or *slippery* commitments, which therefore are not clear commitments at all. One area in my business where I saw myself being slippery was around proposals or anything else of substance that I had to provide to someone else. Let's assume it is Tuesday afternoon of a given week, and a potential client asks me when I can get him a proposal. My typical answer would be "early next week." Obviously, I did not make a clear commitment because it is unclear when the proposal is due. Here are a number of reasonable possibilities for the due date:

- Monday
- Tuesday
- Wednesday at noon (what many would consider the middle of the week and therefore anything before that would be "early next week")
- Well, if it is not done by noon on Wednesday, what's the difference if it is by midnight on Wednesday?

See the many problems with this lack of clarity? I cannot be accountable because I did not make a clear commitment, yet I could fail to meet the potential client's expectations (because of my own lack of clarity) and thereby lose an opportunity, hurt a relationship or at least raise questions with the potential client.

As I became more conscious, I started to realize how I unconsciously kept things vague, so I started paying attention to it and changing my behavior. Specifically, I made conscious efforts to be specific about my commitments—even down to the hour—and I made this clear to the people to whom I was making the commitments. Instead of saying that I would get something to them by early next week, I would pick a date *and a time.* For example, "I will get the proposal to you by Tuesday at 4:00 p.m." This clear commitment set me up to be accountable *by choice* and helped me to be focused and prioritized in order to honor that commitment. While I still sometimes find myself going slippery, my personal and conscious commitment to clarity is proving to be the remedy for my own slipperiness.

In what ways are you slippery with your commitments and promises? Write down two or three ways in which you know you are already slippery (at work, at home or otherwise). Please be as specific as possible:

Now write down one specific thing that you can do differently in order to shift from slippery to self-accountable for each of your current *slippery ways.*

Conscious leaders are aware of and acknowledge their slippery ways in order to change those ways, thereby modeling personal integrity and self-accountability in ways that others will see and follow.

Personal Responsibility and Ownership

The last of the core foundations of self-accountability is personal responsibility and ownership—*of everything*! While some people see this level of personal ownership as being hard on themselves, conscious leaders embrace the idea that accountability, change in behaviors and ultimately changes in communication, relationships and outcomes all flow from a deep level of personal ownership and responsibility. They also embrace the idea that transformational change comes not from big steps, but from little acts and shifts which compound and build on each other. Thus, conscious leaders know that every little shift in accountability is a further sharpening of their leadership edge, which translates into profound impact on others and downstream. Conscious leaders also know that their people are not perfect, and more importantly, they know that they themselves are not perfect (far from it). Rather than look for outs, excuses or circumstances (or other people) to blame, conscious leaders step right into their own mistakes in judgment, choices and actions.

While many of us think that we are self-reflective and working on ourselves, conscious leaders take this thinking even further and put it into action in assessing everything—every situation and every outcome that does not go as planned or come out as hoped. This deeper self-assessment process is true even when another person is taking responsibility or other people are willing to put the responsibility (or blame) on outside circumstances or situations. Conscious leaders do not accept this even if it is partially true or substantiated because conscious leaders know that they cannot change or predict outside circumstances. They can change only themselves.

I believe in the power of questions—the right questions—to change our answers, our insights and our outcomes fundamentally. I also know that conscious leaders are experts at questions and use them in many different ways (see Chapter 11 for an in-depth discussion of the power of questions). With respect to self-accountability and personal ownership, the core question for conscious leaders is "What can/could I do differently?" As noted above, this is the "go-to" question even when someone else is taking responsibility for the situation or outcome.

Remember the leader in Chapter 2 that insisted on learning what he could do differently in the future even when the other manager took full responsibility for the miscommunication? Conscious leaders want to steer the conversation toward a more collaborative discussion of how mutually to avoid or minimize the situations in the future. The conscious leader thanks the other person for taking responsibility, but also insists that they explore ways that the leader can be different in the future. Conscious leaders know that communication is a two-way process and that therefore there will always be improvement opportunities on *both sides* of the communication. Conscious leaders invoke questions such as "In what ways could I be clearer in the future?" Can you see the difference—conscious leaders default to "I" and "we," while unconscious leaders default to "you" or "they."

> With respect to self-accountability and personal ownership, the core question for conscious leaders is "What can/could I do differently?"

The Accountability Imperative

Yes, we have a cultural and business crisis with a lack of accountability. We do not understand accountability, are hesitant to make clear commitments and actually avoid making commitments in order to avoid being accountable. We are not doing enough of the right things. We make unconscious promises without ever considering our other promises and priorities. We make promises and do not honor them. We rely on others to do what they say they will do, but they come up short—and we say it is okay. We fail to do what we say we will do, and it is okay. Are you getting the picture?

Conscious leaders, in contrast, embrace self-accountability as a new and more authentic way of living and leading. While we are currently experiencing an accountability crisis, there is a simple solution to the crisis. It may not always be easy, but it is simple.

- Commit to personal integrity.

- Be intentional with your commitments.

- Make clear and specific commitments.

- Embrace self-accountability with support.

- Beware of covert contracts and your own slippery ways.

- Inject personal ownership and self-assessment into your leadership.

The time is now for this shift back to self-accountability.

This is your crisis, and you have the opportunity to change things *for the better*. The shift to self-accountability is a shift that will make a difference in your business and in your life, and that shift happens as a result of small shifts in your thinking, in your consciousness and in your actions. As a conscious leader, are you willing to commit (clearly and unequivocally) to this shift to becoming consistently and predictably accountable? This commitment level will in turn create an environment where your modeling of self-accountability will certainly support and empower others to make that same accountability commitment and shift.

If you are so committed, then take the first giant leap in that direction right now. Write down the name of one person with whom you will speak and inform him or her about your commitment to self-accountability. Ask that person to watch and observe you and support you in this shift with direct and honest feedback about your level of self-accountability. In fact, if you want to make the leap even bigger, then pick someone from whom you are *least comfortable asking* for support, perhaps even someone

on your team or who reports to you. Who will you choose? _____
_____.

This is a great step into your own self-accountability—accountability in all things and in all ways!

CHAPTER 5: ACTION HERO (THE ACTIONIZED™LEADER)

"Remember, a real decision is measured by the fact that you've taken new action. If there's no action, you haven't truly decided."

Anthony Robbins

Several years ago I had the opportunity to sit down and speak with Nido Qubein, owner of several businesses, President of High Point University, corporate Board member of multiple companies, and highly sought after business and motivational speaker. After just a few minutes of learning and understanding how much Nido does and is involved with, I was exhausted. I thought I had a full schedule, but Nido's schedule made mine look easy. I could not fathom how he was able to navigate successfully his many commitments and a schedule that would tire most of us. He is engaged in so many different things that it is difficult to imagine how he even begins to manage them. Naturally, especially since I am the question guy, I asked Nido how he did it. While some of his answers were expected—focus, good time management, avoiding distractions, delegation, etc.—one of his key answers was profound in its impact. Nido's core comment was that he and his team are passionately committed to taking action and getting things done. It was that simple.

Nido went on to say that while strategies and plans are important, he does not want to hear any of the following from his team members:

- "We're planning to …"
- "I've got a plan to …"

- "We're hoping to …"
- "I'm going to try to …"
- "We're working on a plan …"

You get the point. Rather, Nido is primarily interested in hearing one thing from his team—what are they *doing*, what have they *done* and what *actions* are they taking? Execution, action, implementation, doing—that is Nido's preferred organizational language. Yes, even Nido would say that strategies and plan are valuable, but he knows that they can often replace, delay or block action. This focus on action is the higher realm of conscious leadership, where leaders are *actionized* (for themselves and in their expectations of their team members). Are you ready to get into action?

Actionized Leaders

If you have not seen that word before—*actionized*—you are not alone. You will not find the definition in any dictionary, nor will you find any generally accepted usage of the word. In this context, I created it to apply to and define one of the key elements of all conscious leaders. Conscious leaders are *actionized* because they live in a state of almost constant action. Yes, they think things through and ponder options, but they are self-aware of how easily pondering can become procrastination. Conscious leaders also deeply understand how easy it is for themselves and team members to get lost in planning at the expense of action and execution. They know that quick action can sometimes result in mistakes or bad decisions, but they better know and embrace this theme: *We often forget that not making a decision is still a decision—and it is almost always the wrong one.* Action wins every time, and conscious leaders know this and model it in and through their leadership.

Many years ago I was having breakfast with David Akers, who has since become one of my dearest friends. David is a serial entrepreneur and one of the most creative and innovative thinkers and problems solvers that I know. In short, David is an idea guy. He loves ideas. It was during our first

> Rather than focus on or worry about labels (e.g. great ideas), conscious leaders are zealously committed to turning good ideas into great outcomes.

breakfast that I said something to David that is now permanently stuck in his mind, almost to the point of being annoying. In fact, when I said this to David, he questioned it and almost got angry because it was contrary to one of his core passions—ideas. I shared an idea with David, and he quickly responded that he thought it was a "great idea." I then told David that I did not believe that there was any such thing as a "great" idea. When David naturally set out to defend the existence of great ideas, I explained as follows:

> "There are no great ideas. There are only good ideas that are actually executed and become great in and through their execution and implementation."

In fact, I still assert that labeling any idea as "great" is likely the kiss of death and may literally assure that it does not become a reality.

Think about it—when do the best or "great" ideas come up during a meeting? At the end of the meeting, when there is never enough time to discuss it, flesh it out and develop an action plan around it. Everyone talks about what a great idea it is and then when you meet again, you collectively discover that nothing has happened to turn that great idea into reality. What happens then? Do we develop the action plan and assign responsibilities to assure that it gets implemented? Of course not because, after all, it is a great idea and it will happen because it is such an amazing idea. Sound familiar? I see this phenomenon of the death of great ideas all the time with teams, organizations and even individuals.

Rather than focus on or worry about labels (e.g. great ideas), conscious leaders are zealously committed to turning good ideas into great outcomes.

They know that strategic plans have value and a place, but the biggest gap in any organization is not the lack of planning or a bad plan; it is the lack of execution (action) to turn the ideas, strategies and plans into outcomes.

I am a big movie fan, and this theme of action always reminds me of the movie *The Untouchables* (1987), starring Kevin Costner and Sean Connery. Several times in the movie, Sean Connery's character (Jimmy Malone) challenges Kevin Costner's character with this question: "What are you prepared to do?" In the movie, the challenge is about whether Kevin Costner's character (Eliot Ness) is willing to do what needs to be done, whether it is taking on Al Capone or avenging Jimmy Malone's death. For the longest time, I thought that the key word in this phrase was "prepared." Was he prepared to take it far enough? Would he follow through? Was he willing to match Al Capone's acts of violence with equal or greater acts of violence? I now see that while preparation and willingness is important, the "do" was even more important. As a leader, you can be prepared to do many things, but nothing changes or happens unless or until you actually *do something*.

If you have any doubts about the difference between intentions or decisions and actions, then consider the types of conversations that occur every day between friends, co-workers and partners.

Challenger:	"Why didn't you take the garbage out?"
Intender:	"I'm going to."
Challenger:	"Did you get the food for the party tonight?"
Intender:	"I'm planning to."
Challenger:	"Do you have the report for me?"
Intender:	"I'm going to do it tomorrow."
Challenger:	"Did you finish the proposal yet?"
Intender:	"It's on my to-do list."

Obviously, we do not have to look far or long to find hundreds of examples to highlight the difference between intentions or plans and actions with implementation.

Conscious leaders model doing and action in ways that everyone can see and personally experience. Think about leaders that you have known in the past. Did they "show" you decisiveness or did they demonstrate it through their actions? I am not suggesting that conscious leaders do everything, but their leadership is modeled through their actions. Just as they do with personal accountability and alignment, conscious leaders desire to be judged on whether their actions align with their words. If they make decisions, they want to put those decisions into action, either themselves or through empowered delegation. In most organizations, it is a short list of people that get to see decisions being made, but everyone can see people and decisions *in action*. Action is what people are looking for to be inspired and engaged. People do not care about how "great" the idea is; they want to see action, and conscious leaders are actionized for all to see.

Conscious Leaders Are Purposefully Actionized

At this point, I am guessing that you might have some challenges for me bubbling up inside you. One question you might have for me is this: "Jeff, are you suggesting that leaders and their teams should just run around and do things? Isn't that an even bigger problem resulting in lots of activity and not much productivity?" My answer is a little yes, but mostly no. Yes, activity for the sake of activity can be a horrible trap and create its own form of delay or execution obstacles; however, the concept of being *actionized* includes the additional element of purposefulness flowing from the heightened levels of being awake and aware that are inherent in conscious leaders.

In today's world, it is easy to be busy, and busy typically has no connection to productivity, effectiveness, profitability or satisfaction. The state of being busy is much like a drug—it makes you feel good (better than doing nothing), but it is often not purposeful or effective. Personally, I have been working at giving up the word "busy" for the past year, realizing that being busy was not moving me forward personally or professionally. Conscious leaders are very aware of the allure of busy (just doing) and instead focus on being purposefully in action—in other words, actionized.

This past summer, I was experiencing a rare feeling—stress. That may sound odd, but I am rarely stressed, and I will be talking about one of my stress reduction strategies later in this chapter. In this case, I was feeling stressed, and I felt overwhelmed with too many things on my plate. My initial response was to do more—just as I always do—and I began doing just that. The result: I was just as stressed and perhaps even more stressed. What? I was doing things, but I was not being purposeful with my actions and doing. I was falling into the trap of merely doing, rather than purposefully or strategically doing.

After a couple of weeks, I shifted gears. I looked at my many "to do" lists and realized that there were a lot of decisions needing to be made on my list—things that were lingering in my head and taking up space and time on my list and in my thoughts. I decided that I needed to make more decisions and take action, which I did. I started making decisions, got into action and started to feel less stress. I even started to tell people that the key was making more decisions, and I shared a new stress reduction formula:

Make more decisions + act on decisions = Less stress

In retrospect, however, I was not completely clear on what I was creating and experiencing. Yes, I was making more decisions, but it was the *execution* of those decisions that was reducing my stress. For example, one item on my list was to decide if I was attending a certain conference. I could have decided to attend, but only when I took action to implement that decision did the item come off of my list and therefore get out of my head. I could have made a long list of "decisions," but until I acted on them (got actionized) they would continue to occupy and even interfere with my thinking and my emotions. The stress started to fall away when I put my decisions into action—when I modeled being actionized.

Conscious leaders do not care what you have decided; they care about what decisions you have put into action. Likewise, conscious leaders do not talk about their decisions; they show you what they have done to actionize their decisions. Thoughts and decision in action is what engages people and teams. This is also what gets things (the right things) done and what creates change and new outcomes.

> Likewise, conscious leaders do not talk about their decisions; they show you what they have done to actionize their decisions.

Conscious Leaders Acknowledge Their Failures to Act

If you are like most people, you have some level of attachment to lists ("to-do" lists, project lists, etc.). If you actually love lists, then you might be one of those people who make lists and then add things to their lists (things they do that were not already on their lists) just so that they can mark them off on their lists. Do not worry—lots of people like you and me love this practice. While to-do lists, project lists and the like can be valuable, I have come to realize that there is a fundamental flaw in such lists, one that you must be aware of in order to avoid falling into what I call the "list trap."

Much of my business coaching work includes an element of accountability. My clients set goals (action goals) and make commitments to themselves (and to me), and I periodically check in with them to see if they have done what they said they would do. Simple, right? Perhaps not. I have discovered a blind spot of sorts with to-do and project lists, one that can actually keep you off course from your objectives and goals by giving you an "out" (an excuse for not completing tasks and not doing what you said you were committed to doing).

Here is how it typically plays out:

Jeff: You committed to follow up with Steve, and it was on your list of things to accomplish by this session. Did you get it done?

Client: No, but it's still on my list.

I would then ask questions about what may have gotten in the way of honoring this commitment, what choices the client made that interfered with getting it done, the impact of not getting it done, etc. A couple of weeks later, we have another session, and the same scenario plays out. The client did not get the item on the list done. This process can go on for a short or long period of time, but at some point I will challenge the client and suggest that he or she acknowledge not having done it and not intending to do it. I also suggest that he or she should probably remove it from the list.

It is amazing how much people will NOW seek to protect and preserve that item on the list. When I suggest removing it, question why it is still on the list or state that the client has failed to do it, I hear all of the "stories":

- No, I'm still going to do it. After all, *it's still on my list.*
- I will still do it. I have just been busy.
- I didn't fail to do it. I just have not done it yet.

Are you seeing what I started to see? The existence of the item on the list is an out on any accountability. The person also (through this subterfuge) does not have to admit having failed to do something that he or she said was important and had committed to doing. In this way, the existence of items on your "to do" or project list can actually inhibit the execution of those items unless you are willing to be honest with yourself about what you have not done.

At some point in time (and conscious leaders reach this conclusion earlier), you have failed to do something on your list and you must either decide to do it now or choose to take it off your list and acknowledge that you failed to do it, no matter what the underlying reason was for not getting it done. Conscious leaders are truth-tellers to themselves, admit their failures to take actions that they have committed to and then, most important, take that action or consciously decide not to do it. They know that gray exists everywhere, but they view actions (being actionized) as black-and-white scenarios. Do it or do not do it *on purpose.* You may fail to do something that you are committed to doing or that has already been decided, but be conscious and intentional. Otherwise, it is another example of failing to take action consistent with your commitments. Are you prepared to take such personal ownership and responsibility as a leader, in your organization and in your life? Are you prepared to be this internally honest? Are you prepared to acknowledge your failure and either get it done or decide to move on?

What Is the Next Action?

Conscious leaders also adopt (and encourage others to adopt) their own language of choice and leadership. Above, we discussed one of the challenges with "to do" lists, and another significant shortcoming of most lists is that they are project lists, not action lists. We could spend an entire book on this concept, but I will instead refer you to David Allen's book, *Getting Things Done* (2002), which offers an in-depth approach to productivity and stress reduction. For this book and point, I only offer you David Allen's different approach to "lists," observing that the trouble with lists is that they are project-oriented (which most people struggle with), not action-oriented. David invites a new phrase—Next Actions—

into the discussion, and conscious leaders are believers in this language (or their own version of it).

Rather than talking about or jotting down a long list of things to be accomplished (end goals, objectives or outcomes), the concept of "next actions" focuses solely on actions that need to be taken (specifically, the next action) to move any project, initiative or objective forward. While we all want to focus on getting the ultimate thing done, conscious leaders know that we get big things done or achieve objectives only by consistently, predictably and accountably taking the little actions that build up to and create the objectives or goals. Much like Nido Qubein's fanatical focus on what people are getting done and accomplishing, conscious leaders enlist "next action" thinking to assure that they and others are getting things done. "Next action" thinking also requires you to focus on true *action* items. If you cannot take action on something without the need for anything else (e.g. research, resources, input, thought, etc.), then it is not a next action. Only when you are down to raw action have you found the realm of next actions from which all outcomes erupt.

Try it out now. What are three actions you can take to move toward becoming or deeper into your journey as a conscious leader? Remember, these must be physical actions you can take, and thinking alone is not an action. If you need to think about something, then an action would be to schedule time on your calendar to think about that specific topic. Write three actions down now and include a definitive date by which you will take the listed action:

1. _____

2. _____

3. _____

Yes, in some ways the foregoing is like other time management and accountability ideas you have seen or read before, but here is the difference.

Conscious leaders literally adopt new words and language to support their own awareness and consciousness, and "next action" thinking is one example of this type of purposeful shift. In addition, conscious leaders ask others to support them to be accountable as leaders so that they are best positioned to remain in integrity for their decisions.

It may sound overly simplified, but that is just what you need—simple over complex—in order to get your teams, your organization and yourself back on track and make the right things happen. We have become a culture of people more comfortable with thinking about things (sometimes endlessly) rather than taking action. When we take action, we risk failure. When we think about things, we delay decisions and actions. Thinking about things is safe (or seems safe), while taking action *seems* risky. While thought is one element of decision making, it is only one element. And as we discovered above, decisions without action are nothing—literally.

Stress Is a Drug

Knowing how much we all love control, we can learn a valuable lesson from conscious leaders—a lesson that not only enhances our influence and control, but which also dramatically reduces or eliminates our stress. I have recently heard it said that there is good stress and bad stress, but I am not a believer. That seems to me like a theory designed to justify our stress so that we can stay stressed. Some claim that good stress helps us stay focused and maintain a sense of urgency, but conscious leaders embody focus and a sense of urgency *without the need for stress to get there*. Think about it—do you know anyone (including yourself) who has ever woken up in the morning and said, "I hope I have some stress today" or "I could sure use some more stress today so I can get more done?" I certainly do not because we all know that stress is something we want less of, not more of. If I have to get stressed to be focused and start acting with urgency, then I am out of control (of myself), and I am largely unconscious.

Consider it this way: If you need to be stressed (so-called "good stress") in order to be focused or to act with a sense of urgency, then you are saying that you cannot be focused and act with urgency *without stress*. In this sense, stress is your drug of choice, and it is addictive. We have become a culture of medicators. If we are overly stressed (so-called "bad" stress), we relax with alcohol or other drugs. If we have trouble sleeping (often due to stress), we take sleeping aids. If we are unhappy in our relationships, we self-medicate with alcohol, drugs, infidelity or pornography. We are a heavily medicated society and relying upon supposed "good" stress in order to be focused and effective is a part of the self-medicating mindset. Rather than relying upon the false truth of "good stress" to help you focus or get more of the right things done, instead embrace different ways of thinking in order to be focused and effective *without stress*. My inability to focus or act with a sense of urgency is the outcome of what and how I think (often about myself), and rather than medicate with stress—stress that will always spiral out of control—I choose to work directly on those things that impede my focus. This is precisely the type of inside-out growth that is at the heart of conscious leadership.

What is offered below is a simple formula that I use to accomplish these four things in my life and leadership:

1. Reduce or eliminate stress;

2. Make more, swifter and clearer actionable decisions;

3. Create more clear decision points for myself and for others; and

4. Embrace more tangible and impactful control for my business, my teams, my relationships and my life.

How does that sound? Would you like to have some of this as a leader and in living your everyday life? It really is simple, even if it is sometimes challenging. After all, creating what you desire involves taking personal responsibility and ownership of your outcomes, and this ownership creates the risk of failure and removes the option of blaming others or outside circumstances.

At a client team session, I made the comment that I rarely experience stress, and one of the team members sarcastically said, "Why don't you show us how to do that!" Up to this point, I knew that I was experiencing very little stress (even in the midst of setbacks and periodic chaos), but I had not yet figured out the "how" of what I was achieving. I instinctively told him sure, and then set out to share the solution with him and their entire team. The following formula is the outcome of that process.

The formula involves a few critical questions to ask yourself about every situation, challenge or opportunity that you confront. The most important and starting question is this:

Is it important?

Simple, I know, but most of the time we do not ask ourselves this question before we start down the road of trying to understand, solve, fix, change or stress out about whatever "it" is. In my work with clients, it often takes my outsider perspective and questions to help people see that the issue they are fixated on (and which is consuming them, their time and their psyche) is not important and not worth thinking about, let alone solving. Here is the truth: *not all situations or circumstances need to be fixed, solved or even given thought!* Conscious leaders understand this reality and are more discerning in the moment to avoid charging down rabbit holes to fix or change things that are not important (or not important enough) to warrant their valuable time and attention.

Our culture has evolved (more accurately devolved) into one in which we react to people and situations (almost always to our personal and professional detriment), without ever asking whether it matters enough for us to give it another thought. This is where conscious leaders learn to be cautious in seeking outside input because so many people will

> Our culture has evolved (more accurately devolved) into one in which we react to people and situations (almost always to our personal and professional detriment), without ever asking whether it matters enough for us to give it another thought.

tell you that you are justified in your thinking when you are being distracted by people and situations. One question that I ask myself and others when I am getting caught up in ruminations and ponderings: Why do you care? This question will stop you and others in your tracks so that you can make a choice (a decision) about whether to continue with it. When you answer this question (or cannot answer it), then it is time to put down the issue and let it be because *it is not that important.*

One typical outcome when I ask people this question is that they realize that they are burning time, brain cells, emotions and energy on a topic that is not important or, worse, relates to a situation or person that they do not even respect. Talk about a waste of breath and precious time—being upset, stressed or concerned about a situation involving an issue or a person that is not important to you. My questions will often get people angry with themselves when they realize that they have been wasting their time and energy on situations that are not what they appeared or which are driven by people who do not warrant the investment. Make no mistake, people are important, BUT we can also choose not to get caught up in other people's games. We do not have to accept what people try to give us to deal with.

Let's make this really simple: If a person, situation or challenge is not important to you, *then let it go!* Drop it. Leave it be. Do not pick it up. Do not accept delivery. And remember, not everything is important. When we do not do a good job at prioritizing, we fall into the trap of believing that everything is important, just with different degrees of importance. Conscious leaders are more discerning than that about importance and prioritization, knowing that at some point there are limits to time, energy and resources. They do not want to waste any of these on things that do not matter enough to take precedence over other priorities. You must also be careful not to fall into the trap of believing what appear to be the obvious answers to our questions of "Is it important?" and "Why do I care?" At first blush, many situations seem to matter because they are related to things that are important in your life—your business, your relationships, your family, etc.—but it is only when we go deeper to the next level of questions that we can assess if the specific situation itself is important (even if it might generally relate to a category that is important).

A perfect example is a person's job. Employees often tell me that they are hesitant to do or say something because they might get fired— the ultimate risk for an employee. However, when I turn the question back to them and ask, "Do you believe that you will be fired for doing something, saying something or not doing something?" nearly 100% say "No." In their heads (their initial reaction or thought), the risk of firing came right to the surface, but when they think about it even briefly, they realize that this either is not a risk or it is not the risk that they are really worried about. This is the difference between conscious and unconscious leaders—conscious leaders ask themselves better and deeper questions to understand more fully the upsides, the downsides and the relative importance of each topic or issue.

If the issue is not important, then you move on and let it go, but what if it really *is* important? What then? We then go to another simple question:

Do I control it?

This question may be a little more complex than the first, but the question is simply whether or not you have the ability to directly control the outcome, situation or result *on your own*. If so, you alone have the control, and you are not dependent on anyone else for help or support unless you need it or choose to ask for it. Using the language of conscious leaders, if you have ownership of the outcome (or the actions to move toward your desired outcome) then you control it. Hopefully, you know what is next if you control it—*Take Action*! This is where the Nike slogan springs to life—*Just Do It!* If you have the ability to control something directly and choose not to take action (or not to take swift enough action), then shame on you for staying stuck or not getting the different results you desire. You have no one to blame but yourself when you control things but choose not to take action.

Even worse, we sometimes choose not to take action and then complain and stress about the situation, challenge or outcomes. Talk about insanity—wasting precious time and energy (with stress or worse) when you have the ability to take action. There are no guarantees of results or outcomes—you may take action and not get your desired results—but stressing over situations where you have control while not taking action is the ultimate of unconscious living and leadership. If you are not prepared to take action that you have the ability to take, then drop the stress, worry and over thinking—just let it all go *by choice.*

What if you do not control it (directly and solely)? What now? Again, simple—you ask yourself one more question:

Do I have the ability to influence it?

This is perhaps the most challenging question because there are so many different ways that you can influence a decision or an outcome, yet it is still a question that you can and must answer. Failing to ask and answer this question is akin to choosing to take your business or your life off-course without a thought, and it can result in not having time and attention for things that are truly important to you because you are distracted by something that you may not even have the ability to influence.

Let us start with the easiest answer—no, you do not have the ability to influence the situation, decision or outcome. Things are now super simple—drop it immediately. If you do not have the ability to control directly or indirectly influence something, then it does not warrant another iota of your precious resources of time, energy and thought. Much like worrying about things that are not important, worrying about or working on things that you have no ability to influence is absurdly insane (both personally and professionally). I know you will find that you have at least some ability to influence most things, but if not, then let it go as soon as you can. Drop it right now. Conscious leaders are keenly aware of this reality and quickly drop things that they have no ability to control or influence *so that they have time and energy for things that they can control or influence.*

Now we are at the end of the process—it is important, we did not have the ability to directly and solely control it, but we have some ability to influence it. What now? We take action to lay the groundwork for a clear "yes" or "no" by whomever directly controls the outcome, knowing that we do not control the answer or the outcome. You may not like it, but if you do not control it, then you only (at best) have the ability to influence it. My research and experiences have shown me that most people (mostly unconsciously) do not set things up for a clear *yes* or *no*. Instead, the lack of a clear decision point is the bastion of people who want someone to blame, and so we rely on assumptions and past history or experience to conclude that things will not change, *so we choose not to do anything* except blame someone else or outside circumstances when things are not as we want them to be.

This is a common scenario that I encounter when I work with teams. They are quick to tell me what is not working, but when I ask them if they have done everything that they can to change things, their answers are fuzzy. Alternatively, they claim to have done everything that they can and tell me that the leaders won't listen or are not willing to change things. Not surprisingly to me, when I talk to the leaders they tell me that they have not been asked those direct questions. When I then go back to the teams, they tell me about prior experiences from the past and often with other leaders or decision makers (aka old stories) or just tell me that they "know" the answer will be "No." This culture of assumptive "no" is where I challenge the teams or any person, which is often why organizations invite me in to work with their teams.

I am not suggesting that problems, defects or missed opportunities are always the fault of one side or the other. In fact, it is almost always a shared responsibility, but if a team or team member has chosen not to take action to get the desired changes or different outcomes, then there is only one person to blame—the person or team that has chosen not to take action. This brings us to the classic definition of insanity, one that is often attributed to Albert Einstein: "Doing the same thing over and over again and expecting different results." If you are unwilling to take action to bring a question or an issue to a clear yes or no point for the person who has the direct authority to decide, then you are wasting yourself, your time and your psyche. This approach is crazy, and I do not hesitate to point out this absurdity to people or teams.

Here is an updated definition of insanity:

> Stressing over something that is not important, that you do not control or that you do not have the ability to influence (or that you are not willing to take the action necessary to influence).

Even if you are convinced based upon past experience that you will not get the answer or decision that you want, it is still a choice as to whether you take action to find out for certain. If you are not willing to take that action, then let it go. If you are prepared to take action toward a definitive yes or no, then take the action and get your clear decision. Conscious leaders seek out, create and support others in creating clear decision points in their businesses and in their lives.

You may be thinking, "Why would I or others choose not to take action toward a clear yes or no?" Once again, it is rather simple: If I do not take action towards a clear yes or no, then I can live with my assumptions, avoid taking the risks associated with the action AND blame someone else for the situation or circumstance that I do not like. This scenario is regularly played out with people and organizations. It is like a legal drug where you can avoid the risks but keep the blame card in your pocket. It is all too comforting for people, yet this approach does not change things. In fact, it almost guarantees that things will not change.

This is where courage becomes one of a conscious leader's pieces of armor. Conscious leaders would rather have a clear no (even at their own risk) than leave important unresolved things as they are. Additionally, if conscious leaders choose not to take action to create a definitive yes or no, then they drop the blame and worry and let it go by choice. Conscious leaders do not always take action (they are as imperfect as anyone else), but they acknowledge that what they do (or do not do) is the outcome of their choices. Thus, conscious leaders are always in control of the situation, of their response, their attitude and their stress (or lack thereof).

> Conscious leaders seek out, create and support others in creating clear decision points in their businesses and in their lives.

Are You Ready to Take Action?

We have now set the foundational framework for conscious leadership—awake, aware, authentic, accountable and *actionized*. All are critical ingredients for conscious leadership, yet the proof is in the implementation. The rest of this book is about two things: 1. Different ways of thinking *that you put into action*; and 2. Different ways of being *that show up in your actions*. All talk and no walk is not the way of the conscious leader, and your life and your business will change based only upon the new actions you take from your place of consciousness and purposefulness. If you have made it this far in this book, then you are ready—you are getting it and are open or even desiring to be a different type of person and leader. You are on the brink, but if you stop now, then the beginning of your journey was all for nothing. You can choose to stay as you are and to continue with the outcomes you have been achieving to this point in your business and your life. I honor your choice, but make no mistake—it is a choice, and you are at a critical decision point. It's time for a clear "yes" or "no." Are you in or out? If you are out, then put down the book and walk away from this new way of being. If you are IN, then strap yourself in, swallow the red pill I offered you at the outset, and let us take the deeper dive into you and your conscious leadership.

CHAPTER 6: STAND FOR SOMETHING (THE PURPOSEFUL LEADER)

"Doing the wrong thing perfectly is perfectly wrong."

Bill McDonough

The prior chapter focused on new, different and impactful ways of leading and living, but some of the biggest obstacles to these shifts are the beliefs you hold about yourself, about business and about life. The core of these beliefs is reflected in your stories, which are covered in the final chapters of this book; however, *what* you as an aspiring conscious leader believe and even *how* you believe will have a significant impact on your leadership effectiveness. Those old beliefs and stories often will either block your way or minimize your acceleration. In contrast, as you shift your beliefs and make the decision to have and live according to consciously chosen beliefs or values, then you create your own foundation for change and impact.

Critically, conscious leaders believe in something and are zealously focused on deciding what is right and then following through by doing and living out what is right. Conscious leaders are more focused on effectiveness (consistently and predictably getting the right things done to create impact) than on efficiency (doing things well or quickly). Conscious leaders have not only beliefs, but also values and personal missions that they live out every day in their words and, more important, in their actions.

Now that we have the foundational ingredients for a conscious leader (set forth in the foregoing chapters), we begin to explore the different ways of being that conscious leaders model and demonstrate. These are the things that show up in a conscious leader's behavior so that you can *see conscious leadership in action.* Much like the inside traits of conscious leaders we've already discussed, the new ways of being build upon that foundation and upon each other like the bricks in a building. Each trait or way of being is integrated with every other, so that they support each other, build upon each other and accelerate each other.

Not surprisingly, one of the first core traits of conscious leaders revolves around values, but these values play out in a clearer, more tangible and more actionable way in conscious leadership. Many organizations and leaders have or at least talk about values, missions and visions. Many people (including perhaps you) claim to have and talk about values or core values. Conscious leadership, however, takes these concepts to a whole new level in terms of priorities, aligning values, modeling values and integrated decision making. In this chapter, we explore what it means to live out conscious leadership with your organizational and personal purpose, mission and values—in essence, living and leading on purpose.

Right Over Best

A core identifier that makes conscious leaders different is that they are passionately committed to figuring out what is right before they figure out how to do it. They are passionate about the right thing, including the why of what they do and the purpose behind what they do. The purpose, the why and their rightness are not just parts of their strategic plan—these are the essence of what they do and who they are. The strategy and tactics follow all of that. Conscious leaders start with what is right—always! Think about this fundamental shift to doing first and foremost what is right (which is often not about right or wrong, but more about values and alignment), rather than what would traditionally be called "best."

Conscious leaders understand that the best solution, direction or action includes and is actually guided by what is right—for a person, a team, an organization and for a leader. Conscious leaders also deeply connect with the reality that doing what is right typically also has significant intended and unintended consequences

> Conscious leaders understand that the best solution, direction or action includes and is actually guided by what is right—for a person, a team, an organization and for a leader.

beyond the decision, the team and the organization. Thankfully, more organizations today are being intentional in supporting community initiatives, but conscious leadership goes much further than merely making donations or even volunteering. This model invokes the mantra that doing right (and thereby doing good) creates positive impact far beyond narrow decisions, strategies and tactics.

That is the challenge and opportunity of fully stepping into and becoming your own conscious leader. It is not a part time job, a sometimes tactic or flavor of the week or month. Conscious leadership is a personal commitment, especially when it comes to values and purpose. Certainly, none of us are perfect in our consciousness or our leadership, but conscious leaders are intentional about the path they choose and purposeful in choosing to live as a conscious leader each day (not just talking about it or doing it only when it is easy or convenient).

Does this mean that conscious leaders *always* do the right thing? No, they do not. Sometimes even conscious leaders go unconscious or get off-course with their thinking, decisions and actions. There are also times when conscious leaders choose a path that is not fully aligned with their values, "why" and purpose. The difference with conscious leaders, however, is that when they decide to stray from what is right, they do so awake, aware and conscious that they made a decision. It is not an unintended consequence of some other decision or choice. While there are always variations on the theme, conscious leaders go through a step-by-step process that looks something like the following:

- What is the situation, opportunity, challenge, problem, decision or choice?

- What are our core values, personal why, mission and purpose?

- Does the proposed solution, strategy, choice, tactic, path or decision align with our values, personal why, mission and purpose? If yes, then full speed ahead.

- If not, then choose a different path *unless there are compelling reasons to proceed or take action outside of our core values, personal why, mission and purpose* **AND** I (the conscious leader) am willing to be personally accountable for the decision and the outcomes.

Wow—now that is a difference in assessing, prioritizing, choosing, deciding, acting, being and leading.

How many people do you know—maybe you yourself do this—who are constantly focused on getting things done or getting better at things? Of course, most of us want to be more effective and more efficient. How many companies talk about, "We're going to be fearless or flawless in our execution," but do they ever ask the question *why? What are they doing and why? What is the right thing to do, what is the right thing for them, what is the right thing for the organization?* Conscious leaders live in alignment. They figure out what they believe, and then they make sure that their actions and their words align with those beliefs, or they consciously choose not to be in alignment, knowing the potential outcomes and the slippery slope that this creates.

I once had the opportunity to hear a speaker who, as my dear friend Tom would say, "singed my eyebrows." Within a few minutes, he had me hooked into a new way of thinking. His name is Bill McDonough, and some people would call him a sustainability expert. Not even close. To call him a sustainability innovator is to damn him with faint praise. What this man is doing with sustainability is flipping the whole model.

The first thing he said that resonated with me was this: "The problem with sustainability is it's all about making things less bad. And making something less bad is not good." Wow! There's a paradigm shift.

And then he said this—I wrote it down and I will never forget it: "Doing the wrong thing perfectly is perfectly wrong." Bam, that perspective hit me like a ton of clarity bricks. I thought about myself. How often do I get caught up in what am I going to do, my to-do list, my goals, etc.? I have to get better, more efficient, more consistent and more effective. Yes, these are important, but am I doing the right thing? Am I being who I am meant to be? Am I living what I claim to be, which is awake, aware and conscious?

Check in on these questions with yourself. Amidst all of your thoughts, planning and efforts towards getting better at what you do or how you do it, are you giving thought and effort to who you are, who you choose to be and how you choose to live? How often do you think about and assess your core values? Do you even have them—written down—so that you can quickly and confidently recite them and use them in making daily decisions? Conscious leadership is not just about the big stuff and the big decisions; it is actually more about the little things and little decisions you make every day, the daily choices you make that define who you are and what you stand for. In fact, what do you stand for? More specifically, do you stand *for* anything? If you cannot immediately articulate what you stand for, then perhaps you do not stand for anything.

When you make decisions, do you first determine what is right? Is your focus on the right things, values and purpose, or are you narrowly focused on getting better and making better decisions toward your personal or business objectives? Conscious leaders lead with what is right. Rather than focusing on doing things well, conscious leaders commit to *getting it right* and *then* figure out how they will do what is right very well. When I started my first job many years ago, one of the senior people had a quote on the wall that I still remember to this day:

"Do what is right and let the consequences follow."

This is the mantra of conscious leaders. Traditional leaders tend to focus on the consequences (the desired outcomes) and then design a strategy and tactics to achieve those consequences. Conscious leaders are committed to the rightness and alignment of their decisions and actions, often allowing the strategies and tactics to flow from the rightness and alignment. In addition, conscious leaders understand that in many cases different and better outcomes and consequences can be created when you start with what is right and good. Being committed as much or more to doing what is right than to outcomes is the path of the conscious leader.

Conscious Leaders Start With Why

Without using the words *conscious leadership*, best-selling author Simon Sinek speaks directly about this core trait of conscious leaders. In *Start With Why: How Great Leaders Inspire Everyone to Take Action* (Penguin Group 2011) and his highly watched TED video, Simon makes the case that the key difference between great companies and leaders and everyone else is clarity about their *why* (their purpose) and commitment to living out that why as the driving force of innovation, team engagement, customer attraction and retention, and business success. He also argues that the same is true for individuals as leaders of their own lives. Citing business success stories and community impact stories, Simon demonstrates that organizations that start with why (at the center of their business model) excel and surpass all the rest.

Simon Sinek also validates the concepts we have already discussed about alignment and commitment to what is right in having core values and beliefs and modeling them as leaders, personally and professionally. He defines the "WHY" as follows:

"Very few people or companies can clearly articulate WHY they do WHAT they do. By WHY I mean your purpose, cause or belief—WHY does your company exist? WHY do you get out of bed every morning? And WHY should anyone care?"

What about you? Do you have a personal "why" that resonates to a level that it inspires you to keep going even when the going gets tough? Does your organization have a core "why" that is at the heart of every decision, strategy and tactic? Are you or your organization vested in a "why" that you will protect and preserve against all challenges, internal and external?

If you are feeling like "the Why" is a big concept, then you are getting it. Clarity on and commitment to your "Why" is a game changer and a difference maker for you in your life and for your organization. How big is it? It is THE thing. As Simon urges,

"People don't *buy what you* do; they *buy* why you do it.

And what you do simply proves what *you believe*."

Are you visualizing this concept? If you have a core why and build your actions or business around that why, then the why (what you believe) will be visible to everyone. Transparency in action!

This type of commitment to a why and *living it* goes far beyond a strategic plan, a mission or vision statement and a rah-rah planning retreat. Most organizations (but not all people) begin with some sort of mission, vision or purpose—and perhaps even a why—but most let their why fall to the wayside. Great leaders and great companies do not let that happen. In fact, it cannot happen if you keep the why (and everything related to it) at the top of your mind and at the forefront of your planning not only every year, but every day. Indeed, if you are not invoking your why every day, you are missing opportunities and perhaps allowing your why to slip out of your business model completely.

> Clarity on and commitment to your "Why" is a game changer and a difference maker for you in your life and for your organization.

Maintaining your organizational why takes a commitment from the leader and from the team. It is easy to let things slip, especially once things are working well or when things start to get off-course. When things are going very well or when they first start to unravel is when the risk of being or going unconscious is the greatest. During challenging times, it is easy to fall back into a reactive mode and do what seems to be the easiest or the quickest solution. Conscious leadership, however, does not take any more time, only more attention and awareness and courage—courage for the person with the title "leader" and, often more important, courage for the people *without* the title to raise their hand and say, "Wait a minute. Is this the right thing? Is this consistent with our values and our why?"

What is your personal "why" important? This need for a clear why is just as pressing for you and for every individual, not just business owners, organizational leaders, managers and others with leadership titles. You need to have a why in your life, something that inspires you to make the most of every relationship and everything you do. In fact, no need to stop with a personal why. You can and should also have a personal mission statement—a clear statement of your mission in life. I did not have a personal mission statement until a few years ago, when I attended a retreat weekend hosted by the Mankind Project. My personal mission has evolved a bit and gotten clearer, and today it stands as follows:

> I co-create a world of people healing themselves, both through
> my storytelling and by modeling authenticity, vulnerability
> and unconditional love.

This personal mission is at the core of my business (integrated and aligned) and my personal life (part of my core values). And my WHY: To help people be and achieve all that they can and were meant to, personally and in business.

Having a personal mission statement and why then allows me to ask several critical questions to assess (at any time) if I am on course or off course:

- Am I living my mission and my why?
- Is this decision in accordance and alignment with my mission and my why?
- In this moment, what does it mean to live my mission, why and values?

Without a why and a personal mission statement, you cannot assess your life or your path. You have nothing to measure against, and you are left to ask vague questions such as "How am I doing?" But how are you doing against what measure and compared to what?

Your personal and organizational why has nothing to do with winning or beating someone else. It has everything to do with meeting or exceeding the guidelines of your own inner compass (your why), even as you raise that bar throughout your lifetime. You are your own competition, and conscious leaders not only understand this but model it in their leadership. You can do the same as the leader of your own life.

A couple of summers ago, I read Walter Isaacson's biography, *Steve Jobs* (2011). As I went deeper into the world and mind of Steve Jobs, I discovered that at the core of it all was clear purpose and passion. From the beginning, Steve Jobs and Apple set out to create and define the future— not to follow trends or even customer demands. When asked whether Apple had done market research to determine customer wants and needs, Jobs said that customers could not know what they wanted when it did not yet exist. Steve Jobs and Apple were committed to creating things that didn't exist. This clarity of purpose was fueled by Steve Jobs' personal and infectious passion for creation. This was the core "why" for Steve Jobs and Apple, and it served and continues to serve as the catalyst and foundation for Apple's relentless pursuit to create and deliver the future.

What about you or your business? Do you have a clear purpose or "why" for your business and what you do? Are you and your organization dripping with passion to live the purpose and make your "why" a reality? Do you have a clear personal "why" and purpose?

You are probably wondering or asking why then, if having a clear "Why" makes so much sense and is so impactful, don't more people have a personal mission and "why?" Two simple reasons: 1. Many people are not yet ready to be, or do not know how to be, conscious as a leader; and 2. Even more people do not want to take personal responsibility and accountability for their lives. A majority of people also do not want to be responsible for the outcomes in their lives and prefer to blame other people and outside circumstances. As we discussed in the initial chapters, once you wake up and commit to being accountable, you are abandoning excuses and blame. You are putting away the victim blanket, perhaps forever. If you think I am being harsh and judgmental—tough. It is time for more truth telling in our culture.

The good news is that if you are reading this page in this book, then you are not one of those people who want to ride out their lives at the whim of circumstances. You are here and now reading this section because you are hungry for something more and different in your life, for your business, your teams, your relationships and your family. I recently heard a sermon where the pastor offered the perspective that if you are not hungry, you will not do what it takes. You will not be willing to be unconventional. You will not take action to change things. In short, if you are not hungry, you will not change. We are still in the beginning of what it means to be and live as a conscious leader, and I ask you: are you hungry for something different in your life and in your business?

Peter Finch's famous line in the movie *Network* (1976), "I'm mad as hell and I'm not going to take this anymore," has always spoken to me— especially in the past several years. I am just as mad about how we are living and leading, and I am hoping that you are tired as well. My hope is that you are tired and fed up enough to change things, to choose to be conscious in your organization and, even more important, in your life. Take responsibility. Take action. Wake up and lead your life!

Bringing Values and Why to Life

We have already alluded to it, but one essential element of a conscious leader's commitment to doing what is right is putting it all in action (all the time). There may be times when a conscious leader knowingly takes a different path, but the key word is "knowingly" and after carefully balancing a wide range of factors. Most critically, this means balancing the fact that veering away from your core values and why is often a slippery slope toward being permanently or dramatically off-course (as opposed to a single decision that goes a different direction). Conscious leaders are aware enough to build their decision-making process around their values and their why in order to assure that the values are at the heart of any planning, strategy or tactics process. In this way, you can assure that your values and your why are always the foundation of your decisions.

> Conscious leaders are aware enough to build their decision-making process around their values and their why in order to assure that the values are at the heart of any planning, strategy or tactics process.

In fact, when conscious leaders are tempted to stray from their core values and whys, even if the circumstances pushing such a decision are compelling, they then assess whether the core values or why still fit for the organization. The same is true for you as the leader in your life. While values may not change, their meaning may change as part of your personal journey. In addition, the values may have different priorities or you may come to a different understanding of them for you and for your organization. In any event, keeping core values and whys at the forefront of any strategy or decision is one of the key roles that conscious leaders will play for an organization or team. It is also a vital role that you must play in your own livingship.

To understand what it means to live your values and your why, let us start with an example of ways that organizations do <u>not</u> live them. Some time ago, a client of mine, a large organization, had undertaken an internal team survey to assess how the teams were performing, working together and getting things done. The first question on it related to whether or not the organization's three core values were widely understood and used as guidelines for the business. The team members' discussion of this question yielded the following comments:

- "I thought there were four core values"
- "What are they again?"
- "We used have them hanging up around the building, but I haven't seen them for a while."
- "I don't remember them being discussed in a meeting for a long time."

Can you guess how the teams rated the organization's use of the values in their business? Obviously very low, but the organization was surprised at the results because the leadership team thought that the values were featured in the business. We could talk at length about how this might just be a difference in perceptions, but the core difference is between having values and *living values*.

The organization and the team members mostly knew the values, but they were not integrated into the business operations. They were not regularly talked about and not typically referenced or relied upon in making decisions. Living your values in an organization requires that they be regularly discussed, understood and utilized in planning and decision making. When it is time to make a decision, do you go to your values in order to make those decisions in accordance and consistent with those values? While choice is always at the heart of conscious leadership, living out organizational and personal core values almost takes the choice out of it because choosing not to honor the value means choosing not to be the person or organization that those values represent. There will certainly be times when it is not fully clear which course of action best aligns with your values, but most of the time you will have that clarity, and you must rely on your own personal courage to choose a course that aligns with your values.

One quick test of personal or organizational core values is if they are written down and whether you can easily and fluidly reference them in a way that tells everyone that they are real and that you are committed to them. I am talking about integration of the values beyond memorization, which is demonstrated when your values are supported by real life examples that show the values in action. Another way to test your values is to envision someone asking you this question:

> Can you give me an example of how you put this value into
> practice (personally or in your business)?

Many organizations have values but cannot articulate examples of those values in action. This misalignment exists when organizations do not use the values to make decisions, do not invoke the values in discussions and processes, and do not have an expectation that the values will be living and breathing throughout the organization, its teams and its people. Whether it is at the beginning of a meeting/discussion or at the end of the process, organizations with truly integrated values will always assess in what ways the proposed course of action fits (or does not fit) with the core values and will also seek out and develop courses of action that align with the core values.

If you had asked me over the course of my life whether I had values, I would have naively said yes, believing that I was generally a good person. In truth, there were many ways in which I was not a good person, but that is a discussion for another place and time. The problem was that such general descriptors as *good, principled, ethical, honest*, etc. are not really values, especially when they are not front and center, written down, consciously invoked, and supported by day-to-day examples. Business and life may be complex, but not so complex that your core values cannot be invoked every day for big and even small decisions and choices.

My path to my own core values took many twists and turns, but the path is less important than the outcome: five core values that I use in my life almost every day to make decisions and choices.

1. **Authenticity**–Being who I am and showing up as who I am without pretense, including speaking my truth to clients and people in my life;

2. **Vulnerability**–Being open about who am, what I have been, what I have learned about myself and who I choose to be;

3. **Integrity**–Telling the truth, living my truth and aligning my words and actions with who I have chosen to be as a man, as a business owner, as a father, as a friend, as a partner and as a member of the community;

4. **Fully Present**–Being fully present in every interaction with another person, in person, on the phone or otherwise, so that I can listen deeply and differently as I focus on that person, who they are, what they are saying and how I can help; and

5. **Unconditional Love**–To engage with and interact with people from a place of unconditional love and without judgment on who they are or who they should be (accepting them as they are, even while challenging them to take a look at who they are and where they are).

These are not platitudes or pronouncements. I know them and I integrate them. I go to them when I need to make decisions, whether big or small.

If I need to have a difficult conversation that I am hesitant to have because of how someone might react to or mishear what I have to share, I ask myself, "What would an authentic person do in this situation?" If I am hesitant to be honest with someone about something important which is impacting our relationship, authenticity and integrity dictate that I have that conversation. When I am worried that my listeners might judge me or even reject me if I show them or tell them too much about who I am, how I am feeling, etc., my commitment to vulnerability guides me towards being open and vulnerable despite the risks.

Recently, a friend asked if I would be open to a question, to which I responded that I was and that I would answer the question honestly. I told them that I felt that I had no choice but to say yes because of my core values. When they challenged me—noting my belief that everything is a choice—I responded, "I do have a choice, but my core values dictate that choosing not to be authentic and in integrity is a choice not to be the person I have chosen to be." I integrate my core values and model them in the world when the values are front and center in my communication, my decisions and my actions, both in business and in my personal life.

Take a moment now to think about your core values–what they are or what you would like them to be. This will not be your final list, but just a start into the process of consciously choosing and committing to core values that will guide you as a person and as a leader. List all of the values that come to mind in terms of how you choose to be or would like to choose to be and live. Do not write out long phrases or sentences–keep it simple, knowing that you know what each one means or you will by the time they have become committed values.

Core Values

_____

_____

_____

_____

_____

_____

_____

_____

Once you have this list, the next step is to take your probably extensive list and circle 8–10 words or values that are the most important to you.

Now comes the hard part, but the most important part. Take your circled words or values and narrow them down to 3-5 words. Reducing your listed values down to 3-5 most important ones will be difficult, but it models the thinking that if you stand for too much, then you stand for nothing. It does not mean that you will not live and model the other values, but it does recognize that clarity and conciseness matters when it comes to values that you will use as a guidepost in life and business.

If you are wondering about having separate personal and professional values, believing that they are different, then think again. You are one person, and you as that person show up in your life and in your business. Yes, your business might have different values that are the center point for the business, but your personal core values are applicable for you both in business and in the rest of your life.

Now that you have your short list completed, the next step is to ponder it, refine it and define it. What does each value mean to you? Do not go to the dictionary. The inquiry is not about what the world thinks a word or value means, but what it means to you. Frankly, your values are no one else's business; they are for you and to be used by you, not someone else. Spend some time sitting with these values. Think through what they mean to your deeper self. Do not pick values and meanings that you think will help you be more successful, for those would be false values. Values flow from the truest part of yourself, even if they are aspirational values (i.e. you are not currently or fully living them now, but you are choosing to live them). You do not have to wait until you fully live the values to have them as values, but you do need to be prepared to tell yourself the truth when you are not living in alignment with those values.

This introspective process should also involve thinking through examples (again, for you) of each listed and soon-to-be-claimed value.

Think about some real-life situation when you modeled that value. Think about situations when you did not model that value. Imagine some current situations you are dealing with and how each value would guide you in how you deal with, handle or navigate that current situation. You can and should continue to refine your values and their meaning over time, but I encourage you to adopt fairly quickly (in the next 7 days) a working version of your core values. Start using those values to make decisions and choices, both personally and professionally.

Here comes the scary part: Share these values with people that are close to you or who work with you. Let them know what you are working on for yourself and as a leader, and ask for feedback from them. Tell them you want to know when they see you modeling the values and when they see you off-track from the values. Invite them to ask you questions– even challenging questions–so that you can move toward and into the conscious leader that is already inside you. This act—sharing with others from a place of authenticity and vulnerability–is the way of the conscious leader, and it requires a type and degree of courage that is missing in our culture and organizations. Still, it is time for a change, and the time is now for a new type of leader, a conscious leader who is committed, aligned and willing to model that leadership in an open and authentic way. In other words, *on purpose.*

> This act—sharing with others from a place of authenticity and vulnerability—is the way of the conscious leader, and it requires a type and degree of courage that is missing in our culture and organizations.

As we close this chapter, I am guessing that you are asking yourself a question: What about strategy? Every business leader, book, workshop and training in the past 100 years has included critical elements for having a strategy and a plan (tactics and action). Where does strategy fit with doing what is right in alignment with mission, purpose, values and whys? The answer is simple: Doing what is right is like an overlay on the strategy! Doing what is right or acting on purpose is not a tactic or even a section of the strategy. The strategy must evolve from and around what is right, around the why and around the core values. The strategy for a conscious leader is innately aligned with the why, and the implementation tactics and actions must also be so aligned.

Are you getting the picture? Visualize your business or life strategy laid out before you on a table and then imagine pulling over top of it a transparency (pun intended) of your organizational or personal why, purpose and values. Once it is overlaid, you can see whether the strategy aligns or does not align. The why and the values are there at the beginning, the middle and the end of any decision-making or planning process, whether it be strategic or tactical, short term or long term, problem solving or opportunity pursuing. They are always there and will always remain there. By keeping your values, why, mission and purpose at the forefront, and aligning your strategies and tactics with them, you will be deciding, choosing, living and leading on purpose.

CHAPTER 7: EXPONENTIAL BELIEVING (THE POSSIBILITIES LEADER)

"The art and science of asking questions
is the source of all knowledge."

Thomas Berger

In the old way of leading and being, leaders sought to be visionary. They were known for their abilities to be strategic and develop plans for their team to execute. Leaders were also tasked with empowering and engaging their team behind the shared and common vision, yet the vision was often created without most of the team members participating. Team members were asked to share a vision that they had no role in creating. Today's new leaders—the conscious leaders—have all of these good traits, but they also nurture and develop their ability to be exponential thinkers. This exponential thinking in turn arms conscious leaders with a different way of being—an advanced and more conscious form of thinking out of the box—that helps them to navigate challenges, expand their range of potential solutions and move past the old stories that often hinder leaders, whether in business or in life.

Conscious leaders must shift their thinking and even their beliefs about how they think, create and understand. This chapter is an invitation to expand your thinking beyond the incremental and to embrace an expansive approach to business and life. Rather than seeing the world with a scarcity mentally, conscious leaders create, decide and execute with an abundance mentality. Another important shift is away from easy answers and towards questions as the best way to get better answers and outcomes. Conscious leaders are also committed to letting go of ways of thinking, deciding and leading that limit choices and opportunities. What follows are inside-out shifts in mindset that will unleash your inner leader.

Changing the Way You Think About Everything

You know the old saying: *fake it until you make it*. The premise is that if you pretend that you think a certain way or are a certain way, you will create that reality in your mind's eye, and then your actions will follow what you were faking. My experience and my observation of many people who are utilizing this approach is that it generally does not work. The problem with faking it is just that—you are faking it, and that does not create sustainable changes in behaviors or thinking. If you do not believe in or agree with what you are doing and thinking (or pretending to think), then you will likely lose momentum and go back to doing things the ways that you have always done them. Instead of faking it, the best path is to change the way that you think–to shift your thinking (sometimes in profound ways) to test and challenge theories, premises, perceptions and perspectives.

While leadership is often associated with strategic, blue ocean and visionary thinking, conscious leadership is an invitation to exponential thinking and believing—thinking that is not only different in and of itself, but which also creates more influence for the leader and more impact for the organization simply by virtue of the shift in thinking. Critically, this different thinking must be founded upon something, and that something is your beliefs—beliefs that are at the core of who you are. The trouble with thinking alone is that it is by definition limited to the logical capacity of our minds. Conscious leaders have come to understand deeply that what and how we think goes (or should go) far beyond our logical and rational capacity. Vision is beyond our mind. Dreams are beyond our thoughts. Possibilities are beyond what we can conceive in our minds alone. I am talking about the alignment of our thoughts, our values, our intuition, our emotions, our feelings, our guts, our spirits and even our souls. Enter *Exponential Believing*!

If you want to learn about leadership, life and exponential believing, study Albert Einstein. If you had suggested this to me two years ago, I would have said that you were crazy, and I would not have listened to you. Einstein was a scientist—brilliant, but still a scientist. I was reading the brilliant business minds like Jim Collins, Jack Welch, Tom Peters, Patrick Lencioni, Malcolm Gladwell and Seth Godin. I wanted to access the wisdom, insights and perspectives of the great business minds, not those of a scientist. Now, two years later, I understand Albert Einstein as a philosopher and different thinker on a wide range of topics, many of which directly relate to and impact leadership.

One of my favorite Einstein quotes is the following:

"The world we have created is a product of our thinking;

it cannot be changed without changing our thinking."

Read it to yourself again. Ponder its meaning and impact. Your thinking created the world that you live in, work in and experience. Your Thinking! Thus, whatever changes you desire in your life and in your business are on the other side of changes in your thinking and believing, which includes how you see things, think about things and experience things. This way of thinking, believing and creating change is at the core of all conscious leaders.

Most of you reading this book will remember the powerful Apple marketing campaign of the late 1990's which featured many icons and change agents. This campaign included print, radio and television and was embodied by two words—*Think Different*. It kicked off with the memorable "*Here's to the crazy ones*" commercial. Initially recorded by Steve Jobs himself, but later released with Richard Dreyfuss providing the voiceover for the commercial, its visuals and words were impactful and inspiring. If you have not listened to it in some time (or ever), I highly encourage you to find it on You Tube and experience it. I also encourage you to listen to the version with Steve Jobs to experience his own passion for the concept and message. The commercial featured the following iconic figures: Albert Einstein, Bob Dylan, Martin Luther King Jr., Richard Branson, John Lennon, Buckminster Fuller, Thomas Edison, Muhammad Ali, Ted Turner, Maria Callas, Mahatma Gandhi, Amelia Earhart, Alfred Hitchcock, Martha Graham, Jim Henson, Frank Lloyd Wright and Pablo Picasso—people that Apple referred to as some of the *Crazy Ones*.

Read the script of the famous commercial and you will start to understand what Steve Jobs and Apple were talking about in defining the *crazy ones*:

> Here's to the crazy ones. The misfits. The rebels. The troublemakers.
>
> The round pegs in the square holes. The ones who see things differently.
>
> They're not fond of rules. And they have no respect for the status quo.
>
> You can quote them, disagree with them, glorify or vilify them.
>
> About the only thing you can't do is ignore them. Because they change things. They push the human race forward.
>
> And while some may see them as the crazy ones, we see genius.
>
> Because the people who are crazy enough to think they can change the world, *are the ones who do.*

These are the people that "see things differently," not merely think differently. These are the people that challenge the status quo and ask questions—different, difficult, challenging questions. These are the boat-rockers—not just for the sake of rocking the boat, but to explore and push themselves and others beyond what and how they already thought and believed. These are the passionate change agents committed to making things not just different, but better. These are the conscious leaders, who are willing to take the risks required to change the world for the good, often in the face of many challengers, detractors and even destroyers.

Are you one of the crazy ones? Are you ready to do whatever it takes and change how you think in order to create the desired changes in your business, your team, your relationships—your life? Well, are you?

One of the iconic crazy ones of the twentieth century was Nelson Mandela, and he offered us various ideas on shifting our thinking. In a situation where everyone in the world would have understood a desire to seek revenge and retribution, Mandela ignored over 27 years of imprisonment and literally put it behind him. He left prison and continued his lifelong fight against apartheid (the same fight that had put him in prison), eventually becoming President in the first multiracial election in South Africa. Despite the way he had been mistreated and abused politically and physically over the decades, Mandela's presidency was committed to national reconciliation and forgiveness. He even included on his cabinet and in other roles within his administration many members of the party that had imprisoned him and presided over apartheid. Well known for many quotes and shared perspectives over the years, two of Nelson Mandela's more famous quotes embody the heart of conscious leaders.

The first speaks to the ways that so many people choose—and make no mistake about it, Nelson Mandela was a man and conscious leader that embraced his power of choice—to limit themselves, their objectives and their lives by choosing to play small and to settle in life.

> "There is no passion to be found playing small—in settling
> for a life that is less than the one you are capable of living."
>
> *Nelson Mandela*

Conscious leaders are acutely aware of the risks of settling and of how easily we can fall into the trap of settling, often without even realizing it. With heightened awareness and self-reflection, conscious leaders are hyper-vigilant to make sure that their choices are directed toward and designed to achieve their highest potential and the highest potential of their teams and businesses—and even of the world. Consistent with the theme, conscious leaders are zealous believers in and pursuers of exponential living and achieving—not for the sake of the achievement or perceptions of success, but for the sake of passion and purpose.

Nelson Mandela embodied and modeled this spirit in his life and famously highlighted the exponential believing of conscious leaders:

> "It always seems impossible, *until it's done.*"

Until it's done! So many things in our personal lifetimes and throughout time were considered to be impossible by the masses, yet each one's ultimate achievement sent the foregoing message loud and clear—impossibility is simply a moment in time and a *state of mind.* This different way of framing possibilities is the opportunity that conscious leaders seize upon to push themselves and others past old ways of thinking, doing and even being.

> Conscious leaders are acutely aware of the risks of settling and of how easily we can fall into the trap of settling, often without even realizing it.

One of the most famous examples of how thinking and then outcomes can shift is the first breaking of the four-minute mile. This feat was long considered beyond the capacity of any human being, but the world's perspective shifted on May 6, 1954, when Englishman Roger Bannister became the first person to run a mile in under four minutes (3:59.4).

What the world had believed to be impossible happened in 1954, but what happened thereafter is where the magic shows up. Just two months later, Roger Bannister and another runner both ran the mile in under four minutes in the same race. Just over a year later, three more men had broken the four-minute mile. The impossible had become the possible by virtue of the achievement of the impossible, yet the deeper reality is that the possible was birthed by and flowed from the beliefs of people. Clearly, Roger Bannister believed it was possible, and once the impossible had been achieved, more people achieved it. Did they magically get better, stronger and faster with the attainment of the impossible? Of course not; others followed because the limits of their beliefs had been changed by Roger Bannister's act of possibility.

You might be tempted to dismiss this example as being of limited value because it involves the human body and its limits, but that would be to miss the real point. Roger Bannister's breaking of the four-minute mile barrier is less a story of the potential of the human body and more a story of the exponential potential of the human spirit. It is also evidence of the ways that our beliefs impact our outcomes, especially in the limits that our beliefs create. Conscious leadership is fundamentally a matter of connecting to and unleashing this type of unlimited thinking and believing. Once the four-minute mile barrier was broken, other runners achieved it (in fairly short time) because they now saw it as possible. The conscious leader in this story was Roger Bannister, since it is the conscious leader that believes beyond what others believe, sees beyond the vision of others and expects beyond the expectations of others. You are defined by what you believe is possible, and most people are narrowly or exclusively focused on limits and perceptions of possibilities. Conscious leaders reject this thinking and choose to believe in the possible—exponential thinking and belief in action.

Before we move into a discussion of some specific examples of exponential thinking, it is important that I give you a warning. Consider this your midway-through-the-book caution or resetting of expectations with these truths about the lives of conscious leaders. Conscious leaders ....

- Are the minority
- Stand out in a crowd (for all to see)
- Are rarely popular (because most people do not like change)
- Will be disagreed with and often vilified
- Will be rejected, opposed, challenged and even persecuted

And here is the one critical thing that you must also know about conscious leaders, which you can also choose for yourself: *Conscious leaders do it anyway*! Conscious leaders model the beliefs of Margaret Mead:

> "*Never doubt that a small group* of thoughtful, committed citizens can change the world; indeed, it's the only thing that ever has."

Conscious leaders are rarely backed by the masses (at least at the outset), but they courageously proceed, armed with their different thinking and beliefs, their willingness to take risks and their personal passion for changing things for the better. Are you here to change the world? This is the invitation that I am extending to you IF you are ready and willing.

If I Only Knew

One of my personal building blocks for exponential believing was given to me several years ago by my friend Joe Smucny. We were kicking off our first Master Mind retreat, and Joe made this memorable and impactful comment: "If I'd known what I know now about my potential, I would have raised the bar." Throughout his life and career, Joe has been highly successful, a person who set high goals for himself (or so he thought) and then achieved them. Yet in the rear-view mirror of hindsight, he realized that he could have been more, achieved more and created more impact. I am not talking about having to overachieve or having the mindset that whatever we do is never good enough. Rather, it is about the realization that you have so much untapped potential and that you mostly limit yourself. You do not live up to your own potential because you set the bar too low. Joe talked about the greater impact he could have had in his businesses, with his family, in his community and in the world at large.

The reason most people set their bar too low is simple: we set our objectives based upon who we are today, and we forget that we can (and will) grow and develop (if we're committed to it) into a person that is capable of so much more than we are today. In his Stanford commencement speech many years ago, Steve Jobs memorably spoke about the fact that we cannot "connect the dots" in our lives going forward, but only as we look back and examine our life's path. Joe was connecting the dots in his life that day as he looked back and saw that the goals he had set for himself were formed from what he thought was possible (for him) and were based upon who he was then, not his future and potential self. Imagine the potential that we could all unleash if we were to raise the bar based upon who we know we can evolve to be. If we only knew!

Your Bar Is Based on What You Know (or Have Done)

I have now come to understand that those four words—*if I only knew*—were not only memorable but profound, and that within those four words lies the opportunity to create the life and business you have always desired. These four words highlight many of the obstacles in your life, and I want to highlight three key ways that this self-limiting thinking holds you back. First, most of us set our goals and objectives based upon what we know. As the saying goes, "we don't know what we don't know," and this can often be true of possibilities for us—we don't know what is possible because we do not know what is possible. If we are relying on what we know, we will *always* play small and set the bar too low because until we have achieved something, most of us cannot envision more. Still, conscious leaders see beyond their own limited intellectual views and achieve more because of their heightened self-awareness and awakened way of living and leading. In our ordinary thinking, we set goals based upon what we have done before and what we think is realistic.

Many years ago, I heard John DiJulius say that he never wanted to hear team members say that they had done their best. Wait a minute! He couldn't have said that. He couldn't mean that. I was raised on the principal that if we do our best, it is all we can do. My father shared that message with me, and I had passed it on to my two boys. John Wooden talked about how winning was never the objective at UCLA; the objective was to be and give your best, and then the results would follow. Certainly, I had not heard John DiJulius correctly. But then he said it again and explained. He said that the problem with people giving their best is that it is based upon what they have experienced or achieved before and *what they believe is possible.* Most of us won't set goals or objectives that we believe are impossible for fear of coming up short, yet Nelson Mandela said "It always seems impossible, until it's done!"

Indeed, much that has been accomplished in this world was deemed impossible until it was done. Every invention ever imagined was deemed impossible before its creation or discovery. John Kennedy committed to landing a man on the moon during the 1960's when the space program was in its infancy—which everyone thought was impossible until July, 1969. Martin Luther King Jr. created a revolution that began the transformation of a nation and the world because he had a dream, a dream that many believed was impossible. In 1980, the United States hockey team shocked the world with what is now known as the "Miracle on Ice" when they beat the best hockey team in the world (the Soviet Union). We achieve the impossible virtually every day, yet most of us set our objectives based upon what we have done before *plus maybe a little bit more.*

Imagine if we instead set our life and business goals with an expectation of achieving the impossible or, at a minimum, set objectives so big that they were scary. I often say that if we are not scared, then we have set the bar too low. If we have not set the bar high enough that we risk failing in some way (and often we do fail), then the bar is set too low. Where is the challenge if the bar is too low? Where is the fun and excitement of a low bar? I recently saw this anonymous quote: "If your vision is not intimidating you, then it is insulting God." Conscious leaders purposefully set out to pursue goals, objectives and visions that are intimidating even to them. Conscious leadership is not about setting grand goals without fear, but setting and creating expectations and visions (and proceeding toward them) despite the fear.

> If we have not set the bar high enough that we risk failing in some way (and often we do fail), then the bar is set too low.

Your Bar Is Based on Other People's Bar

The second limiting way of thinking is when we set our bar based upon everyone else. We look at the goals of others, and if our goals are bigger (even by a little bit), then we conclude that our goals must be "good" goals, ones that are aggressive or at least big enough. The problem is that in our culture, most people's goals are built upon a foundation of mediocrity. Most people set goals based upon survival, getting by, okay or just enough. When we have those "huge years" of incremental achievement, the magical 5, 10 or 15% improvement over mediocre, where did it take us? It did not take us where we wanted to be, but rather where it was *safe* or *easy*. Look around you and ask yourself this question: Do the people or businesses that I watch and observe have the lives or outcomes that I want? Without this question being asked, it is very easy to be lulled into thinking that you are doing pretty well in business or life compared to everyone else. But is that why you are here—to play small and to be just good enough? For conscious leaders, playing small is _not_ acceptable, and they trust that the bar is meant to be so much higher—living up to their truest potential. If I only knew!

Your Bar Is Based on Who You Are Today ... Not the Future You

The third and final limiting way of thinking, one that I discovered only in the past couple of years, is that when you set your course, your vision and your objectives, you do so based upon _who you are_ in that moment. You do not expect and plan for the personal and professional growth you will achieve in the future. Admittedly, some people are not growing much (by their own choice to stay as they are), but you can choose to challenge yourself and invest in your growth and development so that you will blossom throughout your life. Who you are today is not the same person that will be achieving your plans and goals in the future. When the time comes to hit your long-term goals, you will be closer to becoming the person you were always intended to be. For conscious leaders, it is less about the objectives and more about the decisions you make about who you will be and whether you will become all that you are capable of and who you were born to be—what I call stepping into your truest essence—_by choice._

You are already living your life. Whether you own a business or work for someone else, whether you are young or old, whether you are a parent or not, whether you are in a relationship or not, we all have one thing in common—we are all living our lives right now. Thus, we all have the same skin in the game, but it is up to each one of you to choose how you will play the game. Imagine the impact if team members woke up every day focused on possibilities instead of being realistic. What if in your heart you believed in unleashing rather than just getting things done? What if your core commitment every day was to transformation instead of just hitting some goals? How would your life change if every day you decided to live the life you were meant to live? Not the one someone else wrote for you or that someone else told you that you were worthy of, but rather, the life that is in your heart.

Conscious leaders know so well the magic that is in each of us and lead their lives and lead others into lives and outcomes based upon the very real existence of this magic. This exponential thinking creates magic in business, relationships, communities and the world. We cannot fully envision our capabilities, but we can embrace the fact that we are capable of more than we believe we are capable of. Some people would ask, "How can I do more than I am capable of when that is all I can possibly know?" Conscious leaders are self-aware enough to see beyond what is known and realistic. Most people live by the credo that seeing is believing, but conscious leaders go the other way (the road less traveled) and trust that instead, *believing is seeing*. If you believe it, you will see it.

As you plot your course into the great unknown that is the rest of your life, challenge yourself, your team, your organization and even your family to raise the bar. Imagine a world without limitations (especially those inside us) and set your sights on transformation and impact, not merely goals and objectives. Instead of asking "can we," ask "what if?" When you reach the end of your journey (wherever it takes you), do you really want to look back and say "if I only knew"? Instead, set sail into the future with an expectation of the *limitless you* knowing that the future you will be capable of so much more than you are today. Tally Ho!

Conscious Leaders Eat Their Cake and Have It Too

You have heard this saying for many years, likely from the time you were a child. You have not only heard it, but it has been drilled into your head as a universal and obvious truth:

"You can't have your cake and eat it too!"

Some suggest that this phrase was first written in the early 1500's, so it has been a part of our vernacular for hundreds of years. Its literal meaning is that you cannot eat your cake and still have your cake. Variations on this theme include the belief that "you can't have it both ways" or that "you can't have the best of both worlds." With all due respect to these hundreds of years of use, I say "Who says you can't?" Why can't you have it both ways or the best of both worlds? Because there is this old saying that says so? Talk about living with someone else's self-limiting belief systems.

The concept that you cannot have your cake and also eat it is based upon scarcity thinking (there is one piece of cake that I can either enjoy or keep), while conscious leaders are possibility and abundance thinkers (I can enjoy my piece of cake AND create more cake for all). If the cake is limited, then we must be careful how we carve up the cake and equally careful to protect our piece of the cake; however, if we are co-creating the cake and making it even bigger, then there will always be plenty of cake to go around to those who are invested in the cake and the process of creating and expanding the cake. This is the realm of conscious leaders.

If the cake is limited, then there will always be a limited amount of cake, and we are collectively doomed by limits. If we base our business models on this limited thinking, then there will never be enough to go around, and every time we give something up, we are doomed to have less. Thus, every time you hire a new employee, that employee is *taking* part of the revenues of the business. In contrast, if the people you hire are investments in the business that will help or allow the business to grow, then technically giving up a part of revenues of the business will allow you to create more business and revenues for everyone involved.

I am not suggesting that leaders should not be thoughtful about the use or expenditure of resources, but I am suggesting that what you believe to be true about resources, markets, relationships and cakes will have a dramatic impact on the decisions you make and the outcomes you achieve. The supposed practical impossibility of having your cake and eating it too is merely a story based upon a belief system. As such, you can choose to adopt this belief system, or you can choose to think and act based upon a premise of abundance and possibilities.

Our culture seems to believe that the world is based upon a principle of equal balance. Consider these different examples:

- There must be good news and bad news (together).
- Don't get your hopes up.
- You should play it safe.
- If it is too good, then it must not be true (because nothing is easy and there are no truly good deals).

Many of these old sayings and beliefs are based upon self-protection to avoid letdowns or disappointments, but what if instead we are *creating* the letdowns by the ways that we limit our thinking and expect too little. What if the key to achieving more is getting your hopes and dreams up even higher? What if the key to achieving your objectives is to raise the bar rather than to lower it? Unconscious leaders like to play it safe and conservative, while conscious leaders set their sights on big visions for themselves and their businesses, and then they take action to create more possibilities. After all, Martin Luther King Jr. had "a dream," not just an idea.

Be Careful What You Believe

Many people believe that doing what fulfills them and is in alignment with their passions creates risks for their families and their ability to fulfill their responsibilities. In other words, many people believe that pursuing your dream puts your family and responsibilities at risk. Many people then (naturally) act according to that belief system by not taking actions to pursue their dreams and passions because of the perceived high risk. But what if the opposite is true?

Assume that pursuing your dreams and passions actually makes it easier for you to fulfill your responsibilities. If so, then doing the "responsible thing"—perhaps staying in a job

> The main point is to be careful and clear about what you believe and then to make sure that your actions (your chosen path) are in alignment with what you actually believe.

that you do not enjoy or which does not fulfill you, but which seems to be secure—actually is a greater risk for you and your ability to fulfill your responsibilities. Isn't that interesting! The main point is to be careful and clear about what you believe and then to make sure that your actions (your chosen path) are in alignment with what you actually believe. The key is that what you believe does matter, and whether you are acting in accordance with those beliefs is even more important.

Both personally and professionally, it is vital that you achieve clarity on what you believe and that you then create alignment by taking action, doing that which lines up with what you believe. Being out of personal and professional alignment is causing us all a great deal of unnecessary stress and keeping many of us from achieving our dreams and objectives. Be careful what you believe, but most important, make sure that what you do is consistent with what you believe.

Consider some other ways of thinking that will typically block our path, each of which is just a story that we have chosen to believe is true.

- Life is hard.
- Business is hard.
- It takes money.
- It will take time.
- Relationships take time to build.

- It won't be easy.
- We're different.
- You don't understand my situation.

Sound familiar? Sound like perhaps something (or many things) that you have said in the past year, month, week or even day? We have all heard the old axiom about being careful what we wish for, but I am suggesting that you need to be careful—VERY careful—about what you say. Not only can what you say become a self-fulfilling prophecy, but even more important, what you say can and will create a story that you tend to trust, believe and live—and it is almost always to your personal and professional detriment.

Think about it; if I say (and thus believe) that something will be hard, then it is pretty difficult for that thing not to be hard. After all, I have already declared it to be hard, and everything I experience is likely to point to it being hard (because I like being right, even when being right is to my own detriment). Likewise, if I say (and believe) that anything will necessarily take a long time to accomplish or achieve, then I have a built-in excuse for it taking a long time.

Even more critically, you will likely act (or fail to act) in strict accordance with the belief that something will take a long time. Thus, you will not have any sense of urgency, and you will believe (falsely) that no matter what you do, how much you do, how fast or effectively you do it, it is still going to *take a long time.* As a result, it is not much of a surprise when things that you think will take a long time actually DO take a long time. It is easy to suggest and then believe that things take a long time because they do, but you also know that there are many times and situations where you or others achieve things or complete things much faster than you ever imagined, which means that there are no absolutes in terms of how long things take to do or achieve. Conscious leaders believe that things will take as long as they take and that time is relative, especially to outcomes.

Likewise, the phrase "we're different" may be the most debilitating phrase in the English language, for as soon as you say it you give yourself a built-in excuse not to learn from others and not to change. Many great and transformational ideas have been successfully executed across organizations and industries, yet when you state (and believe) that you are different, then there is no reason for you to try anything new or to try things that have helped others to be successful because—of course—you are different. In fact, the belief that "we're different" is really about arrogance and ego and is closely aligned with the destructive phrase "We've always done it this way." This mindset virtually precludes change or even efforts to try new things, yet we know that relying on the fact that "We've always done it this way" is a sure way to get and remain stuck, even to the point of utter failure.

Business owners and entrepreneurs are famous (and infamous) for changing the rules, achieving against all odds, creatively solving problems, and doing what no one else believed was possible. As business owners and leaders, you need to be mindful of what you say and what you believe so that you do not fall into the trap of creating a recurring story that matches what, perhaps, you have experienced or even heard before. Likewise, every team member has the opportunity to be a part of creating, changing, and solving, but operating under self-limited statements and beliefs can often be the difference between success and failure. Leaving these limiting statements behind is the way of conscious leaders.

Leadership is defined by actions, not words, yet in this case the "act" of making or accepting self-limited statements and beliefs can be as debilitating and dangerous as any self-destructive activity. Be aware of what you say, what you accept as true, and ultimately what you believe as evidenced by your words and statements. There are very few (if any) universal truths when it comes to life or business. History is replete with stores of men, women, teams, organizations, communities and even nations achieving that which everyone else believed or perceived to be impossible. In order to keep your mind and thoughts open to possibilities, you need to be vigilant about taking care in what you say and thus believe.

Embracing the And/Both of Life

The key ingredient in all of this exponential thinking and believing is the conscious leader's fundamental adoption of the "and/both" mindset, the belief that you can create and/both scenarios and outcomes and you are not limited to one OR the other (i.e. you can have your cake and eat it too). While many of us missed this subtle television message, the Miller Lite Beer commercials in the 1970's were based upon and/both thinking—yes, you could have a beer that was less filling AND that tasted great. More recently, Ford has launched commercials for their Focus automobile embracing the mantra that "and is better" (than or). This thinking is core for conscious leaders.

In the business world, this exponential thinking was introduced to the main stage of business thought by Jim Collins. In *Built to Last* (1994), he offered that highly visionary companies do not

> "[Highly visionary companies do not oppress themselves with what we call the 'The Tyranny of the OR'—the rational view that cannot easily accept paradox, that cannot live with two seemingly contradictory forces or ideas at the same time. The 'Tyranny of the OR' pushes people to believe that things must be either A *OR* B, but not both."

Conscious leaders know that this so-called rational view (where there can be no paradoxes) is self-limiting and is a choice.

F. Scott Fitzgerald said:

> "The test of a first-rate intelligence is the ability to hold two opposed ideas in mind at the same time and still retain the

ability to function. One should, for example, be able to see things as hopeless and yet be determined to make them otherwise."

This ability is the foundation of and/both thinking, planning and executing. Conscious leaders not only simultaneously acknowledge two different beliefs or ideas, but they seek out and create and/both solutions.

Admittedly, this shift in thinking can be challenging because the "either/or" mindset is so ingrained in our culture and ways of thinking. We are

> As a result, you must fight against this self-limiting belief system and surround yourself with people who will help you see the "and/both" opportunities.

surrounded by "or" thinkers who will overwhelm you with "or" options and promptly shoot down your and/both thinking. As a result, you must fight against this self-limiting belief system and surround yourself with people who will help you see the "and/both" opportunities.

I consider myself an "and/both" thinker, but I can fall into the enticing trap of the "tyranny of or." Last year, I was working out of my Raleigh, NC, office for the week and was looking forward to the upcoming weekend. I had planned to stay over for the weekend, and the weather was supposed to be spectacular—sunny and 75 degrees or warmer in January. That same week, my girlfriend was having a challenging and emotional week in Cleveland, and she very much wanted to have me around to offer support. I was torn—enjoy the beautiful weekend in Raleigh or come home early and be there for Jennifer—and I had decided to come back home on Friday to be there for her. On Thursday night I was having drinks with my dear friend Darlene, and I shared my quandary and decision with her. Thankfully, Darlene was there to pull me out of my OR thinking and show me the and/both solution: "Why don't you fly Jennifer to Raleigh for the weekend?" Duh … why didn't I think of that? Simple—because I was stuck in the problem and the self-limiting belief that I had to choose one or the other. Thanks to Darlene's intervention, Jennifer flew down to Raleigh on Friday, and we had a lovely weekend and enjoyed the beautiful weather together—truly an "and/both" or "win/win" solution to a small, but important, matter.

One of the best ways to keep and/both thinking and solutions at the forefront is to invoke it in your questions. Rather than asking "What should we do?" ask "What is the and/both solution?" As I discussed above regarding using the phrase *in what ways* in your questions to stimulate creativity and better solutions, purposefully invoking "and/both" in your questions, problem solving and opportunity pursuits will provide you with better outcomes, longer-term solutions and more satisfaction. Instead of "waiting for the other shoe to drop," conscious leaders strap up their laces and kick-start themselves and their organizations into high gear to achieve ignition, acceleration and exponential results.

Conscious Leaders Are Unrealistic

A recent conversation highlighted for me the need for a dramatic (180 degree) shift in our thinking. I was suggesting a different approach for addressing a business challenge when my friend responded with these words: "Jeff, you have to be realistic." That is when it hit me: *Says who?* Maybe that is a big part of the problem; we are all trying to be realistic when in fact we need to be *unrealistic*. The trouble with being realistic is that it often comes from a place of fear, limitation and feeling powerless. Being realistic also often involves lowering your expectations.

I know, it sounds crazy. Realistic is safe and secure. Realistic is practical and prudent. Realistic is rational and logical. Are you seeing the pattern and the problem? If not, let me lay it out for you—when you live your life and run your business being *realistic*, then you are living and leading as follows:

Safe—Secure—Practical—Prudent—Rational—Logical

Boy, doesn't that get your blood pumping to go out and create, build and achieve? While you should always exercise some degree of prudence and practicality, living and leading *realistically* will likely keep you right where you are. If you want different results, then you must shift to *unrealistic living and leading*!

Contrary to popular misconception, you **do not** have to be realistic. In fact, most significant achievements are the result of being *unrealistic*. In case you missed it, I can assure you that the Auburn Tigers coaching staff was *unrealistic* when they planned for the possible return of a missed field goal by Alabama in the closing seconds of their football game at the end of the 2013 season. The result: an unlikely 110-yard return for a game-winning touchdown to upset their arch-rival, No. 1 ranked Alabama. I wonder if, perhaps, the Alabama team was being *realistic* in not being prepared for Auburn's unrealistic preparation.

The same is true for the breakthroughs achieved, the inventions created, the milestones surpassed, the records broken and the innovation launched throughout history. If you choose to be realistic, then you are choosing to be ordinary, average and okay. Only if you choose to be unrealistic can you achieve, thrive and excel. Conscious leaders are fascinated with being *unrealistic* and managing their reactions to avoid experiencing disappointment even if expectations are not achieved. This part is (or should be) obvious, so what is the fascination with being realistic all about?

One significant thing—avoiding disappointment! Being realistic primarily attempts to avoid being disappointed or disappointing someone else. It is a valid perspective, but consider this: Do you want to live your life avoiding disappointment? Will that approach and thinking take you, your business or your relationships where you want to go? Clearly, seeking to avoid disappointment by thinking realistically is a choice you make, and thus you choose the nature and scope of your opportunities (or the limits thereof).

The other choice we must be aware of—perhaps the less obvious one—is that disappointment itself is a choice. In the conversation I referenced above, my friend was suggesting that people should be realistic (and lower their expectations) in order to avoid disappointment. In typical Jeff fashion, I suggested another option—keep the expectations high, but choose not to be disappointed if the outcomes do not match your expectations. The key shift in understanding is that disappointment is not a natural outcome of high expectations. In addition, there is a difference between *being* disappointed (acknowledging that you did not get what you wanted) and *feeling* disappointment and perhaps sadness or shame (which can linger). The problem is that we have fallen into the trap of believing that, if you have high expectations, you will *experience* disappointment if you fail to achieve them. The cause-and-effect relationship between not getting what you wanted and being disappointed is an old story that is not true.

I have proven for myself that I can set the bar very high, fully commit to the high expectations, *and* not experience disappointment if I come up short. This requires a healthy detachment from the outcomes so that you can focus on the things that you do control, which includes your reactions when things do not turn out the way you planned or desired. This is a vital way of being for conscious leaders—detaching from the outcomes (see next section).

Disappointment is not a preordained outcome. It is a choice you make. You have the choice to be realistic or unrealistic. You have the choice to be disappointed or to see every failure as a learning opportunity. You have a choice about whether you think and plan for possibilities or instead limit yourself to focus on perceived impossibilities. These are the choices you make every day, and your choices determine your outcomes. Conscious leaders choose to be *unrealistic, to risk failure,* and to experience failure with an *attitude of learning* and growth (rather than disappointment). What will you choose?

Outcomes Are Irrelevant

Outcomes are irrelevant!? Heresy, you may say. Of course I am not serious—or am I? Certainly, outcomes are important—aren't they the primary thing that we plan for, strategize about, measure and rely upon? Have you have seen any strategic or tactical plan without outcomes defined, even if loosely? Have you ever seen sales managers encourage their sales team to do their best and not worry about the results or outcomes? Of course, it is absurd to suggest that outcomes are irrelevant, but indeed that is precisely what I am suggesting, and this detachment from outcomes is a core element of conscious leadership. If you are open to a new way of looking at everything you do, then I encourage you to keep reading and to explore the underlying rationale of this "absurd" proposition.

Yes, outcomes and results are important and they do matter. I am not suggesting otherwise. What I AM suggesting is that you need to understand that ultimately you do not control the outcomes and results. Since you do not control them, then they are irrelevant. Instead of focusing all of your misguided energy on outcomes, you should focus your precious time and energy on the few things that you DO control: your thoughts, your mindsets and your actions.

We love to believe that we control outcomes, but the best we can do is seek to drive them, create them or do our best with what we can control and hope that the desired outcomes will follow. We do not like to admit any lack of control, especially when it comes to important things like outcomes and results in our businesses. We want to believe that we control outcomes because that belief feeds our comfort zones. Those comfort zones desperately want to control our outcomes and futures. We say things like "Failure is not an option," yet we know that failure is always a possibility, whether big or small. We say that we can "make things happen," but we do not have the ultimate control over what things happen. We have only the ability to be at our individual and collective best in executing towards our desired outcomes. We often assert that we are leaders that create or drive results, but great leaders actually create or drive teams who execute well enough and fast enough to create the best opportunity for the hoped-for results. In the end, you control everything leading up to the outcomes *except the actual outcomes.*

Why does this matter? Why should you accept that the outcomes are out of your control? Because in acknowledging that outcomes are beyond your control, you can now focus your critical energy on the short list of things (thoughts, mindsets and actions) that you do control. Many clients we work with spend most of their time setting goals (goal achievement is out of your control), declaring objectives (objective accomplishment is out of your control) and defining desired results (results are out of your control), but precious little time focused on the thinking, activities and execution that are essential in order to create the most fertile ground from which your outcomes can spring forth. In following that path, you actually give up control over what matters most (the short list of things you can control) and you essentially rely upon hope as a strategy. Talk about unwittingly giving up control!

The most fundamental shortcomings that we have found with organizations are poor accountability and inconsistent execution (which are things that you do control), yet these core areas do not get enough attention until we shine a bright light on them. This lack of attention is because the organizations' focus is on the outcomes and goals. For example, when you focus on outcomes, what do you tell your sales people when the outcomes are coming up short of expectations? "Do more, sell more." But what exactly should they do be doing differently? No one knows because the focus and

> In the end, you control everything leading up to the outcomes except the actual outcomes.

planning was around outcomes, not the execution activities that would take them to the brink of the desired outcomes. You do not know what to do because outcomes are not an action. You cannot adjust outcomes, nor can you adapt outcomes!

Regaining ultimate control over your business and your life involves three simple steps:

1. Acknowledgment that outcomes are out of your control;

2. Focusing time and energies on the three things you do control (thoughts, mindsets and actions); and

3. Creating a culture of accountability and relentless execution within your organization.

You may not control the outcomes, but you will take back control over the very few things that can lead you to the brink of your desired results. Outcomes are irrelevant? Indeed they are!

Letting Go of Outcomes

Here is where the conscious leader's and/both thinking critically comes into play. You can be detached from the outcomes, understand that you do not actually control the outcomes, _and_ at the same time be committed and actionized towards achievement of objectives and desired outcomes. The key is to be focused on who you are, what you are thinking and what you are doing towards achieving your desired outcomes, but not emotionally attached to the outcome. If you are confused, stick with me; it will hopefully be clearer in a moment. The problem with being attached to the outcome is that your attachment does not change the fact that you do not control the outcome, and your attachment to the outcome actually makes it less likely that you will achieve it (because you energetically push the outcome away).

I came to this personal awareness several years ago when my business was just getting started. If you have ever started your own business, you know that it can be challenging and potentially stressful, especially with respect to the dreaded thing called cash flow. When you have your own business, cash flow is king, and in the beginning business and revenue can be an almost daily stress point. Is there enough business? Will there be enough revenue? Will there be money to pay the bills? Sound familiar? This focus on a lack of money or revenue was precisely the thought that I was facing several years ago.

I had realized that my cash flow a couple of months in the future was going to be short, so I took action to create revenue. Earlier that year, I had put on a couple of public workshops, which collectively had generated a significant amount of revenue. Simple, I thought—I will just schedule a couple of more seminars, and that will generate the needed cash flow. I did everything the same way I had several months earlier. I booked the dates and locations; I did the same marketing; I planned the seminars the same way. One thing, however, was different—the results. Three weeks prior to the seminars, the registrations were terrible and, instead of anticipating significant additional revenue, I was now projecting that I might actually lose money on the seminars.

How was this poor registration possible? Could I possibly have had every single interested person attend the seminars a few months earlier? What had I done wrong with my marketing or message? I was searching for answers almost in a panic mode and certainly from a place of stress, and then the answer hit me—the answer that helped me to learn more from this failure than I would have learned from a success. I asked myself the type of question that conscious leaders embrace: Why? Why had I scheduled these seminars? It took only a moment for me to face the honest answer—I scheduled them to make money and generate revenue. I did not schedule them to add value to the attendees. I did not schedule them to provide a service to the business community or my network. My motivations were all selfish and self-centered. It was all about me.

This realization was fairly easy to uncover, but it took some more digging to unearth the deeper truth. Rather than focusing on who I was and who I needed to be, I was focused on and attached to the revenue outcomes. It was through this self-reflection process that I came to understand my unhealthy attachment to revenue and money. I was chasing revenue, but in doing so, I was actually pushing it away. As I processed and thought about this misalignment in purpose, a visual came to me that I have continued to use to maintain a conscious detachment from outcomes ever since.

Picture yourself with your hands reaching for and trying desperately to grasp or hold onto something, whether it is a goal, an objective, a desire or an outcome. In fact, try it out for yourself—put your hands together out in front of you and reach out as far as you can as if you are trying to grab something. Alternatively, grasp your hands together and squeeze them together as if you are desperately holding on to something (perhaps money). Now feel the tension in your arms, hands and fingers. Feel the stress in your shoulders. Sense how your mind is functioning—is it relaxed or stressed? As I considered how I was attached to the outcomes and reaching for them, it struck me that instead I should be creating an environment where I take action towards objectives, but detach from the outcomes themselves and think about allowing the results to unfold.

Here is the new paradigm that I discovered and embraced that has proven to serve me, my business and my outcomes in a more positive way. I am sure that all of you have seen a leaf floating in a swimming pool— not a leaf on top of the water, but a leaf down *in the water*. What happens when you grab for the leaf in the water? Of course—it moves away from you. You cannot capture the leaf by sheer force or effort. Instead, the only way to secure the leaf is to open your hands, remain calm and let the leaf drift into your hand. You can then gently close your hand around the leaf.

This healthy detachment is the way that I now approach goals, objectives and outcomes. I develop a strategy, supporting tactics and an action plan. I take action towards the goals and objectives, but I detach from the outcome and I relax my outstretched hands and allow the outcomes to unfold for me or in me. This conscious letting go of the need to try to control what I cannot control (the outcomes) has resulted in better, more predictable and more significant results for my business, in my relationships and in my life. When I am leading, doing and living in alignment, on purpose and consciously, the outcomes do occur—but without me trying to make them happen or force them. This state of surrender or letting go is not an easy path for many; we want to believe that we control and can dictate outcomes, but the shift is simple from attachment to detachment.

Conscious leaders know and trust this different way of thinking and believing. Conscious leaders have experienced the positive shift in their results that comes from letting go of the belief that they control the outcomes and instead focusing on allowing, rather than compelling. If you have not already seen one of the greatest positive benefits of this approach, then think about this question: What is your level of stress when you seek to control things? In contrast, what is your stress level when you are detached from the outcomes and trusting your thoughts and actions? Better results, more consistent results and less stress—these outcomes are the gift that conscious leaders experience when they choose to let go and instead trust, allow and breathe.

Welcome to a New Way of Believing

One warning: Conscious leadership, at least for the moment, may feel lonely because you will be in the minority as a conscious leader. It is not yet the norm, but the ranks of conscious leaders are growing every day in big and little ways. As budding conscious leaders, I invite you to embrace a new paradigm for your business and life decisions—*Minority Rules*.

In life and in business, differentiation rules, and <u>the difference</u> is almost always found in the minority approach (the road less traveled). You know that the road less traveled is often the right and best road, yet you probably continue to follow the pack in most aspects of your business and life. You are then somehow surprised when your outcomes mirror (at best) the mediocre performance of the majority. The trouble, it seems, is that you often fail to consider whether or not you want what the majority has or has achieved. When you do consider closely, it is clear that the majority often does not have a "winning record," especially in life. If you want to be different, by definition you must choose to be part of the minority, the group (or maybe the only one) that is thinking differently, making different choices and creating a new path.

> In life and in business, differentiation rules, and <u>the difference</u> is almost always found in the minority approach (the road less traveled).

I am **not** suggesting that the road less traveled or the minority perspective is easy and without challenges. In fact, this road will often have *more* challenges and obstacles, not because it is the wrong road, but because so many people before you chose to take the perceived easier road. Consider this perspective from Frank Clark: "If you can find a path with no obstacles, it probably doesn't lead anywhere." I am suggesting that there will be many people—perhaps the majority of people—urging you to take a certain path, namely the same path that they all took. That path is not necessarily the wrong one simply because others (or many others) have taken it, but you must be discerning and assess who is on that path, what they have achieved, and who they are as people. If they have what you want, then perhaps their road is your road. If not, then tap into your inner courage, sharpen your machete and start cutting through the brush to create your own life and business.

As for me, whenever I discover that I am on the road less traveled, I get excited and feel good about my path. When everyone says that I am crazy, I say, "Yes! Right on track." In a world where it is the minority that have what we want (in business and in life), it is time to step into the light and adopt a new life credo—*minority rules*! This is certainly the path walked by conscious leaders.

History has shown us that the stories that we choose to believe can *become* true and will likely become our current and future reality. Most of us are today the outcomes of the stories that we have chosen to believe about ourselves, about business, and about life. Changing our language, re-writing our stories, and allowing the future to unfold (rather than accepting someone else's history or experience as true), is a sure path to personal and professional empowerment and creating our desired futures. It is time to throw out the old stories and start re-writing our own truth and stories, and this begins with committing to being careful what we say and believe.

Conscious leaders are passionately committed to possibilities and abundance thinking and embrace the power of choosing their beliefs about business, life and the world. No matter what the source or duration of your old beliefs and stories, what you believe to be true today (about yourself, others and the world) is the outcome of choices. Conscious leadership involves being self-aware of your beliefs and ways of thinking, choosing to believe in possibilities and "and/both" outcomes, and taking actions and making decisions in alignment with these core beliefs. Are you prepared to choose your beliefs wisely as a leader in your business and in your life?

CHAPTER 8: TIME EXPANSION (THE TIMELESS LEADER)

"Don't say you don't have enough time. You have exactly the same number of hours per day that were given to Helen Keller, Pasteur, Michelangelo, Mother Teresa, Leonardo da Vinci, Thomas Jefferson, and Albert Einstein."

H. Jackson Brown

I recently saw this quote from management guru Peter Drucker:

"Until we can manage time, we can manage nothing else."

Peter Drucker is indeed a business and management thought leader, but I don't buy it. While time is precious, too much attention has been devoted to managing time rather than embracing the potential to expand time. Rather than working to manage your time, I invite you to commit to time expansion as a surer path to achieving your desired objectives and outcomes. Time management is the realm of tasks and getting things done, while time expansion is the province of achievement and acceleration.

"I wish I could do that … if I only had more time." Sound familiar? My guess is that you have said this or some version of it in the past week. In our fast-paced world, everyone seems to be struggling with not having enough time to do everything that they want to accomplish; however, there are different ways to think about and experience time. While time has a finite element, conscious leaders understand that time is in many ways infinite, and thus it can be created and expanded. What a valuable tool: imagine the leverage and power of being able to create or expand time!

Forget about time management—you have the ability to *create* time. The truth is that every person can create and expand time, and most people already do it without realizing it. Simply by heightening your awareness of your own time expansion and by seeing time differently, you can dramatically add time to your day, week and year. Would that be valuable to you? Conscious leaders understand this time reality and choose to expand time rather than weakly trying to manage it.

Lest you think that I am suggesting that the key to time expansion is embracing quantum physics or some type of magic, I am merely proposing that you take advantage of the time expansion that you are already creating. Think about times when you have a deadline where you are concerned about whether you have enough time to meet it. You are racing toward your deadline and wondering if there will be enough time. Then, out of the blue, another project, deadline or "emergency" is thrown at you—one with a deadline that requires attention during the same time period as your existing project and deadline. In that moment, which deadline do you choose to ignore or not meet? Which client do you disappoint? If you are like most people, your answer is the same: Find a way to get them both done.

Recently, I asked a client this question:

> Assume that you have 10 hours of work to do today that consist of equal one-hour blocks of time. Also assume that you have 10 hours of time available for these 10 hours of work. Now assume that you are given another one-hour project to accomplish in the same 10 hours of work. Can you get it done?

The answer was an unequivocal and rapid "yes." I then asked what his comfort level would be if I added another one-hour project (now up to 12 supposed hour-long projects in 10 hours), and his answer was a fairly confident "yes." When I asked about adding a third additional hour-long project (now 13 supposed hour-long projects), he said that he probably could not get it done.

Interesting, isn't it? This person works hard and diligently, yet he knows that there is always a way to squeeze more output from the same period of time. What about you? Would you be able to accomplish the same expansion of time?

How would you do it? Perhaps you would be more efficient with your time because you were forced to be hyper-focused. Perhaps you would make better choices about the time suckers that often grab some of your time or attention. Perhaps you would do a better job of creating a working environment where you have few, if any, distractions. We all know that we are most effective and efficient when we can work in a focused way. Perhaps you might delegate more or sooner than you otherwise would have. Perhaps you would do a little less research than you would otherwise, but it would be enough. All of these ideas, as well as other strategies and tactics, create time and thus expand time. We all do this, but conscious leaders actuate it and invoke it.

One truth about time is that we adjust what we are doing to fit the time we have. Why do you think people say, "If you want something done, give it to a busy person"? We misunderstand this phrase's meaning. We think it means that the busy person will be more diligent and willing to get more done in a shorter period of time. Wrong. The busy person will be forced to do more and thus automatically become more effective and productive because he or she is already busy. Give most people a job to do and tell them it will take four hours, and it will take them four hours or more to complete. Give them the same project and tell them it will take two hours to complete, and most people will complete it in two hours. Yes, there are times when we set ridiculous and physically impossible time frames, but more often our time frames allow more time than necessary.

Think about this scenario as further proof of how we bend our tasks to meet the available time, not the other way around. Perhaps you or someone you know has had the experience of working full-time while going to school (often at night). Everyone I have ever known who went to school while working full-time talked about having an insanely tight time schedule. They all talked about how great it would be when they finished school because they would get back all of that time that they were investing in school at the moment. But what do you think happened once they finished school or whatever their other time investment was? Did they suddenly have lots of free time to invest in something else, some hobby or interest? No; they found that they were still very busy (see Chapter 12 for a discussion of the "busy" story), and they wondered where all of that extra time disappeared to. This is another example of the expandable nature of time.

Time is the neither the problem nor the obstacle. Thus, time management is not the solution. Rather, the solution lies in changing your relationship with and understanding of time. Time is not what needs to be managed. Instead, you need to manage your perceptions about time. You also need to understand that your choices regarding time are less about management and mostly about expansion of time. Unless and until we harness the potential for time travel, time expansion thinking is the best tool you will ever have for achieving your objectives.

> Time is the neither the problem nor the obstacle. Thus, time management is not the solution. Rather, the solution lies in changing your relationship with and understanding of time.

Leveraging the Flow

One additional strategy for time expansion involves focus and nurturing *the zone*. Professional athletes often speak about being *in the zone*—a state in which an athlete performs to the best of his or her ability *without effort and unconsciously.* Outside of sports, Mihály Csikszentmihályi proposed the concept of *flow*: a mental state where the person performing is fully immersed and focused, fully involved and enjoying the process. The foundations of flow or being in the zone are focus, immersion and unconscious effort, which can only be accomplished on purpose. There are several key drivers that allow conscious leaders to experience this flow more consistently.

First, in a culture that seems desperate to embrace multitasking as a badge of honor, conscious leaders understand that multitasking is an obstacle to the flow. They also know that multitasking does not actually exist, despite its active use as part of our cultural lexicon and its inclusion on many a job description. Dave Crenshaw, in *The Myth of Multitasking: How "Doing It All" Gets Nothing Done* (Jossey-Bass 2008), laments:

> "It's become a heroic word in our vocabulary. There's a cultural pressure to multitask; that's a big part of why people do it. We have all been taught that we can be efficient; we can be productive by being multitaskers. Never mind that this is just not true."

The research continues to debunk the myth of multitasking, more correctly identifying the truth that the brain cannot multitask. While it may seem that you are doing two things at once, you are more accurately taking advantage (but to your disservice) of the power of the brain to switch back and forth rapidly between two or more tasks. You are not multitasking, but rather switching your concentration back and forth at such a high rate of speed that it seems like multitasking (because your brain cannot comprehend the speed).

Some time ago, I saw a statistic that the cost of a distraction—stopping what you are focused on for something else—has a multiplier effect of 6-7 times. In other words, for every one minute that you leave your focused task to do something else (e.g. read an email, answer a phone call, have a conversation, etc.), it takes you six or seven minutes to get back to the focus level you had achieved before the distraction. This impact is increasing to the detriment of people and businesses all over the country. There is ample and ongoing research into the impacts and costs of these distractions, but those details are beyond the scope of this book. For our purposes, simply know that conscious leaders understand the myth of multitasking and instead choose to focus and thus leverage their time, which in effect creates time and increases positive outcomes.

Stop Prioritizing and Start Committing

For many of my clients, a common complaint goes something like this: We don't have time to prioritize because everything is a priority, things are moving too fast and/or all we have time to do is put out fires. Of course, I always challenge the notion that it is impossible to prioritize because, given that time is relatively finite, we are always forced to prioritize, even if we do not realize we are doing it. I do not know what you do or what business you are in, but I am pretty sure that few of you routinely deal in life-or-death situations. Think about the dynamics of a hospital emergency room and the process known as triage, which is nothing more than prioritization based upon real life-or-death scenarios. Decisions (hopefully conscious ones) are routinely made in an emergency room regarding how each patient is prioritized for treatment. If the emergency room professionals can prioritize injuries even in life-or-death situations, then you can prioritize your business deadlines.

In addition, and despite all of our personal and professional bluster about our ability (or perceived ability) to multitask, we mere humans are capable of actually focusing and working on only one thing at a time. As a result, whatever we are focused and working on is by definition our top priority in that moment. Even if we claim that it is not that important (for example, perhaps you are working on something because it is easy to knock out so you can focus on another project), whatever you are working on right now is your highest priority.

Oops—I should have warned you in advance that a lesson was coming, and that was it:

> *Whatever you are doing at any particular point in time is your highest priority in that moment,* even though this is often not a conscious (or highly conscious) choice.

In fact, most of our "choices" about priorities are not really choices at all.

You are probably thinking that I am referring to the many situations where someone else (often your boss) is dumping things in your lap, so it feels as though you do not have any choice in the prioritization of the work. However, I am actually talking about the many situations and circumstances when you are reactive in what you choose to do in any given moment (i.e., you do not think through what is most important, either based upon its value or because of timing). These unconscious choices and the absence of conscious prioritization are not serving you well in your life. Conscious leaders make more conscious choices, especially about priorities.

Ready for another tough lesson? I received this sucker-punch of awareness just a couple of months ago. While wildly imperfect, I consider myself to be fairly aware, pretty conscious and generally purposeful in my choices. I was with a friend of mine discussing the importance of priorities and making conscious choices with our time. In the midst of the discussion, he asked to see my calendar. When I asked why, he said, "Because when I look at your calendar, I will definitively know your priorities by what you have scheduled." Ouch. That was hitting below the belt, but it was a great reminder that my priorities are easy to spot through my schedule and my actions. If I proclaim something or someone important but choose not to invest time in that thing or that person, then clearly that person or thing is not my priority.

A great way to enhance your consciousness in prioritizing and to increase your effectiveness in execution is to ask yourself two questions consistently:

1. Is this project that I am working on right now my highest priority?
2. If not, do I have good reasons for working on something other than my highest priority right now?

By simply asking and answering these questions throughout the day, you will make better choices, and your priorities will be more intentional and purposeful.

Recently, I discovered an even more important concept about prioritization, and strangely enough it really has nothing to do with prioritization. I was having a conversation based on the questions above with one of my leadership coaching clients, and in the midst of our discussion, a question hit me. These in-the-moment revelations or questions are typical for me; in the midst of a discussion or a facilitation, a unique question comes to me which is often just what is needed to create clarity, a unique solution or whatever the client needs. The client was expressing frustration about the many times when someone dumps a project or deadline on him at the last minute, which often requires him to stay and work late. He also talked about how it felt that the priorities were out of his control, which in turn left him feeling out of control in general. Sound familiar to you?

The following is our brief discussion:

Me: Do you have kids?

Client: Yes, two that are school age.

Me: When you make a clear commitment to be there for one of their activities (e.g. sports, music, etc.), how often are you late or do you miss it?

To be honest, I was expecting to hear an answer such as "rarely" or "not very often," but his clear answer was *"**Never.**"* I quickly processed his response and followed up with this comment:

> *"So, when you make a commitment to your kids to be there, you <u>always</u> honor that commitment, no matter what happens at work or what things get thrown at you that day."*

His response was "Yes, because if I make a commitment to my kids, I honor it." I paused for a moment or two and then told him, "You don't have a prioritization problem; you have a commitment problem, because when you make clear commitments you honor them no matter what other 'priorities' get thrown in your way."

I think we are on to something. When was the last time (personally or professionally) that you or someone else you know made a **commitment** and actually used the word *commit* or *commitment*? I am not talking about what you will try to do, try to make or try to accomplish. I am also not talking about being asked to do something and simply agreeing. There is something empowering and powerful about actually making real commitments to yourself or to others because commitments invoke integrity. If I fail to honor a commitment, then I am out of integrity, and for most people integrity (honoring commitments) is important.

This shift in perspective and language has proven to be a powerful change agent in my life. I do not loosely or easily make commitments, but when I make a clear commitment, I will do literally everything that I can to honor that commitment. Make no mistake—I sometimes still make vague, or what I call slippery, promises. But I also and more often say "no," either to the request or to the requested delivery timing for something, which allows me to be in a position to honor the commitments that I do make. This often involves difficult choices, but that happens no matter what—whether we

> There is something empowering and powerful about actually making real commitments to yourself or to others because commitments invoke integrity.

168

are prioritizing, making promises or making commitments—and I am consciously choosing to be intentional about my commitments.

In a culture where accountability is a rare commodity, wouldn't it be grand to have more self-accountability and integrity (people simply doing what they say they will do)? The solution may just lie in embracing commitments over priorities. Imagine the impact in your life if you made more conscious commitments and honored them. Imagine the impact in your business and with your team if people were focused on commitments and their personal integrity. Our objective with our clients is to create, foster and support transformational impact and experience, and commitments and integrity are at the heart of this work. Try it on in your business and in your life—make clear commitments, honor those commitments, experience how good it feels to be in integrity, and watch the results flow in. **Stop prioritizing and *start committing!***

Time Is Not Your Issue

If you believe the rest of the world, there is not and there will never be enough time. Perhaps this has been your mantra in the past: "If I only had more time." If so, you are fighting a losing battle, and you are looking for time in all the wrong places. From the ancient times, it has been clear that time is not something that is lacking or limited, but something that can be created and leveraged. Lao Tzu (from the 6th century B.C.) offered that "Time is a created thing. To say 'I don't have time' is to say 'I don't want to.'" Indeed, your time and what you do with it is a choice, and conscious leaders tell the truth. They choose not to do something rather than bemoan a lack of time for it. There is always time for what you deeply desire to do and want to achieve, but you must be awake and aware, or it will slip through your fingers. It has been said that we waste time by the minute, not by the hour, because we are not focused and committed to that which we have chosen in the moment to make most important.

Each of you has been given the same gift—24 hours in each day. We do not all have the same number of days, either from the beginning or from this day forward. We do not know the number of our days, but we know the number of our hours each day. Do you cherish them? Do you protect them? Do you honor them with your choices? Time (or lack thereof) is never the reason; it is only the excuse we use to attempt to justify our poor choices (or lack thereof) and lack of priorities. Conscious leaders embrace the choices that empower their investment, leverage and gifting of time. They understand that time can be expanded through the gifts and skills of focus, prioritization, leverage and full presence in every moment. If you are here to change things, and I hope that you are, then it is up to you to make different choices with your time so that it is used to fuel your dreams and your impact. If your time is being wasted, lost or slipping away, then now is the moment—your moment—in time to choose to own your time and your investment of it in order to assure that it serves you, rather than you feeling like a slave to it. It is always the right time for the right thing, and now is your time—IF you choose it!

CHAPTER 9: COMPASSIONATE COMMUNICATION (THE CARING LEADER)

"The most basic of all human needs is the need to understand and be understood. The best way to understand people is to listen to them."

Ralph Nichols

If we are talking leadership, then we know that communication is a critical element. Too often, leaders look at communication as an aspect of themselves and of their teams that can "always be better" but needs only ongoing minor tweaks. The type of conscious communication that I am referring to involves breaking down communication and experiencing it (inside yourself and with others) in an entirely different way. As with many elements of conscious leadership, conscious communication involves a great deal of self-awareness and invokes your ability to separate yourself from the situation. This also requires that you have refined (and always keep refining) your level of emotional intelligence, awareness and balance, since some of the biggest obstacles to effective communication are the emotions and "other stuff" that clutter up the communication.

In this chapter, we will be uncovering the selfless nature of compassionate communication, breaking down the pieces of communication and unmasking the many ways that the communicator often gets in the way of his or her own communication and intended outcomes. Some leaders recognize when their communication did not have the intended outcome with the listener, but few are conscious enough to understand that the off-course outcomes are more about the communicator than the recipient and that they, as the communicator, often have the ability to change the outcomes of the communication.

Other-Focused Communication

The first thing that conscious leaders must learn about communication is that it is and must be *other-focused*. Traditional business and leadership thinking primarily focuses on the communicator and on what he or she wants to communicate. While self-improvement of your methods and ways is an important piece of the communication process, it is only one small piece. As has been the theme throughout this book, communication is an everyday practice, and we use it (even if poorly) constantly in our personal lives and our business lives. You could even argue that our communication is more heavily weighted in our personal lives than our business lives. The key point is that conscious and compassionate communication is an art and science that will transform your personal and business communication and as a result will positively impact your relationships and your outcomes throughout your life.

A traditional thinking leader will assess communication this way:

- What do I want to communicate?
- How do I want to communicate it?
- What is the outcome I want from the communication?

Of course, many leaders never think through their communication even to this degree. They will just communicate, in the moment and often simply in reaction to the situation. I am not suggesting that all communication should be delayed beyond each moment to give the communicator time to think it through, but I *am* suggesting that much of our communication would be improved and the desired outcomes achieved if it were more purposeful and less reactionary. You should also know that the speed at which we can process internal questions around communication is faster than you think. What I am suggesting is not time consuming; it is simply a shift in attention and awareness which will enable you to assess the conscious communication elements below promptly in order to be a more impactful communicator.

How many times have you communicated something or communicated in a way that you immediately or later regretted because it did not accomplish your objectives or it had unintended consequences? There will always be the potential for unintended consequences when human beings are communicating, primarily because the communicator and the recipient are rarely having the same communication experience. Conscious communicators, however, are aware of the potential for unintended consequences and therefore are more intentional with their communication (especially in how they are as the communicator) in order to minimize these consequences.

Admittedly, many leaders never include the third question above in their communication (what is the desired outcome), and including this element of considering the desired outcome will have an immediate and positive impact on your communication. If you think about it, this third element is actually the most important element of communication, and it is the sole reason for communication. If you are focused only on wanting to communicate something and how you communicate it, you missed the point. Communication always has a purpose, and that purpose (the outcome, not the communication method) should be the primary focus of your attention and thought.

> Conscious communicators, however, are aware of the potential for unintended consequences and therefore are more intentional with their communication (especially in how they are as the communicator) in order to minimize these consequences.

In sharp contrast, conscious leaders assess communication at a different and deeper level. While the above elements are part of the conscious leader's communication process, the critical element that conscious leaders include in the process is *the listener* (the recipient of the communication). Now there is an interesting concept—consider the listener in your communication. It seems obvious, but most of our communication is actually self-centered in approach, mostly because we have not thought about a different way to do it or look at it.

From Gold to Platinum

For thousands of years, many people in our culture have embraced and sought to live according to a fundamental rule of human interaction. It is so foundational that it has a name that demonstrates its importance—The Golden Rule.

"Do unto others as you would have them do unto you."

While not all people embrace this rule, it is difficult to argue against. It has been interpreted consistently in terms of treating people well, common courtesy and being kind. All good things, but the Golden Rule seems to assume that other people would like to be treated the same way that you would like to be treated. One particular challenge is that the Golden Rule has been invoked (often without conscious thought) into communication. I will communicate with you the way that I want to be communicated with, including the method of communication. If I prefer emails, I will insist on sending you emails even if you prefer communicating by telephone. In addition to my own personal experiences with these communication method disconnections, I hear them played out almost every day.

I was recently facilitating a client's strategic planning session, and the management team was talking about one of their team members (not present) who frustrates them because she insists on having phone calls because she does not like email communication. Consider the dynamics of what is actually happening here. A couple of people on the management team prefer email communication, and they are bothered or frustrated by a team member that will not communicate *their way*. Likewise, the team member insists on communicating by telephone and is likely just as frustrated because the other team members insist on email communication. Obviously (or perhaps not so obvious if we consider and/both leadership), one form of communication should prevail. A typical leader would focus on whose communication preference will prevail, but a conscious leader instead focuses on the ways that none of the communication participants are considering the recipient of the communication.

Several years ago I was introduced to a different way of thinking and being called *The Platinum Rule*.

"Do unto others as they would have you do unto them."

The Platinum Rule invites us to treat others as they would like to be treated. In other words, other-focused.

I first heard about *The Platinum Rule* from Tony Alessandra's book and assessment tool by the same name. The system's concept is that there are four basic personality and behavioral types. If we can assess other people's types and preferences, we can then communicate and interact with them in the way that works best for them, thereby enhancing our outcomes in business, sales and life. The foundation of the entire system is that we should determine what other people prefer in communication, decision making, thinking and interactions and follow their lead. This other-person focus is at the heart of a conscious leader's leadership and communication.

Think about how the Platinum Rule would change the dynamics in the situation described above. Rather than pushing for email communication because they like it best, the management team would consider their desired outcome (effective communication) and choose to communicate in the way that the recipient prefers. Why the way the recipient prefers? Because the purpose of the communication is to create a desired outcome *with the recipient,* and whatever that purpose, the best way to achieve it is to communicate in ways that most resonate with the recipient (from which the intended outcomes will flow). Now when we flip it, the team member should employ the Platinum Rule toward the management team members. When the team members want to have effective communication, the process will best be served by communicating in ways that are preferred by the recipients (the management team members).

This concept goes far beyond the methods of communication (telephone, email, text, etc.) and into the deeper levels of the ways that people receive information. For example, if someone you are communicating with is emotional in decision making and processing, then emotionally based communication will be most effective. Similarly, if the recipient of communication is very logical and organized in thinking and processing, then the most effective communication will be logical, organized and rational. If you are communicating with a big-vision thinker and you insist (selfishly) on only communicating details, your communication will be ineffective and may actually create unintended beliefs and assumptions with the recipient.

Many years ago when I still owned my law firm, I had my team take another assessment tool known as the DISC Profile, which, like the Platinum Rule system, is designed to help leaders understand people's preferences in communication, thinking and decision making. This assessment tool helped one of my associates and me to correct a serious communication challenge between us. I was finding myself very frustrated with him, and I had started to believe that he was not thinking things through (my judgment of him). In contrast, he had begun to believe that

I was a bad listener and perhaps a jerk because I was always short with him. After taking the DISC Profile assessment, we discovered the source of the disconnections in our communication.

He was a detail person who wanted and needed to turn over every stone and consider every possible point in order to reach his conclusions. I, on the other hand, wanted the answers to the questions and did not need to know the details (more big picture and solution-focused). Once we saw these differences between us, we were able to adjust our communication. I told him to do all of the detailed research and consider every point, which fit his preferences. When he communicated with me, however— the goal of which was to get me the information that I needed—we agreed that he should focus on the answers and leave details out unless I had questions. This awareness had an immediate and positive impact on our communication and relationship, all because we then knew and honored the other person's preferences.

As I have become more self-aware of the sources of these communication disconnects, I see them played out over and over in meetings, with teams, in organizations and in personal relationships. People are missing each other, and the communication is failing or self-destructing, along with the relationships. In some cases, the people even are saying the same thing, but do not realize it. In part this is a failure of listening, but in many cases it is due to the different ways that they are communicating. Each person is communicating in ways that work for them, but the recipient's ways of communicating and processing are not aligned with the method of communication. The solution is simple—communicators must focus on the other person in determining what they communicate and how they communicate, all within the desire (hopefully shared) to achieve effective communication.

Think about it—how often do the participants in communication want the communication to be ineffective? Even if you do not agree with what is being communicated to you, you would still want to have an accurate understanding of the communication. In many cases, the failure of the communication process is the reason that the intended consequences on both sides are not achieved. Conscious leaders embrace other-focused communication as a tool to improve communication, but also to assure that the intended consequences are achieved and that unintended (and undesirable) consequences are avoided.

Listening Leadership

A key element of other-focused communication is the recognition (put into action) that the most important part of communication is not what you communicate. The most important ingredient, even if you are the communicator, is *listening* to the other person. Listening is the most fundamental other-focused ingredient in communication. Even if you have something to communicate, your committed listening and focused attention to the other person's preferences will improve the communication outcomes.

When it comes to listening, there is one intention, outcome and skill that is essential and at the heart of conscious livingship—being fully present in every conversation, interaction and communication. Sadly, our culture and society have devolved so that being present in a conversation is not just uncommon but actually extremely rare. While one culprit is the cell phone, the problem exists even more so in our lack of commitment to others. How extreme is the state of distraction? I once posted on Facebook, "Wouldn't it be great if we could all be fully present in our communications?" The most common response was that this would be great, but "It's too hard." What? It is too hard

> When it comes to listening, there is one intention, outcome and skill that is essential and at the heart of conscious livingship—being fully present in every conversation, interaction and communication.

to listen to someone without thinking about something else (typically myself)? It is too hard to shut off and shut out other distractions in order to listen fully to someone and give them the gift of your presence?

It is truly a gift—being fully present for someone else—and a gift that speaks volumes to the person who is receiving it. I have worked hard at being present in conversations to the point that I will not even look around the room when I am talking with and listening to someone else. I look people in the eye, and I maintain that presence throughout the conversation. On a few occasions I have been told that the way I listen is too intense (which is not my intention), but the more common response is people saying that it is rare for anyone to be present and to listen to them the way that I do. By the way, when you are present and listen, you typically remember more of the conversation. You also listen at a different and deeper level, thereby creating greater trust and more opportunities to add value based upon what you heard. Conscious leaders are engaged in their conversations and show up at a level of presence that is rare, but is a blessing to the other person. This is a vital ingredient for compassionate communication.

Let us get back to the cell phone issue. I could be long-winded, but I will choose to be brief: put them away. You are not that important, and you certainly are not more important than the person you are with. Yes, that is the message you send when you choose to make calls, take calls, read or post on social media or even just look at your phone when you are with someone else. This causes a little white lie scenario in our society. If you are with someone and they get a call on their cell phone, they typically will say, "Do you mind if I take this call?" And what do most of us say: "Sure, go ahead." What are we actually thinking? "I can't believe you are taking that call." When you choose to focus on your cell phone when you are with someone else, you are telling that person that your phone and whatever is happening there is more important than he or she is. That is the message.

I talk to many people on the phone, and it is obvious that they are on their computers, reading emails and sometimes actually typing while they are on the phone with me. Let me rephrase that—while they are pretending to be on the phone with me. They are not present. Everywhere around me I see people not present and not engaged in their conversations, typically distracting themselves with their cell phones. You CANNOT be truly listening if you are not present. If you do not have time to be present for someone, then tell them this truth and offer to continue the conversation when you can be fully present. I was recently trying to set up for a speaking engagement while my hostess was asking me questions about the post-event schedule. After a few seconds, I politely told the hostess the following: "I cannot be fully present to you right now, and my personal commitment is to be fully present in my conversations. Let me set up the presentation and then I will be fully present for our conversation." Her response was totally positive, and she even commented about how great it is that I make that commitment and honor it.

You might need help to change your habits. Ask your friends and co-workers to support you by letting you know when you are not fully present. Ask people to help you be more present in your conversations by giving you honest feedback. Simply by asking for this support and feedback, you are telling people that being present and being a better listener is important to you and that they are important to you. These are simple steps, but the steps and the positive outcomes will have a dramatic impact on the quality of your relationships.

A friend of mine, Jack Ricchiuto, wrote that "We listen each other into existence." Think about that—without someone to listen, there is no reason for anyone to speak, and our listening brings them to life and into existence. This is powerful for a leader and is an almost sacred trust, and conscious leaders value people and conversations at this deep level. This is why listening is such an important part of compassionate communication.

Listening also plays a vital role with the other person's questions. All communication should include a check-in to see what the other person heard. Unfortunately, this step is often skipped, assumptions are made and disconnections occur. Even when the check-in step is employed (e.g. "What did you hear me say?") it is often ineffective because it is focused on the accuracy of what was heard (like a recording), rather than the overall context and desired outcome of the communication.

Listening on purpose also lets the other person know that you are engaged and that he or she is being heard. Whether at work or in our personal lives, we will not always get our way, but every person deserves to be heard and should expect to be heard. I always tell the teams I work with that they cannot always expect to get things their way or to have decisions made in their favor, but they have every reason to expect to be heard by management or other team members. Being fully present and listening beyond the words is essential to assuring that the communicator feels heard.

Another impediment to effective and empathetic listening flows from our own ego—the need to be right. Too many of us have a strong need to be right all the time, which means that our "listening" is really designed to help us refute what someone else is saying and to strategize and plan our counterpoints and counter arguments. If you are wondering if you have this bad habit, think about this reality: If you already have your response ready as soon as someone finishes speaking, then it is pretty clear that you were not listening to the person. While you may have heard what that speaker said, you were simultaneously thinking about the ways you wanted to refute his or her positions, contentions, and theories. If you are thinking about your response, then *you are not listening*.

In addition to being unable truly to multitask, it is also true that we are not capable of understanding when we are just trying to be right. Just as important, your desire or need to be right limits your ability to learn from someone else's perspective. If your goal (or need) is to prove the other person wrong, then learning and listening cannot exist. Only when you release the need to be right can you engage in a conversation or discussion and truly listen to other people's positions and perspectives with a sincere desire to understand the people, their positions and their context. It is only when you are listening to understand that you can learn yourself.

Why bother listening? Because empathetic listening will enhance our relationships, personal and professional; because listening to understand will create business relationships that will accelerate our business and our success; and because organizations that effectively communicate (which starts with full-presence listening) are more effective in consistently executing and achieving their objectives. Yes, the world has evolved to the point that listening is a scarce commodity, but you have the opportunity to change that dynamic starting today. I invite you to invest in others, to decide to listen, and to embrace the gift of full presence in all of your interactions and relationships!

Conscious leaders begin with the end goal in mind in their communication, consider the perspectives, preferences and context of the recipient, and communicate and listen in ways that empower and support the recipient. There is no such thing as one-way communication for conscious leaders, whose endgame of communication supports whatever it takes to achieve that desired outcome—and always with a focus on the other person.

The Three Communication Buckets

Have you ever had a situation where you felt that you were outside your body watching yourself in a conversation or some activity? Perhaps you have had this experience in a dream? While it might seem like a bunch of hocus-pocus, conscious leaders have the rare self-awareness ability to step out of situations and even emotions, observe themselves in those situations, and separate the various parts of the situation so that they can be more thoughtful, more intentional (rather than reactive) and more purposeful and strategic with their words, actions and decisions. If you are struggling to follow, stick with me. The examples below will shine a light on this unique

> Conscious leaders, however, do learn how to separate themselves from situations (even when they are in those situations) or at least slow down their thought processes so that they can make more objective and disinterested decisions and choices.

awareness skill that is nurtured and finely tuned by conscious leaders, a skill that gives conscious leaders a magnificent tool for creating more effective and engaged teams, consistent accountability and execution-minded organizations.

In a perfect world, leaders would have the ability to try things out (perhaps via computer simulation) before they acted in order to test how communications, choices and decisions will play out, but that is not reality. Conscious leaders, however, do learn how to separate themselves from situations (even when they are in those situations) or at least slow down their thought processes so that they can make more objective and disinterested decisions and choices. In the heat of the moment or in the midst of whatever is happening, it is easy to make emotional, rash or reactive decisions. Conscious leaders, however, use their self-awareness abilities to essentially step out of the situations or emotions to make more objective decisions.

What conscious leaders are able to do is to separate situations, circumstances and emotions into three distinct buckets:

1. Data (observable and verifiable facts);

2. Judgments (what others, including the leader, decide is true about people or situations); and

3. Feelings (the emotions that accompany the data and the judgments).

Awareness is the key to this unique ability to separate these three elements, because without awareness we lump everything (data, judgments and feelings) together. This lumping often guides us to bad or emotional decisions that are not in the team's, leader's or organization's best interests. The process alone of separating these three elements helps leaders better understand the situation, their team members and themselves. In addition, once he or she sees things separately, the leader has more opportunities to reflect on and assess the reality of the situation or circumstances and to make choices and decisions based upon that heightened awareness of reality.

Let us look at an example of this thin slicing and separation of these three elements. I was working with a leader in an organization (we'll call him Alex) who expressed concerns (showing self-awareness) about how he was communicating with certain team members. His desire was to provide objective feedback and accountability, but he found that he often became frustrated, and this frustration came out in the form of anger (or unnecessarily energized communication). We will talk more about energized communication below, but for this situation I walked the leader through the separation process which he had not been able to do for himself.

When I asked him the data of the situation, Alex shared that three of his team members continued to fail to do specific things that were part of their job descriptions and role expectations. I encouraged him (with my questions) to be specific as to what in this situation was data, which is limited to observable facts, words or events. In other words, data is what anyone else observing the situation would actually see or hear.

The following are examples of data that might apply to a work situation:

- Bob failed to file his daily report by 5:00 pm
- Sarah arrived at the meeting five minutes after the scheduled start time.

- Kyle's written report had seven typographical errors in it.
- Deana failed to call back a customer within 24 hours.

What is often mistaken for data (looking at the foregoing examples) are things like the following:

- Bob files his reports late.
- Sarah is late for meetings.
- Kyle is not careful in preparing his report.
- Deana does not serve customers well.

These are actually judgments that someone might make based upon the foregoing cumulative data, but judgments are not data. You will see below why this distinction is important, but one important difference is that a person can often unilaterally change the data or create new data, but judgments of people and situations are made by other people. As a result, a change in the data may not change the judgments.

Alex was frustrated (his word) with his team members, but he could not understand why he continued to get frustrated and why he continued to communicate with them in anger. Alex knew that his anger was not serving to create the desired changes in behavior, and he wanted to figure it out so that he could be a more effective manager and leader. When I asked Alex why he was getting frustrated and angry, he said that it was because he wanted his team members to "get it" so badly that he became frustrated when they did not get it. I then did for Alex what conscious leaders eventually do for themselves—frame their perspective in a clear statement that allows them to see more clearly what they are doing, thinking and believing. Here is the specific statement that I played back for Alex:

> Your team members are not "getting it," and you get frustrated
> and angry with them because you want so badly for them to
> succeed.

When I reframed the situation for Alex, his response was, "That doesn't make much sense, does it?" Alex was realizing for himself that it did not make sense that he would be angry with one of his team members *because* he wanted them to succeed.

After a few more probing questions (conscious leaders ask themselves these questions and invite others to challenge them with such questions), Alex realized that his frustration and anger was due to the fact that when his team members did not "get it," his job was made harder and he potentially looked bad. Imagine that—self-interest impacting our experiences and our reactions. In other words, Alex's frustration and angry communication were the results of his own self-interest in looking good and not having to make up for other people's failures.

Mind you, there is nothing wrong with Alex's reaction, but his reaction and his resulting angry communication were not helping to fix the problem. In fact, they were likely making the problem worse or at least limiting the opportunities to improve it. Since Alex did want to fix the problems and did want his team members to "get it," he used this awareness and assessment process to understand his underlying motives and drivers, which in turn allowed him to change his communication. Without this awareness, Alex would likely have remained stuck in the same unproductive behavior and communication because in his initial perception, his angry communication seemed to be the result of wanting his team members to succeed. Why would he change his behavior or communication if he thought that it was coming from a place of support and encouragement? The answer is that he would not.

Because Alex genuinely wanted to see his team members "get it" and improve, he then consciously chose to adjust his communication with them so that it aligned with his truest objective—to support, mentor and guide them towards improvement. While this awareness does not guarantee that Alex will never go back to the more unconscious form of angry communication (we will talk more about anger awareness and communication below), Alex is growing in his personal awareness and the ability to use this tool to separate himself, his drivers and his emotions from situations in the future.

Perhaps even more critically, by learning to separate the data from the judgments from the emotions, Alex and other growing conscious leaders can develop the ability to experience their reactions and emotions (whatever they are), but separate them from their decisions and communication. When everything is all lumped together, there is no opportunity to separate anything, and decisions, perceptions and communication are often reactive, unconscious and off-course. The mere ability to separate the elements into their own categories then allows a growing conscious leader to slow down the assessment and thinking process, to be more thoughtful (even in the midst of chaos), to make better decisions and to communicate more effectively.

Picture it this way (using the Alex example). Alex's team members fail to perform as expected. He is frustrated and angry, but he is aware enough to discover that his frustration comes more from how their performance impacts him than from caring about them. Alex wants to support them and help them improve. He is aware of his frustration and anger, but he realizes that communicating or holding someone accountable through the anger is not going to be productive. As a result, Alex *chooses* to communicate with his team members about the data only and from a place of support, rather than from his judgments and emotions. Think of it as Alex saying to himself, "Hmm. I'm angry. I don't want to communicate that anger because it won't serve me, my team members or the organization. I'll acknowledge the anger (and learn from it), but I will put my anger aside and communicate with the team members from a place of supportive accountability (see Chapter 11 for more on Stickless Accountability). This process of awareness, probing internal questions and separation helps conscious leaders be most effective in their decisions, their mentoring, their managing of people and their communication. In this way, conscious leaders are more consistently and predictably intentional, purposeful, thoughtful and strategic with their decisions and choices.

> This process of awareness, probing internal questions and separation helps conscious leaders be most effective in their decisions, their mentoring, their managing of people and their communication.

Unenergized Communication

Earlier, I mentioned the concept of energized (versus unenergized) communication, which is an important awareness and skill development opportunity for any leader. I developed the concept of energized communication after struggling with leaders and teams to clarify the emotions that were being included in their communication. The deliverer of the communication typically proclaimed that he or she was not angry, but the receiver of the communication was adamant that the communicator was "upset" or "something." Instead of focusing on the communication (or lack thereof), on the disconnect or the underlying issues or behaviors, the parties to the communication were overly concerned about figuring out the whats and whys of the emotion (or whatever it was) that was underlying the communication.

Clearly seeing that the focus was misdirected, I developed the theme of energized communication, which is the almost vibrational energy that accompanies much communication (verbal and written). This extra energy is essentially the current on which the message is carried and, too often, the focus of the listener/receiver is on the energy, rather than the message itself. Likewise, when the communicator denies that there is anything extra happening, the communication gets even further off-course (or even spirals downhill) because the separate parties are not in agreement about the energy.

As leaders become more aware, they can become better and better at identifying the extra energy, separating it from the messages and communicating as cleanly as possible. This separation greatly enhances the quality of the communication (on both sides), resulting in more effective communication, fewer disconnects and enhanced relationships (personally and professionally). By dropping the need to label or identify the extra energy, the parties to the communication (whether one-on-one, small groups or teams) can better and more deeply commit to the communication, to mutual understanding and to moving through and beyond whatever the core issues are that necessitated the communication.

Interestingly, when we drop the need to label or judge the emotions (the extra energy), all of the parties to the communication become more readily able to acknowledge that there was something extra in the communication, even if it was unnamed. I have found that people are willing to take ownership of the extra much more easily when it is just called energy than when it comes with a label (often someone else's negative label). For example, I found that if a team member took issue with the undertone of some communication, that member would typically label it (often as frustration, anger or worse). The communicator, when challenged with these labels, would often deny *the label*, but neither party to the communication was getting to the core issues. The disconnects often ended up being more about the extra in the communication, thereby negating the purpose and objectives of the communication itself. No wonder people are so frustrated with communication.

When reframed as just "energy," people are much more open to acknowledging that there is something extra, as long as they do not have to accept the labels on that extra. Conscious leaders work to become aware of the extra energy and to minimize or eliminate it from their communication, knowing that this extra energy never serves to enhance the communication or its outcomes. They also seek to model this awareness for their team members and mentor them in embracing the same awareness and approach to communication so that the entire team, group or organization can move into more effective communication.

The process for breaking the communication into its elements of the data, the judgments and the emotions works hand-in-glove with the concept of energized or unenergized communication. This separation of the elements actually can reduce or sometimes eliminate the extra energy (whatever it is), thereby further facilitating the communication process (both delivering and listening).

The other valuable outcome of this level of awareness is that the awareness itself—just paying attention to the energy that we are experiencing with or about a person or situation—actually reduces or eliminates the energy. Imagine a conscious team member feeling the need to communicate with another team member about some issue, challenge or disconnect. By purposefully observing any feelings or energy with the person or about the issue, the team member can begin to assess and debrief himself about the energy. For example, if the team member breaks out the pure data (facts only), that person might realize that there is no reason to have extra energy towards the other person based solely upon the data. With this realization, the team member can then explore within himself or herself the source or cause of the extra energy, which often relates to prior interactions with the other team member, an existing disconnect or relationship gap or even something else going on in the first team member's work or life that is sneaking into and complicating the real issue.

If the team member does not consciously work through the extra energy, there is a substantial likelihood that the short-term communication will be ineffective at best or create even longer-term disconnects, relationship gaps or team issues. How often have we heard or said ourselves that we are okay with the message, but we take issue with the *way it was communicated?* By observing and demystifying our energy and emotions around communication, we can create a fundamental positive shift not only in the process of communication, but in the ultimate ends for which the communication was intended. In other words, the things that we want to stop, change or improve actually are addressed more consistently, more collaboratively and more effectively. Now that is one big win for (and from) awareness!

Compassionate Communication Leads the Way

At the outset of this chapter, I talked about the ways that conscious leaders look at communication: other-person and outcomes focused. This is the new way of communicating being embraced by leaders—effective over efficient; selfless over selfish; balanced over one-sided; unemotional over emotional; impact over process. Conscious leaders make different choices in how they experience other people, including how they communicate. They also recognize that the recipient's communication experience is the most important part of effective communication. The interesting dichotomy is that conscious leaders look inside themselves to be more effective in communication and step into the shoes of the recipient to create a collaborative communication experience (even if the recipient is not engaging in the communication in the same way as the leader). You cannot control how someone else experiences your communication, but you can take your own steps in that direction by investing in understanding, committing to being present for the other person and focusing on the desired outcome for the communication.

In short, conscious leaders are willing to take themselves *out* of the communication in order to invest more fully *in* the communication. Conscious leaders are able to embrace different perspectives and go within at the same time as they step outside of themselves. This is one of the impactful traits that conscious leaders develop and refine, knowing that they cannot succeed without other people, and thus communication is the path to their desired outcomes, both personally and organizationally.

CHAPTER 10: COMMUNICATION TOOLBOX (THE INFLUENCING LEADER)

"Trust is the glue of life. It's the most essential ingredient in effective communication."

Stephen Covey

What's In Your Communication Tool Box

Stephen Covey left us so many gifts through his books and teachings, and one that has always stood out for me is his tree-cutting wisdom: "Always make sure to sharpen the saw." Covey was focused on the critical need that we all have to take care of ourselves in order to be best able to live, lead and achieve. This book is all about this type of internal shifting and sharpening. Similarly, Abraham Lincoln famously said: "Give me six hours to chop down a tree, and I will spend the first four sharpening the axe." Honest Abe was speaking more about the importance of regularly sharpening our tools for whatever task is ahead of us, and that is my invitation in this chapter.

The prior chapter on Compassionate Communication is focused on different ways you can think and communicate as a leader. These mindset and approach shifts will prove to be highly impactful as you seek to accelerate your personal and professional communication in terms of effectiveness and outcomes. To go along with these different mindsets and ways of communicating, you will need a new communication toolbox filled with razor-sharp communication tools to help you be at your most effective in every aspect of communication. Stephen Covey was clear about the essential role of trust in communication: "When the trust account is high, communication is easy, instant, and effective." Thus, trust is the missing link in most communication disconnects, both personally and organizationally. In this chapter, we will explore several unique communication twists to help you be your most effective as a communicator and as a leader, with trust as the foundation.

The Truth Arrow

During a retreat I attended several years ago, a team was discussing the obstacles to effective communication, including the ever-present challenges of engaging in honest and direct communication with each other. The most fundamental obstacle to this type of direct communication is a lack of trust. While organizations and teams do not want to admit it, they often do not trust each other with respect to feedback, honest communication and accountability. Think about it—if I fully trust that any feedback, accountability or even constructive criticism is intended solely to help me improve or improve the team and the organization, why would I take it personally (ignoring for the moment the way that it might be communicated)? The answer is that I would *not* take it personally, I would not be defensive, and in fact I would be grateful for the feedback, even if it might be considered negative or critical. The most natural response to direct feedback in a trusting relationship is "Thank you." After all, we would all want to know if we are not performing up to expectations, if we are not understanding the expectations or if we are not on the same page with another team member.

The problem is that we often do not trust the motives of the deliverer of the feedback or criticism. We believe that person's motives are not supportive or team-oriented, but instead self-interested or even selfish. In addition, the communicated feedback often comes with that pesky extra energy, and this can cause the receiver of the feedback to make judgments about the source or underlying basis for that extra energy. No wonder we do not do well with direct and honest communication and feedback.

We could spend an entire book on the topic of trust gaps within teams and organizations (and we will talk about trust in some other contexts later in this book), but the other issues we identified during the retreat discussion were the extra energy and what happens when direct communication does not happen in a timely fashion. This discussion led me to the creation of the *Truth Arrow* (see figure below), which explains many of the dynamics that occur when people and teams fail to communicate promptly with each other, causing disagreements, disconnects or misaligned expectations.

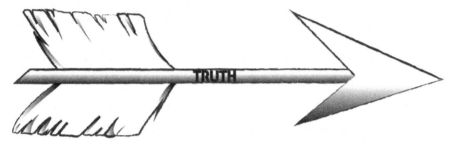

In a perfect world (or, I would argue, a more conscious world), we would all share with each other our perceptions of the truth. Let's face it—there is very little that is truly objectively true, especially when we are discussing people's interactions and communication. In my perfectly conscious world, the issues would arise, we would speak our "truth" to the other person and, whether or not the receiver of the "truth" agreed, he or she could engage in an open discussion so that both parties would have clarity about the communication and about the underlying issues. This "truth" is the shaft of the arrow and could be delivered in a fairly even-handed and simple fashion—much like handing the other person the "arrow of truth." Unfortunately, this often is not how the communication experience unfolds. Rather than having that prompt and direct communication, the party with something to communicate does not share what he or she has to say for some time, and that is when the wheels of communication come off.

They say that time heals, but that is often <u>not</u> the case with unshared communication, especially when it relates to anything that might be deemed critical, negative or implying any type of shortcoming. Apparently, the act of communication is like releasing the air out of a balloon that is overly inflated. The release of the air through communication tends to minimize the energy, but when the release does not happen, then the air continues to build, and that is when the extra stuff really starts to surface and even expand.

When the direct communication does not happen, the person with something to say often stews and the information swirls. While that person waits (for whatever reason) to share, things continue to build and build, and it is during this time that the following can emerge:

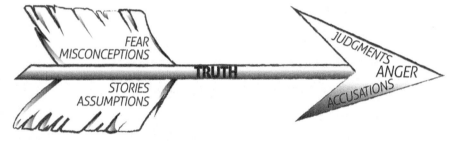

By the time that the "arrow of truth" is delivered, it is armed with a nasty point loaded with all of the foregoing judgments, stories and accusations. Instead of merely delivering the truth arrow to the recipient, the speaker is now firing a poison-tipped arrow at the other person, with or without warning of what is coming. Not surprisingly, the recipient then does what many of us naturally would do: we deflect, defend, protect and perhaps even begin firing back our own judgment-filled arrows.

Can you imagine any healthy communication going on here? How about the level of listening? How about the desire to seek mutual understanding and to resolve the core issues? None of that exists because the sole focus is now on the other person, the judgments about that person and his or her motives, and the desire to win the argument. Perhaps even worse, one common form of defense by the recipient is to shut down and not listen (or just pretend to listen). Without attempting to judge who is right or wrong in this communication breakdown, one thing is clear—productive communication is decidedly <u>not</u> the outcome. As for the underlying issues, you can guess what happens with them—they go unresolved, at least in the long term.

Despite the many obstacles to healthy and direct communication, your ability (as well as that of others) to be more aware, to observe your actions and your emotions, and to break down communication into its different parts can and will create a whole new model for honest communication. Communication where:

- The parties are mutually committed to the process.

- The parties are willing to listen to each other.

- The parties seek to understand each other and the various perspectives each person brings to the table.

- The parties are able to communicate the essential information *without* the extra energy and emotions that block effective communication.

- The parties trust each other enough to be open to hearing each other.

If it sounds impossible, then perhaps you are considering the possibilities through the old way of being, where communication is largely unconscious. The new way of being and leading by the conscious leader can create precisely this type of encouraging, supportive and open communication environment. These same conscious leaders can and must model this level of awareness and openness to other members of the team—they must walk the talk—so that the rest of the team can see and experience the positive outcomes and experiences from this type of more purposeful communication.

They Are Your Emotions

One of the fundamental truths that conscious leaders embrace about emotions is that their emotions are their own and that no one else and no situation can *make them anything* or force them into having any emotion. This self-ownership of emotions is one key difference between conscious leaders and others: Conscious leaders look inside for the answers, rather than blaming others and circumstances for their emotions. So often we make excuses and blame others for *our emotions*, whether the topics are big or small:

- My boss makes me so mad.
- That person who cut me off in traffic made me angry.
- My son made me feel bad.
- My daughter made me feel guilty.

Do any of these sound familiar? It can be easy to believe that someone else is always responsible for every emotion, situation, or outcome that we experience. Still, this belief alone completely leaves us powerless and at the whim of circumstances—a far cry from maintaining the control that we seem to desire. In the words of Eleanor Roosevelt, "Nobody can make you feel inferior without your consent."

In the past couple of years, two things have hit me:

1. My belief that other people *made* me feel certain ways was not true. In fact, others do not do (and cannot do) anything to me to *make* me feel anything—what I feel,

> One of the fundamental truths that conscious leaders embrace about emotions is that their emotions are their own and that no one else and no situation can make them anything or force them into having any emotion.

experience, and achieve comes from inside me.

2. The only way to be truly in control of myself and my future is to accept full responsibility for my life, including accountability to myself for my emotions and my circumstances.

Wow—what a shift this has been, especially in a world where blaming others is not only easy, but the apparently preferred mindset in our culture. This attitude is pervasive even in our personal relationships and our business teams.

Before you give up on me and stop reading, I am not suggesting that other people do not have an impact on our lives, our emotions, and the results we achieve. They certainly do. As the saying goes, "It takes two to tango." It also takes two to ruin a relationship—and a team to mess up a project. The fact is, we do **not** have the ability to control others; we do, however, have the ability to change ourselves, our perspectives and our behaviors—but only when we accept full responsibility for our lives, our emotions and our results. In the wisdom of George Costanza, "It's not you, it's me."

Yet, in choosing to focus on that which we do not control (other people and outside circumstances), we give up on that which we have the most control over in our lives—our choices (see Chapter 2). It is fascinating to me how often and how persistently people hang on to the need to point the finger of blame at others, especially when it comes to their emotions. I recently gave a speech on this topic, and much of the feedback was along the lines of, "I liked your speech, but I don't agree with you that the emotions are mine." When I ask people who object in this way for examples, they typically fall back on cultural norms and stories: "Of course I would be mad if someone did or said this to me." Of course? What does it matter what others (or even the majority) might do? The fact that many people would respond the same way as you does not prove that your response is reasonable or correct, just culturally acceptable.

In *Road House* (1989), Patrick Swayze plays a "cooler"—essentially a head bouncer who is hired to turn brawling bars into reputable places. When he is hired to clean up the Double Deuce, he calls the existing employees together and shares his simple message: "Be nice until it's time to not be nice." When an employee asks, "What if somebody calls my momma a whore?" Patrick Swayze's character (Dalton) responds, "Is she?" His point is profound—that what others do to us or say to us is not personal; how we receive it inside makes it personal. His point to the employee is that if what someone says is not true, why would you be angry? Unfortunately, our society has so embraced the idea of blame that we allow other people and circumstances to upset us, anger us, sadden us, or get us off-track, and then we blame them for our emotions and responses. As a result, we never look inside at the parts of us that are angry, sad or off-track. Until we take this look inside (and ignore what society says is normal), we have virtually no chance to change our responses and our lives.

As I share this message with others, I regularly encounter objections. People are hesitant to believe that other people are not the cause of their emotions or outcomes. Of course, it is very logical to conclude that someone *else* must have made me angry, but let me invite you to see the words or actions of others as merely the trigger for <u>our own</u> inner emotions. I was recently presented with an effective visual for this idea. It is called *the sponge and the ink*. Like a hand squeezing a sponge full of ink, the words and actions of others only help release emotions that are already inside of us. While others can trigger things in us, the reactions and emotions we feel inside are our own. In other words, the ink that comes out belongs to the sponge, not the hand doing the squeezing. The reaction or the emotion is <u>our ink</u>.

My personal transition to living by the belief that my emotions, reactions and outcomes are my own came about a couple of years ago when I was very upset with one of my sons. After several weeks of not being able to see him because he was very busy with the things going on in his life, my emotions were bubbling and boiling over. I felt a combination of anger, disappointment, incredulity ("How dare he?") and sadness. When I finally had the opportunity to see him, I told him that I could not spend time with him then because of all of the emotions rolling around inside me. I unleashed on him a torrent of all of the foregoing emotions with harsh words, tears, and intensity. I finished it off by saying, "You've made me feel like a piece of crap."

I stormed out the door. By the time I had taken the 30 steps to my car, I had had my epiphany. As I sat down in my car, the truth and clarity hit me like a lightning bolt: He could not *make me* anything. Not mad, sad, scared—not *anything*. Yes, I was feeling all of those emotions. Yes, he had been a trigger. Yes, he had been rude, had ignored my desires to spend time with him and, in my estimation, had been inconsiderate in his communication, all things that he could change (and I believed he should change) and which were within *his* control.

At the same time, my emotions came from inside of me. I immediately began to assess why I was feeling sad, angry and disappointed, which I traced to the parts of me that were already feeling alone and unloved. Certainly, I could have justified my emotions as logical and appropriate, but in doing so I would have put all of the blame on my son. In that scenario, my emotions could improve only *if he changed.* Out of control? Yes. Sound familiar? Certainly. Perhaps a recent experience with your work team? You are waiting for someone else to change in order for you to feel better, be less stressed, be more productive, etc. In choosing to look inside for the source of your emotions and disconnects, though, you have the empowering opportunity to work on and through whatever is at the core of your emotions, your stress, or your disrupted productivity. Then, you can change this "trigger" in the moment and in the future. Talk about being *in control.* From that day forward I have consistently (though not always perfectly) looked inside for the source of my emotions and reactions, thereby moving ever closer to the control we all seek.

The mindset of looking first and primarily within for the source of your emotions applies equally to other situations in our lives. Yes, other people can have an impact on the things that we achieve (or fail to achieve), but one truth never changes: We do not have direct control over other people's actions, inactions, or behaviors. When I blame others for my outcomes, I give up not only control, but the ability to change the one person that I do have control over—me! The other problem with blame is that it is awfully convenient and much easier than taking personal responsibility and living in accountability for my own outcomes. Thus, blaming can be a convenient habit that gives us temporary pleasure since it allows us not to look in the mirror and face the things that we did (or did not do) that created the outcomes we have.

While some people have argued that they can do both—blame others and look at their own actions–I have found that this is an almost impossible balance. After all, if I am blaming, why would I look at myself? In addition, if I have already blamed, then will I really see my own role fully and honestly? No; that is why I have chosen to invest my time, energy and efforts on the only person that I have a real opportunity to change—again, me!

They Are Your Filters

Whether you have good vision or poor vision and whether you need prescription eyewear or not, I imagine that each of you has at some time had an eye examination. You know the drill—you look through a piece of equipment, and the doctor adjusts the lenses in order to determine when you

> You apply individualized filters in the communication process, and these filters have a dramatic impact on how you hear or experience the other person.

can see better or worse. The examination often also includes a test where different colored filters are used to check for color-blindness and to see how the different colors impact your vision. The essence of this process is that as the lenses and filters are changed, they impact what you see and how well you see it. In other words, they impact your visual experience.

Why am I talking about eye examinations? Because each of you essentially does the same thing in communication, especially when the communication or situation is energized, challenging or off-course. You apply individualized filters in the communication process, and these filters have a dramatic impact on how you hear or experience the other person. These filters often drive your judgments about the communication, the situation *and the person* (almost always unconsciously). However, when you are more aware of the ways that you are using filters in your communication, you can choose to not to use them or to shift your filter to one that better serves you, the relationship, the communication and your desired objectives.

Let us take a look at what I mean by these filters and how they get in the way of healthy and effective communication. I was working with a coaching client (we will call her Pam) on team communication issues, including the ways that she reacted or responded to other people on her team. In the hope of better understanding the extra sources and drivers of the reactions, I asked Pam to list the names of five team members with whom she regularly communicates. I then asked Pam to give me a brief description (not more than a couple of words) to describe the best and worst aspects of each person. While traditional communication training often focuses on the positive, I have found that the identification and acknowledgment of the negative aspects in our relationships is critical to making adjustments and improvements because it is the so-called negative aspects that are most likely getting in the way. This is particularly true when evaluating yourself in terms of the ways that you communicate (or fail to communicate) with other people.

Pam came up with the following list of filters:

	Positive	Negative
Tom	Thorough	Irresponsible
Kris	Open-minded	Over-analyzing
Len	Honors Commitments	Sticks His Nose in Things
Terry	Perceptive on Details	Never Good Enough
Kathy	Understands Business	Self-Righteous

These were the primary filters that Pam had and used for each of her team members.

I then asked Pam this additional question:

When you are frustrated, angry or otherwise energized with each of them, *which filter are you experiencing them through?*

Pam quickly acknowledged that when the communication was not working or when she had negative reactions to the team members, she was certainly "hearing" or experiencing them through the negative filter; Pam was quick to suggest, however, that the use of the negative filter was *because in that moment they were communicating or acting consistently with that filter.* In other words, Pam was suggesting that the other person was dictating which filter she used in the communication. Then I shifted gears with Pam and told her that she was wrong: while the other people may have acted or communicated in ways that were consistent with the filter, Pam as the other participant in the communication still *chooses the filter.*

I then played out this example with Pam. I asked her to imagine that she was interacting with Tom and that Tom was engaging in behavior or communication that Pam would consider to be irresponsible. I then asked Pam what would happen to her experience of Tom if she were aware in the moment and chose to experience Tom and the communication through the filter of Tom as someone who is thorough. While this can be a difficult concept to grasp immediately, Pam got it right away and said that *if* she communicated with Tom and saw him as someone who was thorough (a positive trait in Pam's mind), then it would markedly improve the communication *even if Tom was acting in ways that might be deemed to be irresponsible.* In other words, like Pam, you can choose how you experience someone else, and that choice is yours alone to make. It is not the automatic outcome of how the other person chooses to communicate or interact with you. You choose the filters, and thus you have the ability to determine the communication experience. You may not control the other person, but you own the choice of filter.

I recently shared this concept with a friend who struggles with communication with her business partner, and we went through exactly the same exercise regarding her partner. She identified what she perceived as the worst trait of her business partner (controlling) and the best trait of her business partner (giving). When I shared with her about the role of filters in communication and that these filters are her choice, she was at first hesitant, but she seemed open to thinking differently about the communication and her partner. She was also clearly committed to improving the working relationship with her partner. The next day, my friend sent me the following email:

> "Jeff, I believe you changed my life yesterday and I truly mean that. I am going to start listening to conversations with a different filter. It really makes a lot of difference."

Indeed, they are **your** filters and **you** have the unique ability and opportunity to choose which filters you will use to listen to and communicate with other people, in business, in relationships and in every aspect of your life.

If you want to improve your communication and general experience with every person in your business, on your team and in your life immediately, then identify your opposing filters for each person and consciously choose which filter you will listen and experience them with in the future. You will see immediate and positive improvements in all of your communications and relationships, even if the other person does not change. That is the beauty of owning and choosing your filters on purpose.

Conscious Leaders Flip It

No, I am not talking about flipping pancakes. I am talking about an impactful tool to use in communicating with others and with yourself. The process is quite simple, but the insights it provides are amazing, both for yourself and others. The flip process is simply a matter of inviting someone to see a situation from another person's perspective (using a question), and you can also learn to extend to yourself that same invitation to see another perspective. It is basically a process for being able, in the moment, to get inside another person's shoes—that is, his or her context and experience. There is nothing terribly new about this approach, but the newness comes from the fact that we do not usually make a practice of flipping our perspectives for ourselves or helping others to flip their perspectives. Instead, we tend to tell other people exactly what they should think or how they should see things, and that approach does not work.

The Flip is simply a matter of asking yourself or another person to see the other side of things and to experience things as another person. Let us look at a couple of specific examples, personal and professional. I was working with a client—James—on improving his listening and communication skills. We were discussing a specific situation where James had given input to another team member that had not been well received, and James did not understand his team member's reaction. In James' view, he had just shared information, but his team member had gotten defensive. I set up the Flip by asking James to state (for me, but mainly for him to hear) the context for the conversation, both his context and his team member's context. This context clarification is an important step because even if you think you know the context, saying it out loud really helps you to understand it, especially the context of another person. We often miss pieces of context when all we do is think about it in our heads, and speaking it out loud helps us hear things differently.

I then asked James the Flip question:

> Imagine that you are your team member and he communicates with you exactly the same way that you did with him. How would you receive it and react?

It may be difficult to believe, but this very simple two-step Flip process—identify the context for both parties and then put yourself in their shoes—usually results in new and valuable awareness. In this case, James' answer was that he would not have liked the approach, and he even listed the reasons why (this is the third step in the Flip process). In listing the reasons, James more fully understood his team member's perspective and James gained his own insights into himself. Even if James still disagreed with the team member's response and reaction, the Flip process helped him to understand it and the team member. It also gave him insights into how to change and improve his communication approach in the future, all with greater awareness of how it might be received.

You might be thinking, "Doesn't going through this process take up valuable time?" or "Wouldn't it be easier if people just got a thick skin and didn't take things personally?" Yes, it does take a little time, effort and self-reflection. And yes, it would be great if everyone were fully open to feedback and direct communication and never misheard anything. Good luck with that strategy, but it is not a strategy—it is a hope that is not realistic in human interactions. My flip to you is to suggest that if communication is really valuable (which it is), then it deserves the investment of a little additional thought and awareness. In addition, the people that you work with and have relationships with deserve to be understood, and the investment in understanding will pay big dividends in your ongoing work, relationships and communication together. The time for the Flip is worth it.

You can work the Flip on yourself using the same question format either to understand your own reactions better or to understand another person's reaction. My girlfriend and I will often involve the Flip in our discussions or even arguments. For example, imagine that I am

> This opportunity for creating self-reflection in another person or within yourself is why the Flip is so powerful. It allows for better understanding of other people, their positions and reactions, and the understanding comes through your own eyes (which makes it more likely to be "heard" and to stick).

suggesting to her that I would like to have more communication with her about a certain topic, but she is questioning either my reaction or the need for the additional communication. In the midst of the discussion, I can ask her the Flip question: "If I had not communicated this additional information to you, how would you feel?" Rather than telling her how she would react or feel, I ask the question in the hope that she will better understand my position *through her own eyes.*

This opportunity for creating self-reflection in another person or within yourself is why the Flip is so powerful. It allows for better understanding of other people, their positions and reactions, and the understanding comes through your own eyes (which makes it more likely to be "heard" and to stick). Once you have established the use of the Flip, you can actually use it in your conversations. In a friendly way, before I ask the Flip question, I might say to the other person, "Let's flip it." The Flip is a powerful and non-threatening tool for enhancing empathy, understanding, awareness and communication.

Make It Bigger

The other process that conscious leaders use to enhance understanding and communication is the "make it bigger" process of taking information and presenting it in a "bigger" way, without embellishing it. In this process, the information is accurate, and you can get buy-in from the other person on the accuracy of the information, but you exaggerate how the information is being conveyed in order to help someone see the true impact of his or her communication or actions. Because the "make it bigger" process is also relatively non-threatening, it can open the door to deeper understanding and stimulate change more effectively than confrontational methods.

Here is a quick example. I was having a discussion with someone about her use of her cell phone to check emails and post on social media while in meetings or conversations with other people. She was somewhat aware of this behavior (we had talked about it before), but when I brought it up she gave me a long list of reasons that she had to be so accessible and responsive. Rather than challenge her "reasons," which would not have helped the discussion or been heard, I turned her reasons into an exaggerated example—I made it bigger. Here is what I told her:

> I want you to imagine that you have a piece of paper that you carry around—much like an oversized business card—and on that card are all of the reasons that you are on your cell phone when you are with other people. The paper will have a warning at the top that says, "I want you to know in advance that I will be on my cell phone during our meeting and that I will not be fully present in our discussions for the following reasons."

Obviously, no one would carry around a note like this, much less give it to people at meetings—this is the exaggeration part. I then told her that this is precisely the message she is communicating when she is regularly accessing her cell phone when she is with other people. She provided the reasons, so she cannot dispute or disagree with the reasons. While she might question the conclusion, most people will recognize its accuracy or concede that people would (or at least might) form that conclusion. I just made it bigger to get her attention.

A great use of making it bigger is to help someone see the reality of messages that they are communicating to other people by their words, actions or approaches. I often use the "make it bigger" approach with clients who are telling me the reasons that they do or do not do something that might benefit their clients. Recently, someone told me that he does not share certain information with clients because he cannot trust them. I then suggested that he send out an email to his clients (I made it bigger and somewhat ridiculous) to inform them that he is not sharing information because he does not trust them. I was not suggesting that he actually send out such an email, but thinking about that idea helped the business owner to see that he was not fully considering his clients in decisions.

In this context, I am not talking about using bigger words but about turning ways of thinking or acting into "bigger" forms to highlight how off-course they are. Here is one more example to clarify what I mean by making it bigger. I was in a meeting where a business owner was talking about a pain-in-the-butt client—his largest client—and feeling that there was nothing he could do about it. I said that one option was to choose not to do business with him, and he said that firing the client was not an option. I believe that saying something is "not an option" (versus "It is an option, but that option does not make sense") is a very limiting way of thinking and can become a habit. The absence of perceived options can also become your normal way of thinking, assessing and making decisions.

In response, I said: "Would you fire the client if you found out he was sleeping with your wife or had beaten his children?" The owner said, "Of course, yes." I said, "Therefore, firing the client is an option if the reason is good enough." This opened up the discussions to a wider range of options because I "made it bigger" in order to highlight the existence and range of choices. The point of the "make it bigger" approach is not necessarily to identify realistic options or choices. Rather, it is designed to remind you that you always have choices, even if they are not easy or good choices. Armed with this awareness, you can then go through your process of assessment in the context that everything is a potential choice and then refine your long list of choices down to the choices that are best within the context.

The goal with the "make it bigger" process is not to tell people what they should think or to convince them to see something your way. It is simply a method for helping someone to see a situation or behavior differently or more fully, allowing them to make more conscious decisions about their words, actions, behaviors and decisions going forward. The "make it bigger" process is not about changing minds but about helping to create more conscious decisions. These conscious decisions themselves, and even simply the fact that more conscious decisions are being made, are a win for every leader, organization, team and person.

Sharpening Your Communication Edge

The foregoing communication tools will help you achieve your objectives, enhance your relationships and expand your influence, all of which are leadership and *livingship* essentials. Unlike traditional communication tools, they address the heart of communication disconnects and improvement opportunities—trust, understanding context, emotions and perspective shifting. Whether you are seeking to transform your business, your organization, your relationships or your life, nothing will change—yes, I said *nothing* will change—unless and until you become your best in communication.

Rather than trying to figure out how to get other people to listen differently, conscious leaders are committed to improving and shifting the ways that they communicate in order to achieve the desired communication outcomes. The tools discussed above <u>work</u> and are based upon a collaborative approach to communication, which after all involves two or more people. The idea of one side or another trying separately to improve communication has limitations. The foregoing also encourages direct and honest communication that is delivered without the extra stuff (mostly emotions) that typically limits or dooms this essential communication. It is time to embrace new ways of communicating without excuses and without expectations, which empowers the communicator to have direct impact on the communication outcomes. Let the sharpened communication begin!

CHAPTER 11: QUESTIONS ARE THE ANSWER (THE QUESTIONING LEADER)

"The wise man doesn't give the right answers.
He poses the right questions."

Claude Levi-Strauss

Among the many impact-creating traits of conscious leaders is this: *They stop talking* so much and instead question their way to influence. They understand the power of questions. Not statements. Not presentations. Not affirmations. Questions, for they are unique in their ability to ignite the flame of our own intellectual, intuitive and emotional brilliance. While statements are intended to communicate what one person believes to be true to another person, questions are intended to unleash a person's internal reflection, assessment and self-discovery, and this inside-out type of learning is what matters and sticks. When we ask ourselves and others questions, we open the door to heightened awareness, accelerated creativity, hyper-engagement and new levels of innovation (in big things and in small things).

Going back to the Albert Einstein well of wisdom, here is what he said about questions:

> "If I had an hour to solve a problem, and my life depended on the solution, I would spend the first 55 minutes figuring out the right question because once I did that, I would have the solution in five minutes."

What? No "let's get right to the solutions"? No "let's do a brainstorming session for action items"? No "let's create a team for problem solving"?

Instead, Einstein invites us to **stop** and first figure out the *right question.* Once we have the right question, we will have the solution.

People are always looking for answers. They want to know how to improve themselves and fix the various problems inherent in their businesses or their lives. They want to know how to get more clients or customers or how to increase their revenue. They want to know how to improve profits. They want to know how to deal with the economy. Yes indeed, everyone is looking for answers—THE ANSWERS—to help them create positive change. Many times, however, the problem is that they are asking the wrong questions. In order to get the right answers, we need to be asking the *right questions.*

Study after study has demonstrated the power of our minds to solve problems, whether the solutions involve complex analysis or simple creativity. Our brains are hard-wired to answer questions. Whenever we hear a question, our brains immediately (and without conscious thought) begin to try to answer the question. In fact, we cannot stop our brains from trying to answer questions. Unfortunately, we too often forget or ignore the power that our brains have to solve problems. Even more frequently, we miss opportunities within ourselves and within our organizations by failing to ask the *right question.* The creative power of the question is precisely what Einstein understood and integrated into his world.

Influence Is Asking the Right Question

Given the power that we have (individually and collectively) to answer questions, solve problems and create solutions, ultimate power is not in the answers but rather in the questions–the *right questions.* The problem is that in facing challenges or opportunities, we too often jump into the obvious questions with little or no thought, and we fail to invest time in developing the right question—the question or questions that will drive us toward the right answers and the right solutions.

I am often asked *a question* such as "What is a great question?" but these inquiries are missing the point. The focus is not on the right list of canned questions (although you can learn to deliver some good ones over time), but rather on the *right question* in the particular, specific context you are dealing with. It is not about finding a right question that universally applies, but rather learning to "listen for the question" in all situations and interactions. The concept and process of listening for the question is what Einstein was describing when he talked about investing most of his time in determining the *right question.*

In What Ways Can You Empower Your Questions?

Another impactful shift in questioning was shared with me many years ago by a fellow member of my Master Mind group. We were doing what we thought was brainstorming for another group member to answer this question: "How can I grow my business?" (a clear example of a wrong question) We had spent about a half-hour on this question, and we collectively had come up with less than a dozen ideas, none of which were particularly exciting. One group member then shared a question shift that she had recently discovered, which was that "how" questions are necessarily limiting. When we ask "how" questions, how many answers are we looking for? The answer is <u>one</u> because once we have one "good" answer, then we have technically answered the question of how to do or accomplish something. Thus, "how" questions do not support or encourage creative thinking, brainstorming or innovation. Instead, "how" questions invite us merely to come up with a short list of possible answers until we find <u>one</u> that sounds pretty good, and we have then *answered the question.* Now we think we can stop looking for more answers. "How" questions do not allow us to tap into the true genius and creativity of our brains and minds.

Instead of "how" questions, we were introduced to a shift to *"in what ways"* questions. Here are some examples of "how" versus "in what ways" questions:

How can we grow the business?	*In what ways* can we grow the business?
How can we increase client satisfaction?	*In what ways* can we increase client satisfaction?
How can we create team engagement?	*In what ways* can we create team engagement?
How can I improve my relationships?	*In what ways* can I improve my relationships?

Here lies the power of *in what ways*. Rather than looking for one (perhaps *the* one) good answer, *in what ways* automatically takes our minds to possibilities and creative solutions in volume. During our Master Mind session, the shift from *how* to *in what ways* took us from a few okay ideas to a whiteboard (8 feet wide) filled with over 150 ideas, from which our group member selected a combination of several to put into action. All of this came from changing a couple of words in our question, and conscious leaders understand that changing a few words can have profound impact. We often answer questions based upon existing resources (or perceived resources and limits), but the *in what ways* question invites us to create without limits or filters. If we are working to brainstorm and come up with many ideas, then we need to change the question to one that automatically stimulates our creativity—*in what ways*.

> We often answer questions based upon existing resources (or perceived resources and limits), but the in what ways question invites us to create without limits or filters.

The Question Is The Answer

Anyone that knows me knows that I *LOVE* questions—the power, the guidance, and the insights that good questions deliver, and the positive ignition and impact that good questions can bring to a team, an organization, and especially an individual. My premise is that the *RIGHT Question is the Answer!* When we invest in determining the right questions, they will provide us with the right answers, answers that will propel us and our organization to where we want to go. I have invested thousands of hours in my lifetime figuring out right questions. I pride myself on my questions because questions are not so much about the intellect, but more about your intuition and instincts. Questions and conscious leaders are about listening. Conscious leaders hone their listening skills and their intuition to help guide people with questions and to help people, including the leader himself or herself, see things they could not see without those questions.

Questions are one of my gifts. In my work with my clients, I rarely tell them things. I rarely give them advice. I ask them questions to help them see something that they could not see because they are stuck in the old but true saying, "I don't know what I don't know." It is called a blind spot for a reason; we need someone else to help us see it. Conscious leaders use questions to help people see their blind spots, and they understand the power of getting to that right question—not necessarily the first question. In fact, the first question you come up with is probably not it. It is the fourth, fifth, tenth, or fifteenth iteration when you say, "There's THE question." And what happens is that when you ask the question—when you get to that right question—then all your gifts take over. Your brain, logic, analytical skills, intuition, heart, soul, spirit and gut—they all conspire to answer that question. But they need the right question, and conscious leaders get that.

One key arena where conscious leaders leverage the power of questions is in meetings. Much like Einstein's suggested approach, I often work with leaders to create questions for meetings rather than agendas. I also often have invested big chunks of the beginnings of meetings to discussing, identifying and refining the answer to *what is the right question*. A great way to plan for or start a meeting is to ask, "What is the right question that we are here to answer today?" This question by itself automatically gets us thinking about the *right question*. As noted above, I will always look for the *in what ways* question over *how* and *what* questions. This approach also gets the entire team collaboratively creating the right question, which gets everyone on the same page. If your objectives are not aligned, you will either discover this when you talk through and refine the right question or you will get yourselves aligned on the right question as a result of this process.

Because the positive impact and power of questions comes in their context—that is, their specific relevance and value surfaces only in each specific situation and context—it is impossible to come up with lists of right questions. Let us consider, however, an illustrative example. During a meeting, the president of my client company was seeking input and suggestions regarding two possible strategic partnerships. He had gone through the pros and cons of each potential partner, including what he perceived to be the relative risks with each one. The question he was posing was the following: "Which strategic partnership should we pursue?" Right away, we see a problem with this question because it is a "which" question that automatically seeks one right answer. While the company and president *might* have to make a choice between the two options (to learn why the choice is only a "might," read on below about and/both thinking), the framing of the question was limiting from the outset.

I listened to the discussions, including some additional questions to the president, for 30 minutes, and then a different question hit me. I then asked the President to imagine that he had selected strategic partner A, which was the direction he seemed to be leaning, albeit with some significant hesitations. Next, I told him to imagine that it was three years in the future and that the partnership had failed. I then added this question: If the strategic partnership with partner A has failed in three years, will you be surprised, and if not, why not? This question helped—actually, it forced—the president to examine his own concerns and hesitancy more closely. He immediately answered that he would not be surprised if it had failed, and he had three core reasons that it would have failed. From this awareness, he quickly decided to proceed with strategic partner B because the question had helped him to realize that what he was terming minor concerns were actually core disconnects between his company and strategic partner A.

The Power of Questions

We all have the power to implement positive change, whether it is in our organization or in our own lives. That power lies within us, within our powerful and creative minds. We need to feed our minds with the right questions. It has been said, *"If you build it, they will come,"* but also remember that if you ask the *right question,* then the right answers and solutions will also come. Indeed, ***power is asking the right question***, and conscious leaders know this and live it, personally and professionally.

Questions are also the avenue to helping others (team members, friends, family, partners, etc.) experience their own awakening and clarity. As we will discuss in more detail below, questions have three critical aspects that do not exist with statements:

1. Questions are indefensible.

2. Questions are supportive.

3. Questions invite self-assessment and reflection.

While statements and conversations have the potential to create the second two elements, statements can be and often are defended against, and questions are still the most valuable in supporting another person. Most important, questions are the only method for helping others to discover their own answers and insights, and inside discovery is the best way to achieve sustainable change. Through questions we invite people into greater self-awareness, enhanced engagement, greater creativity and personal empowerment to change themselves and their outcomes.

Why do we ask questions? This may seem like a silly question (pun intended), but it seems that we often ask questions without knowing why we are asking, or perhaps worse, we ask questions with a narrow focus on only one thing—obtaining information. Some time ago, I had the opportunity to participate in a unique event for people to share and gain insights into questions. This engaging session highlighted two things for me: 1. how little attention most of us give to the questions that we ask, including the superficial nature of our inquiries; and 2. an approach to questions that I believe can, if adopted, dramatically change the nature of our interactions, our relationships and our growth.

The *Merriam-Webster Dictionary* defines a question as "an interrogative expression often used to acquire or test knowledge." Too often, this is the full extent of our own questions–a superficial inquiry designed to elicit information or, perhaps, knowledge. This approach, however, misses the mark because it wastes an opportunity to create real engagement with, between and among people.

What I have discovered is that when we ask good, deep questions (at the most basic level), we must focus on three distinct and intentional elements:

1. **Seeking to Understand**—More than simply trying to obtain information or even knowledge, the search for understanding takes questions into often unexplored and untapped areas about and within people. The search for understanding encompasses information and

knowledge, but it also includes the vital context for that information and knowledge, and this context is where relationships are built, ideas are birthed, and collaboration is nurtured.

2. **Seeking to Know**—More than seeking merely to gain knowledge, this is the intentional and purposeful desire to know the person to whom you are directing your questions. This provides the bridge for real relationships to begin and to grow. We all know that people can create and achieve great things together, but this is only achieved when people can connect at a level beyond the superficial. The desire to know the person to whom you are speaking demonstrates the ultimate commitment that one person can make to another and provides a foundation for genuine relationships and resulting synergies.

> What ties all of this together is a simple concept—a clear and unequivocal commitment to helping others, whether to overcome their obstacles or achieve their goals.

3. **Seeking Opportunities to Help**—Beyond gaining information and knowledge, even beyond gaining understanding and knowing the person to whom you are speaking, the ultimate goal of any question is and should be to find some way to assist the person. If we only understand and even know, but we fail to identify and act upon opportunities to help, the process is incomplete. If we seek only to understand and know, then our questions are about us, but if we also seek to find the opportunities to help, then we become selfless and tangibly demonstrate our commitment to another person. This commitment to others is the foundation of relationships that can and will overcome obstacles, achieve objectives, and accomplish impactful change.

What ties all of this together is a simple concept—a clear and unequivocal commitment to helping others, whether to overcome their obstacles or achieve their goals. This commitment to become an investor in other people is what transforms a mere inquiry into a catalyst for positive change. Most important, we must care about the answers to our purposeful and intentional questions.

Seek to understand people, context and situations; seek to know people and their needs; seek opportunities to help. This simple formula can change our questions into transformational dialogues. The question is whether we are willing to ask the right questions—and care about the answers. Below we will take an even deeper journey into questions and the unique impact that questions can have in relationships, team dynamics, communication, coaching and personal growth and development.

Questions Are Indefensible

One of the most unique aspects of questions—one that conscious leaders leverage for themselves and others—is that questions are indefensible, and our brains automatically and honestly answer every question that is asked. In sharp contrast, people can, will and often automatically do reject or defend themselves against statements. Many leaders work on their communication skills by learning how best to deliver information (statements), while conscious leaders work on their questioning skills in order to create the positive outcomes that questions can deliver.

I stumbled upon this truth a couple of years ago. I was listening to a speaker at a conference who had written a book on raising children. What he had learned from his own research is that people (actually our brains) immediately, automatically and honestly answer every question that is presented. Even if we do not know the answer, the brain will try to process to an answer until it realizes that it does not have the information or ability to answer it.

If a question is posed and your brain senses that the information needed to answer it is stored somewhere, then you will keep thinking about it—your brain will actually search for it until it reaches a point of giving up. That giving up point may take some time to reach if you know the information is somewhere in your memory. Think of those times when you are discussing movies or television with friends, and a question comes up such as the name of a movie, the name of an actor or actress, etc. Your brain instantly grabs for the information, and if you do not have an immediate answer, the brain then automatically goes searching for the answer because it senses that the answer is somewhere in your memory banks. This process all happens automatically and can be a great asset when asking yourself and others questions.

Getting back to the speaker and raising children, he discovered (based upon brain function research) that when he told his children things, they could reject his comments and assessments. However, if he asked them questions (not rhetorical questions, which are just statements with a question mark at the end), he could communicate his message without them being able to reject it or defend against it. His example was a situation where his teenage son was not taking care of his household responsibilities. His statement to his son might be: "It's not fair that you have the benefit of everything that your Mom and I do for you and around the house, but you cannot take care of your few responsibilities." Rejected and ignored. Now to the question approach:

Do you think it's fair that your Mom and I provide you with everything you need, but you don't take care of your few household responsibilities?

Even if his son *says* that he thinks it is fair or otherwise gets defensive, the question was still answered honestly and automatically by his brain. In other words, the message got through the lines of defense. Of course, the desired change in behavior may take more than a few questions, but the point is that questions, unlike statements, cannot be defended against by the person to whom they are directed.

For this reason, I encourage all of my clients to develop the habit of converting statements into questions. It takes time and practice, but anyone can develop this conscious leadership skill. There are two great ways to develop and enhance this skill. First, prepare your questions in advance of planned conversations. Let us assume that you want or need to have a conversation with someone, whether it is in a personal or business context. Step one is to write down all of the things you would like to say (in other words, your statements). Step two is then to convert all of the statements into genuine questions (again, rhetorical questions do not count).

Imagine that you want to tell a team member that his or her performance is not meeting expectations. Here is the statement version:

Your work on the VIP project was not acceptable.

Even if supported by the facts, this statement represents the speaker's judgment of the team member's performance, and it will often be received or heard as a personal judgment about the team member's character or worth, not just their performance. In other words, there is a risk that the team member will "hear" that he or she is not acceptable. While we could blame the team member for receiving the information this way, the trouble with constructive criticism for many people is that it is often just critical and laced with the personal judgments of the person giving the criticism.

Because you desire to have your feedback be received and heard, you want to turn this statement into a question, but your initial impulse will be to take it only far enough to be rhetorical question—a statement with a question mark at the end:

Don't you think your work on the VIP project was unacceptable?

Or this way:

Do you think your work on the VIP project was acceptable?

These are still not the types of questions that will generate the positive impact and outcomes that conscious leaders are seeking for themselves, their relationships and their team members.

In order to offer support that provides the listener genuine opportunities for self-reflection, assessment and personal ownership of the solutions, here are some examples of better questions:

- What did you think of your work on the VIP project?
- What specifically did you do well on the VIP project?
- What specific improvement opportunities surfaced on the VIP project?

If the person is not aware enough or is unwilling to answer these questions honestly, then you have additional development work to do with that team member. You can also continue with more questions to help that person better see the impact of his or her performance:

- What was the impact of your performance on the VIP project on the organization, your team or other team members?
- Were there any unintended consequences from your work on the VIP project?

These questions are invitations for the team member to self-assess, self-evaluate and self-identify improvement opportunities, which you would then follow up by asking that team member what he or she can and will do to make those improvements. When we tell people what they need to do differently or to change, this approach often fails; however, when we help people take personal responsibility for being different or changing their performance, we create opportunities for true and sustainable change in people and in outcomes. This is precisely the impact that conscious leaders seek to create through the use of questions.

The second opportunity to develop this skill is to practice the statement to question conversion in meetings or other conversations. When you are participating in a meeting, discussion or conversation (even if the topic is unrelated to you), write down the statements that come to mind, and either in the moment or later, write down some questions that you could use instead of the statements. I sometimes forget how long it took me to develop my questioning skills and gifts, but I recognize that the transition to questions is not a "throw the switch" shift. For most people, it will take time, attention and effort to convert to a questioning mindset. In fact, one person who reviewed this book before publication suggested that this chapter on questions should be the last chapter because it is the most difficult shift to internalize and implement.

I also know that the key beginning point is to value the shift and be committed to it. For many people, this commitment comes fairly easily because they quickly recognize that the statement approach is not working and not serving them, others or their relationships. For those that are unwilling to change and want to stick with the easy approach of making statements and judgments, they will struggle to become the conscious leaders they could be, and perhaps they will not fit on your team or in your organization.

The same is true with our personal relationships—we can only invite others into a new way of looking at themselves through questions. They must choose to accept the invitation and to take more control over and personal ownership of themselves, their lives and their outcomes. Living in a state of questions is not for everyone, and conscious leaders self-select this way of being and leading; it is not and cannot be thrust upon them.

Questions Are Supportive and Invite Self-Assessment

One of the great benefits of questions (over statements) is that questions—appropriate and genuine questions—are inherently supportive in nature. Statements usually represent the telling person's perceptions and judgments of another person, their actions or their performance.

Additionally, statements can include the telling person's opinion about a situation or what they think the listener should do. We often call this "giving advice," and I continue to be amazed at

> One of the great benefits of questions (over statements) is that questions—appropriate and genuine questions—are inherently supportive in nature.

how many people in how many situations purport to tell others what they should do (or not do), what they should feel (or not feel) or even that they are being silly or ridiculous. No matter how you frame it, this approach will often be perceived by the receiver of the advice to be arrogant and self-centered.

Recently, I was involved in a conversation with a small group of friends, and one friend was authentic enough to share that she was hesitant about a business opportunity because of her own internal self-doubts about whether she is good enough. This was a vulnerable sharing by any standard, and yet one of the people in the group jumped in and offered this: "That's crazy. Why on earth would you doubt yourself? You can do anything that you want. Just do it." The person offering this perspective hopefully was well-intentioned and wanted to support this woman, but the support was given in a way that minimized what the woman had shared. I could see her start to shut down. When I talked to the woman who expressed her inner doubts later, she said that she felt like the other person was not listening, did not hear her and did not understand her situation. She was looking for support in a different way, but the "support" she got from this other person was old-school buck-up-and-do-it advice.

Certainly, it is sometimes helpful to have people who believe in you, who tell you how good you are and assure you that you can do anything that you put your mind to; however, when someone is willing to acknowledge the things that are getting in the way, it is naïve to believe that a pep talk will fix everything. In these cases, support may come in offering questions to help the person process his or her emotions and the situation, rather than in coming to save the day with the answers to everything. It is far too easy to tell people what they should do and to give advice, and this approach often does not help people build their own confidence and clarity around a course of action.

Even challenging questions that may be uncomfortable can be highly supportive because they give the recipient the opportunity to better understand themselves, their situation, the underlying causes and solutions that will stick. These questions also give them the opportunity to personally commit to the process of evaluation and change. I recognize that not everyone is ready for and open to these types of internal questions, so I always ask permission: "Do you mind if I ask you a question?" I sometimes find that people did not fully understand what my questions might bring to the surface, but I let them decide where the questions end. In other words, they decide how far and deep the questions will go, but I will not decide to stop the questions just because they might be deemed challenging or upset the person. Questions offer the unique opportunity for people to gain a deeper understanding about how their thoughts, beliefs, actions or perspectives are helping them or getting in their way in life or business. For this reason, questions provide a form of developmental support that statements cannot duplicate.

As already suggested, the other great trait of questions is that they (by their very nature) invite the recipients of the questions to self-assess and self-reflect. Questions also help recipients to increase their own awareness of underlying causes or drivers and also to discover their own personal paths to change. Good questions play the vital role of setting the stage for these looks in the mirror and for a deeper understanding of the root causes of challenges.

I often tell people and potential clients that they are not paying me for my advice or ideas but for my questions. I believe in the power of questions to open eyes, shift paradigms, and identify the path to visionary objectives, and I also believe that the best advice is the advice not given. Instead of advice, I will offer questions to help my clients see for themselves what they need to see in order to change their business, their leadership, their teams or themselves.

The trouble with advice (even if good advice) is that it must make the following journey in order to create impact:

- Idea received by listener
- Listener decides that they like the idea
- Listener makes the idea their own
- Listener decides to take action on the idea
- Listener commits to the desired change

In contrast, if I ask questions that help listeners discover causes and ideas for themselves, then their path to change is much shorter:

- Listener develops their own idea
- Listener decides to take action on their idea
- Listener commits to their own desired change

This difference is not only about time and speed, but more importantly about the degree of the listener's engagement and commitment to change. Many of other people's ideas never get executed due to lack of full commitment to and ownership of the ideas, but when someone develops the ideas himself or herself (and understands the underlying causes and issues related to the desired change), the potential extent and likelihood of the execution is greatly enhanced. If positive change is your objective, then questions are the right route to get you there.

Questions and Stickless Accountability™

As I shared earlier, in my work with hundreds of teams, one theme is consistent–100 percent list lack of accountability as one of their top three challenges, and 80 percent of the time lack of accountability is listed as the number-one improvement opportunity for the team and organization. This data demonstrates that we have a significant accountability crisis in our culture and in our business worlds. The primary reason for this crisis is that we misunderstand accountability, and we do not know how to deliver it in a supportive way. Instead, we believe that accountability is about punishment/consequences, rather than mentoring and supporting people's growth, development and change.

We are all familiar (perhaps too familiar) with the carrot and the stick motivation theory. I hear this phrase thrown around in businesses of all shapes and sizes, but I am convinced it is time to lose the stick—in fact, to lose the carrot and the stick. If you are familiar with its origins, "the carrot and the stick" theory revolves around motivating a mule—yes, a MULE! Thus, the theory begins askew because it treats team members as stubborn mules who will be motivated only by simple concepts of rewards or punishment. Frankly, this approach to people does a great disservice to our team members *and* it ignores some basic flaws in the carrot and the stick theory itself.

I do not know about you, but I do not see a carrot as much of a reward. Carrots are okay, but how many people really crave a carrot? I know what you are thinking: "But Jeff, we are talking about motivating a mule, and mules love carrots." Interesting thought, but the carrots-are-not-so-great analogy is dead on with businesses where the supposed "rewards" are often not that motivating because they do not get people excited.

Similarly, who really wants anything to do with a stick? At best, the stick will be used to poke me or hit me over the head (or somewhere else). Or perhaps the stick will be poked in my eye or up my … never mind. My point is that the stick represents punishment, and there is no reason to believe that people need to be punished in order to execute and achieve. My apologies to those who seem to think that punishment works, but the truth is that it NEVER serves to get team members engaged. More importantly, the mere idea of using a "stick" is one of the key reasons that businesses struggle with holding people accountable. Since accountability is deemed the same as punishment, many businesses do a poor (or horrible) job of holding team members accountable.

Enter a new, simple and effective approach to accountability, an approach that not only avoids the need for the stick, but can accelerate any business by improving communication, clarity and execution.

This new approach—I call it *Stickless Accountability*, has three key elements:

- Crystal clarity of expectations (especially the what and the when)
- Clear ownership
- Simple and supportive accountability

Consistent application of these three ingredients will provide any organization with predictable and effective execution, resulting in organizational acceleration.

It sounds simple—***crystal clarity of expectations***—but clarity of expectations is a big miss for most businesses for two

> Consistent application of these three ingredients will provide any organization with predictable and effective execution, resulting in organizational acceleration.

reasons. First, most businesses assume that they are already clear with expectations, which makes change unlikely since they think they are already doing it well. Second, they may have a misguided view of what clarity is in terms of expectations. Here is a test: The next time you have a meeting, ask every person to write down exactly what was decided, who is responsible for it and when it will be completed. Like the old telephone game, you will find that the expectations are probably anything but clear. We live in a world where vague is acceptable (a great way to avoid being held accountable), and we are so used to this vague approach that it takes heightened awareness and commitment to shift an organization into the realm where crystal clarity of expectations is the norm.

When it comes to this crystal clarity of expectations, the expectations must be clearly defined regarding what is to be done or accomplished and exactly when each part of the project will be completed. Nearly everything that happens in a business is initially defined as a project, but it is critical to break projects down into the actionable parts, what we referred to earlier as *next actions*. Each next action should then be given definitive deadlines. This precision is essential to keeping projects on track and on time and for providing meaningful accountability check-ins throughout the process. Otherwise, we know if we are on track only at the very end of the project—in other words, when it is too late to make adjustments and corrections. Most of you will find that your habits are built around project thinking and planning, and you will need to be diligent in shifting over to an action plan approach to projects, commitments and accountability.

Even with crystal clarity of expectations, it is essential to add the ***clear ownership*** ingredient into the mix, since ownership is another often-found gap in organizations and teams. While many people may have responsibilities with respect to a project or initiative, and many people may have ownership within the project, there can only be one person who has ultimate ownership of a desired outcome. This simplicity allows leadership and management to go to one person to determine the status of a project and to hold one person accountable. Yes, others will in turn be accountable to this one "owner" of the outcome, but the ultimate owner of an outcome must be clear in order to execute simple accountability. When the time comes for accountability, management must be able to go to one person, the owner of the outcome, to ask the simple questions that make up simple accountability.

Finally, we come to the linchpin—***simple and supportive accountability!*** This form of accountability is NOT about punishment, consequences, blame or shame. Instead, it is about supporting your team in an environment of high expectations. The vast majority of people want to honor their commitments, especially when the culture of a business makes it clear that honoring commitments is a matter of personal integrity. Ask a room of 100 people if they want to be seen as a person of integrity, and you will get nearly 100% in agreement. Integrity is important for most people, and we must connect accountability with a sense of maintaining personal integrity. When most people make clear commitments, they will do whatever it takes to honor those commitments because they are "all in" with their own personal integrity.

With this backdrop of personal integrity, accountability can be simple and massively effective—and it all happens with questions. It plays out like this:

> "Susan, you committed to completing a draft of the project
> plan by the end of the day on August 1st. Is it done?"

Susan can have only one of two answers: yes or no. If yes, then Susan would be praised, congratulated and encouraged to continue her impressive performance.

If her answer is no, then the next *question* is:

> "What prevented you from honoring your commitment?"

The conscious leader would then follow up with more questions, all designed to help the team member better understand his or her choices, especially the choices that got in the way of honoring the commitment. I will sometimes specifically ask this question:

"What did you choose to do instead of honoring your commitment?"

Notice that in this form of accountability, there is *never* a need for statements. You use only questions, all designed to help the *other person* see how their choices led to a failure to honor their commitment. The questions are also designed to help team members be able to consistently honor their commitments in the future—to do what they said they would do. Additional supportive questions include something like this:

"What do you need in the way of support to help assure that

you are able to honor your commitments in the future?"

All are questions and all are supportive. This same accountability model and approach can be used with someone else, even those who do not report to you. Reporting lines (and the ability to hire, fire or reprimand) are related to consequences, but the accountability process is far more than just consequences.

While some people may try to resort to blame and excuses, this supportive accountability model forces people instead to face and own their choices. What choices did they make that kept them from honoring their commitment? We also need to find out if they needed something else in terms of resources or support to honor their commitment. If so, they need to answer for why they did not seek what they needed before they failed to honor the commitment. Note: the use of the word "commitment" is intentional because it heightens the personal sense of ownership of the promised actions or deliverables.

Notice that the entire process of accountability is based upon questions–no statements whatsoever–and is delivered in a supportive way to help people do a better job of honoring their commitments and being self-accountable. If the people on your team do not want to be accountable, then you have a bigger issue, and you probably have the wrong people on your team. It is that simple. There are plenty of good people who want to be accountable, especially if that accountability is designed to be supportive and to help them achieve their personal and organizational objectives.

Simple accountability is mostly about setting clear expectations not only for what must be done (and by when), but also that ownership of a project or outcome has real meaning (not necessarily just real consequences—i.e., the stick). Many people are uncomfortable when they are held accountable for their commitments, and this is healthy discomfort. I recently sat in on a team accountability meeting where a team member who had not done what he committed to do quickly and jokingly asked if the meeting could "move on." Why? Because being held accountable is uncomfortable, especially when you know with the simple accountability model that your failure to honor a commitment constitutes being out of integrity. The stick/punishment approach is about shame and belittling, but simple accountability is about empowering team members to step into their own personal integrity.

In case you are wondering, there is another bonus to *Stickless Accountability*: It attracts and engages team members who want to be a part of an organization that is raising the bar and seeking to achieve great things. One of the biggest complaints I hear in organizations is from the people that are viewed as high achievers by the business. Their complaint is with the lack of accountability. They hate the idea that team members are not required to make clear commitments. They hate the fact that team members are allowed to fail to execute without being held accountable. And they feel this way because the high performers almost always have their own high personal expectations, so they are often the most self-accountable. Even the high performers want to be held accountable for their own commitments. Thus, a natural outcome of implementing *Stickless Accountability* is that you build a team of engaged high performers who ultimately become largely self-accountable.

Imagine what embracing *Stickless Accountability* could mean for your organization—with crystal clarity of expectations, clear ownership and simple and supportive accountability. You would more consistently do the right things correctly and on time, thereby creating a model of predictable execution and ultimate acceleration, all while building an amazing team. What are you waiting for? Throw away the stick and the carrot and implement *Stickless Accountability*. You will love the results!

> Imagine what embracing Stickless Accountability could mean for your organization—with crystal clarity of expectations, clear ownership and simple and supportive accountability.

Questions as a Way of Life and Leadership

Obviously, I believe in questions. I live them for myself and for others. I see questions as the secret weapon in building teams, creating change, deepening relationships and for personal transformation. If there is a silver bullet for business, relationships and life, it is questions—insightful, intuitive and probing questions that help us see things and people (including ourselves) differently, see possibilities and see solutions that will really change things and accelerate people, teams, organizations and relationships.

Questions are also a choice—a choice that requires you to give up your need to know, give up your need to provide answers, and give up your need to be the wise advice-giver. Conscious leaders are self-aware enough to keep their egos in check so that they can selflessly support others in their personal or professional journeys. If you have a compulsive need to tell people what to do and to get the credit for your great ideas, then questions will be a challenge for you. Questioning involves giving up the need to be the person with all the answers. I choose to be the person with all (or at least many of) the questions, with a genuine desire to help others find their own way.

I trust questions, and conscious leaders trust questions—starting with the questions that they ask themselves. They also surround themselves with people who will ask them the challenging questions and support them by pushing them beyond their initial answers. It takes courage to be a questioner of this type, and conscious leaders model this courage by being willing to pick away at problems, obstacles and challenges to find deeper truths and more meaningful and sustainable changes. This is the way of the conscious leader, and the question for you is simple: Are you willing to give up all you think you know so that you can better serve yourself, others, your teams, your organization and the community at large?

CHAPTER 12: PUTTING DOWN THE OLD STORIES (THE CHALLENGING LEADER)

"The key to wisdom is this—constant and frequent questioning, for by doubting we are led to question and by questioning we arrive at the truth."

Peter Abelard

Are you ready to question everything? Conscious leaders are ready because they recognize that assumptions are dangerous, and it certainly is a dangerous assumption to believe that things stay the same. It is also dangerous to assume that what has worked before will always work in the same way. Finally, it is dangerous and erroneous to assume that you will always be the same person in the future that you are today. Given the reality of change inside us and all around us, it is essential to embrace the "question everything" mindset.

Conscious leaders also embrace the need to question everything because much of what we think and do is not working, and questioning is your opportunity to take positive action to change your life, your business, and your outcomes. We have already debunked a number of stories or beliefs that conscious leaders can let go of and thereby create personal, team and organizational change (e.g., the false sense of control, stress, priorities, time, etc.). In this chapter we will explore and debunk a number of additional stories that get in the way of leaders, teams, organizations and lives. This chapter is focused on the cultural, belief and created stories that we described at the outset of this book. Along the way, I will be planting many seeds for your continued growth and development as a conscious leader.

I have a simple belief that is the foundation for my personal growth, as well as my work with my various clients:

> You've spent your entire life achieving according to "stories"—what you believe to be true about business, life and yourself. Some stories are true and empower you, but many are blocking your path. Your transformation will be the outcome of facing, debunking and rewriting the stories that no longer serve you.

This core philosophy is the reason for my title in my business—*Chief Story Debunker*. I am not suggesting that all stories or beliefs are false or wrong, but rather that every story needs to be questioned and challenged. You must also explore the ways that your stories "serve you," but in ways that are not in your best interests.

We are creatures of logic, and therefore, for all of our human emotions and reactions, we do or choose not to do things for rational reasons. Thus, anything that we do (or fail to do) is driven to serve some part of us or some story inside us. Even if the behavior seems not to serve you, you must look deeper to find the parts of you that it does serve in order to break out of the old behaviors and thinking. For example, if I ask someone who is trying to quit smoking how the smoking serves him, the typical answer is that it does *not* serve him. He will tell me that it is negatively affecting his health, finances, family, relationships, etc. But there is still some part of him being served, or else he would stop doing it! While there is certainly an element of physiological addiction to nicotine, the emotional addiction is more powerful. The smoker must confront the internal attraction to smoking in order to let go of it. Perhaps the smoking is calming. Perhaps it feeds the part of that person that wants to be included, so he or she smokes with other people. Whatever the issue or question, conscious self-leadership always involves going inside yourself to discover what is driving any behavior or thinking that you want to change. The deeper the inquiry and answer, the more impactful the shift in thinking and behavior will be.

The Trouble With Stories

The trouble with unhelpful stories is that they seem to be true—or at least have a great deal of cultural, habitual or anecdotal support. Some—like the notion that you cannot have your cake and eat it too—have longevity on their side. Remember, however, that long-existing beliefs or stories are often more the result of no one challenging the belief than of the validity of the belief or story. That is where you come in, as the conscious leader—your vital role is to be willing to ask these three questions about your stories and those of others:

> It may not always be easy, but the debunking process is simple, and you can also seek out the thoughts and, even better, the questions of others who can provide you with the all-important outsider's perspective.

1. Is it verifiably true?

2. If not, and thus knowing that it is just a story, does it fit with and serve who you are choosing to be as a person and as a leader?

3. If it does not serve you, are you willing to put down the story or rewrite it?

Once you answer these questions, you are in a position to make a decision—either to embrace the story or to take action to put down the story and eliminate it from your thinking, processing and decisions.

It may not always be easy, but the debunking process is simple, and you can also seek out the thoughts and, even better, the questions of others who can provide you with the all-important outsider's perspective. One caveat—knowing that most people are living with stories that they have never questioned, be prepared to evaluate carefully the feedback you get from others, especially when the feedback comes in the form of their own statements, opinions, perspectives and beliefs.

That is why I have surrounded myself with people who are more likely to ask me challenging questions in a supportive way, rather than people who I believe "know" the most. In fact, "knowing" itself is one of the stories that you must challenge and beware of, because in assuming that you already know (or that someone else knows) you are opening the door to the ongoing proliferation of a story or belief that no longer serves you. Conscious leaders are willing to give up what they think they know in order to allow themselves to experience the state of not knowing so that they can rethink and reconsider.

What Tunnel?

Let us look at a specific example of letting go of old stories. A couple of months ago, I was visiting my friend, Karen, in Charleston, South Carolina—my favorite place in the world. We caught up on life. We talked about what was going on, what was working, things that weren't working, opportunities, challenges—the good, the bad and a little ugly. At the end, Karen said this to me, almost with a tired expression: "You know, Jeff, I wish the light in the tunnel didn't always seem so far away." And in that moment, I had a vision of clarity, and I said to Karen, "What if there's no tunnel?" She looked at me and said, "What are you talking about?" I said:

> What if there's no tunnel? What if we're already in the light? What if the idea of a tunnel is a story we created or a story someone else gave us that said that everything always has to be out of our grasp, everything always has to be far away, and everything has to be hard, take a long time and involve massive change. Maybe that's all a story—a story designed to protect us, to keep us safe, to keep us from taking risk, to keep us stuck.

Karen looked at me and said, "Wow, that would change everything." I said, "Yes, it would."

Think about it. Have you ever heard someone say that the light in the tunnel is so bright that he or she has to wear shades? I never hear anyone claim to be excited finally to be in the bright light near the end of the tunnel. No—that damn light is always off in the distance at the *end of the tunnel.* Don't we ever make progress? I shared this perspective with my Master Mind group a few weeks later and their response was identical—if there is no tunnel, then that changes everything. And that is precisely the point of and reason for challenging stories and beliefs—the stories are often in our way and *they are just stories.*

I start with this story because I believe it is about changing everything. Every single one of you, at this point in your life, is living, being, doing and leading according to a bunch of stories that you have chosen to believe are true. I am here to tell you that they are just stories. Instead of accepting the stories and living according to those old stories, the opportunity for every one of you is to say, "I'm going to pick and choose what stories serve me, what I decide is true." I admit that this thinking is a little different—some people might say crazy, and I have certainly been accused of that over and over—but to me the process is rather simple: I choose to question everything—not to unthinkingly accept anything that involves a belief, rule, structure or way of thinking.

Are they all wrong? Of course not. Do I reject everything? No, but I question everything. I ask these questions: "Is this really true, or is it just a story? Am I choosing to live with that story? Is that story serving me?" I believe that we all have choices every day, and one of the most important and (for many) unexercised choices is the choice of what stories and beliefs you will accept as true. The stories that you believe are true very much matter in your businesses and your lives. You must choose wisely, for these stories and beliefs will not only define you, but will likely determine whether you see possibilities or impossibilities, whether you live fully or with an internal governor, whether you experience life or survive it and whether you flourish or simply get by.

The Busy Story

Over the past year, I have come to see that there is one especially insidious story that lives in our culture and is blocking us or dramatically slowing us down. As a result, for the past year I have been diligently working to give up the word "busy." *Busy* has become such a cliché and cop-out word in our culture that it has no meaning. Everyone is "busy." What is the preoccupation with being busy? I have concluded that it is yet another way to avoid telling the truth or focusing on what is really important in our lives and businesses.

It has been a challenge to give up the word because it is a word that I used to use regularly. The overuse of "busy" is so prevalent that people struggle with what to say when it is not part of the conversation. When people ask me if I am busy, I typically tell them that I gave up the word, and they do not know what to do with the conversation when "busy" is not part of our common language. It is also a challenge because so many people use the word, ask me about it ("Are you busy?") or assume it about me ("It seems like you're busy."). It certainly makes for interesting conversations when someone asks me about being busy and I tell them that I am working to give up the word.

First of all, if they do not know me well, then the idea of giving up a word is strange enough. The people who know me are not surprised because they know that I believe in the power of words to empower or disempower. Second, most people are confused as to why I would want to give up a word, especially the word *busy*. When they ask me why, I give them the short version—I realized that it no longer served me and in fact was keeping me off-track personally and professionally.

I even struggled in the beginning with what to say instead of that I am "busy." After a short time, I became more comfortable with telling people that I gave up the word "busy" because I was overusing it, that it is overused in our culture and that it no longer has any real meaning. When they ask what I use instead, I tell them that I ask myself more meaningful questions such as:

- Am I focused?

- Am I working on things that are important (versus just staying busy)?

- Am I happy?

- Am I productive and effective?

- Am I profitable?

I explain that these words have more relevance and meaning, especially in my business.

It is funny what you hear when you change the conversation this way. One of the most often-asked questions that I hear is: "So you

> What I had come to realize is that the word and idea of being busy is easy and is not a worthy measure for me in any way, personally or professionally.

can be busy without making money?" I almost laugh out loud when I am asked this, and I usually respond that it is *easy* to be busy and not make money. In fact, I can be busy and unprofitable without any effort at all, which surprises some people—except the people that own their own businesses because they immediately get it. I discovered that the word "busy" was disempowering me (or falsely empowering me), and I chose to eliminate it from my vocabulary.

What I had come to realize is that the word and idea of being busy is easy and is not a worthy measure for me in any way, personally or professionally. In fact, busy is the easiest state of being that we have in our culture because you do not even have to have a full schedule to be busy. Busy, it turns out, is a state of mind—one that is fabricated for most people (we will explore why below). I rarely meet anyone who does not describe himself or herself as busy. Employees that work 9 to 5 jobs are busy. Business owners are all busy, even if their businesses are not performing well or even failing. People I know who have very little business are busy. Retirees are busy, even though they no longer have a full-time job. People who are both working and going to school look forward to the time when they will be only working, and yet when they finish school they are immediately busy again. About the only people that I can think of that truly are not busy are in the ground.

The Busy Drug

We all know how to be busy, but do we know how to be productive? Do we know the ways that the busy state of mind is keeping us from achieving our personal or business objectives? I think not, which is the reason for this discussion in this book on conscious leadership. I recently came across a great quote from Rob Bell:

"Busy is a drug that a lot of people are addicted to."

It certainly is a drug and a highly addictive one, since we have equated busy with successful, profitable, meaningful and valued. The whole world is busy, but is anyone getting anything done? Is anyone accomplishing their goals and objectives? Is anyone prioritizing and working on what is most important for them or for their business? With few exceptions, the answer is no–there is a whole lot of busy and not nearly enough execution, impact and achievement.

Not only is the word or concept of busy addicting, but people everywhere are using it (unconsciously) to hold themselves back and, in some cases, to keep them from pursuing some of the most important things, projects or ideas in their minds and hearts. This is what I hear from many people that I meet and interact with when I check in on things they are working on:

- "How's the book coming?"

    Answer: "Not much progress. I've been busy."

- "How's the new marketing campaign going?"

    Answer: "Slow. I've been busy with other things."

- "How's the new website coming along?"

    Answer: "Way behind schedule. I've been busy."

- "What's the status of the new blog?"

    Answer: "I did a little writing, but I've been busy with other things."

- "Have you planned your family trip for the year yet?"

    Answer: "Not yet, but I will. I've been busy."

- "What's the status of your retreat or big event for the year?"

    Answer: "It may not happen this year. I got busy with some other projects."

- "Did you hire that new salesperson?"

    Answer: "Still working on it. Things have been busy."

- "How is the plan to spend more time with your kids going?"

    Answer: "Fair. Things got busy at work."

You get the picture and hopefully the point. Everyone is so busy with what they are already doing that no one has time for anything new or even for things that they have decided are important. In many cases, people are working on things that they would rate as much less important (thereby staying busy) while not making time for things that they have clearly stated are more important, even high priorities in their personal or professional lives. Crazy, right?! Or perhaps not so crazy.

Why would someone work on less important things and get so busy with them that they would not have time to work on more important things? Simple—because there are blocks (mostly inside us) to the new and more important things: blocks such as uncertainty, fear, risk, other people's voices, internal voices from old stories or the lack of a clear decision. These internal impediments will control our lives and our outcomes unless and until we choose to face them, challenge them and move past them, and *busy* is the excuse we use to justify not facing them, doing what we are doing and not doing what we said we wanted to do. After all, if I am busy, then that is a "good reason" for not getting to what I said was a priority. If I have a good reason (let us be honest–an excuse), then I do not have to change anything. Do not worry, you say to others and to yourself—I will definitely get to those important things when I am *not so busy*.

Good luck with that strategy. That is the same as the *someday* strategy. That is another word that I have removed from my vocabulary— someday—because I realized that it literally does not exist. As of today, someday is in the future. Yet, when someday supposedly happens, it is now today again. Are you following me? Someday is always in the future (apparently much like the light at the end of the mythical tunnel), and I can never get there. In reality, I either take action today towards my dreams or objectives, or I do not. Those are my two choices today, and "someday" is not a real option.

"Someday" is also an excuse that allows us to avoid admitting that we have failed to take action on our projects, ideas, initiatives or dreams. Sometimes we have to admit that we have failed at something in order to be motivated to look at it differently, to assess whether we are fully committed to it and to find the motivation to take action. We use "someday" as a cop-out, which is what I often find with my coaching clients that have made commitments to themselves and to me. When I ask them why they did not honor the commitment, they like to say that they did not fail to get it done. They just have not gotten it done *yet*. In fact, they use their to-do list as their excuse for non-action. "It's right here on my to-do list," they say. "It is not that I did not get it done, because it is still on my to-do list and I still intend to do it." Well, that is another interesting story that keeps people stuck in someday and keeps them from getting things done now that will best serve their business or their life. Oh my, those stories that keep us firmly stuck where we are.

Think about this typical in-your-head conversation. "I want to write a book, but I am busy with work right now. But I will write it someday." Do you know where the somedays are piling up and continuing to pile up? In the cemeteries and urns, where so many people's hopes and dreams for someday have gone to rot for all eternity. If that seems harsh, then good—maybe it will get your attention and the attention of others and create a sense of urgency.

I recently came across the book *The Five Regrets of the Dying* by Bronnie Ware (2012), and the number one regret of the dying is this: "I wish I'd had the courage to live a life true to myself, not the life others expected of me." Sadly, this finding does not surprise me or anyone else that I have shared it with, and yet people are continuing to live a life that will lead to this very same regret. Why aren't we changing if we know this regret and we are already living with it? And the second most common regret of the dying: "I wish I didn't work so hard." Translated a different way—I wish I had not been *so busy*.

Earlier this year, I was talking with a friend of mine about several passionate dreams she has for her life, including creating a forum for women to find personal and spiritual transformation. These are the things of her dreams and deepest desires, but she was not making much progress with them. She was busy with her main business. I know her and her business well, however, and while she had lots to do, her business was not thriving to the point that she did not have time to work on this other project. When I asked her why the dream project was not getting much attention, she answered "Because I've been busy with my business."

I asked her a few clarifying and challenging questions, and after several inquiries peeling back the layers of the onion, she said this: "Do you think I'm staying busy with other things to avoid working on the dream project … so that I can avoid the risks and hesitations I have with the dream project and have a good reason [that I'm busy] not to make it happen?" My response: "What do you think?"

Well, what do YOU think? Does that make sense to you— that a person would stay busy to avoid working on something that he or she says is important because of hesitations about it? I said

> As a conscious leader, you have the opportunity to help people put away stories that no longer serve them, and busy and someday are two of those stories.

earlier that we are creatures of logic and rational behavior, even if it does not appear so at first glance. Being busy is one example of that truth—it is seen as an acceptable excuse not to do what I said I want to do or was meant to do. In addition, since *busy* is acceptable and a recognized state of being, I do not have to explore what might truly be keeping me from working on the new thing, and I can stay blissfully guilt-free in the place of no change and "someday."

If you take nothing else from this discussion, remember this:

> Busy keeps you from doing what you're meant to do, and no one is ever too busy doing that which they are meant to do or destined to do. Busy is everything else that keeps you from living and creating your dreams!

As a conscious leader, you have the opportunity to help people put away stories that no longer serve them, and *busy* and *someday* are two of those stories. Start with yourself—honestly assess the ways that you use *busy* or *someday* to keep you from doing what you believe you should be doing or want to do. Once you have identified the true causes for your hesitation or delay, determine if you are prepared to shift your thinking and to take action consistent with your desired path. If the answer is yes, then take that action and create the change and new outcomes you desire. If the answer is no, then be honest with yourself and acknowledge that you are choosing not to take action towards what you had described as important. Conscious leaders are honest with themselves and then with others about the choices they make, and they do not rely on excuses or stories to justify their lack of action or inconsistency.

You can then offer this same type of support and challenge to others so that your leadership will help others to get to their own inner truths, to understand and own their choices (and the consequences thereof) and to be self-accountable for what they are achieving or not achieving in their businesses or in their lives.

Stories and Excuses

Like the ways that people use *busy* to excuse their lack of attention to things that they claim are important, you also have to be highly aware of other ways you can use your own stories to excuse your inconsistent behavior. Don't forget how easy this is to do or that this behavior may very well send unintended messages to people that you care about, including your children. My Dad taught me a strong work ethic. In fact, I would say that my Dad is a workaholic, and I picked that trait up as well. I know it is important to work hard, but I have to be very careful that I do not let work consume me and become an unhealthy habit. When I was married and working as a lawyer, I worked long hours. In addition to my long work hours, I often attended evening events for the purposes of networking and growing the business. When I was working in these jobs and roles, my "story" was that I had to do this to be successful, and I often communicated this to my wife and my sons: "I'm sorry I can't be home, but *I have to work.*" And that is what I believed—that I *had to* work the long hours and attend the events in order to be successful. One of the big problems with stories is that there is often (if not always) a big helping of truth in them.

Yes, hard work is important and a strong work ethic is a good habit, but anything taken to the extreme can be unhealthy. How many men and women have gone to their graves (often literally dropping dead at their desk) in service of the mantra that hard work is the key to success? Thus, there was some truth to my story in that hard work was one of the ingredients of success for my business, but hard work is relative, and who is to say how much work is too much work? I have also now embraced the reality that I have choices in my life, and, in truth, in those days I was choosing to work the long hours and attend the evening events. I did not have to do it, but I was choosing to do it in order to get something that I wanted. What I now know, however, is that there were unhealthy drivers to my hard work that I now consider to have been *excessive* work.

I now understand that one of my core messages and inner stories was that I was not worthy of love and therefore not worthy of good things. Since I saw myself as not good enough, I had to find ways to feed the wounded parts of me with things that made me feel better about myself, such as working harder than anyone else. I measured my self-worth by the number of hours that I worked rather than the value that I added. All of this was done unconsciously at the time, which meant that I had no awareness that my inner stories and insecurities were driving my decisions and behavior. Since the connection between my inside stories and my actions was all unconscious, I could not see it and therefore could not change it. Only since I have woken up and become aware of my inner story drivers have I been able to begin to take ownership of my choices and change my behavior (or at least understand these unhealthy inner drivers and how they work).

I specifically remember when I started to get a glimpse of how off-course my workaholic actions were. I was sitting in my office and working on an appellate brief that had to be filed the next day. It was after 2:00 a.m., and I was cranking away on the brief when I decided to take a breather, pushed back from the desk, and had this conversation inside my head:

Damn, I am good. It's 2:00 am, and I'm cranking away on this brief and doing great work even at this hour. Everyone else left hours ago, and I'm sure my opposing counsel is not working. I'm here outworking everyone and doing good work even at this late hour.

In the midst of patting myself on the back, what I had said to myself hit me in a different way, and I focused on the following: *Everyone else was gone and had been for hours, and everyone else had been home with their families that night, including most likely my opposing counsel.* In that moment I started to get it—that I was valuing myself by how hard I worked, not by how well I worked and how much value I added. It made me feel good to work until 2:00 am, but I was missing out on many things, including my family.

I would love to say that from that moment on I was a changed man. I was not, but it was the beginning of many shifts for me. One year later, I began a three-year workshop program that I was drawn to in search of balance and more family time, which ultimately led me to decide to leave the practice of law in search of my true passion and path. However, that moment at 2:00 am working at my office was the start of my awareness around my choices to work rather than be at home or even do something for myself. Up to that point (and this is part of my ongoing journey of growth and healing), my life was mostly driven by what I perceived as an absence of choices, by doing what I thought I *had to* and by the feeling that I had no choice.

Sadly, too many of us live life based upon a long list of *have to's*. These are the things that we mistakenly believe we *have to do* because someone else or society said so. How about you? Do you feel that your life is all about what you "have to do"? It is very easy in our culture to play the role of the victim and claim that you have no choices (or very few choices) in what you do, how you do it, when you do it, etc., especially when it comes to

> Conscious leaders are awake and aware enough to catch themselves using stories and to help others around them to see their own excuses dressed up as stories, even if those stories hold a great deal of truth.

time with your family. But "I have to" thinking and living ignores the power of choices and leaves you at the whim of the world and what other people want from you. I have discovered that most of my perceived lack of choices was false and that my acceptance of the "have to" was more about my inner stories than anything that was happening around me or that I thought was happening to me. When I finally chose to be in control of my life, the key to that path was owning my choices, understanding that nearly everything in my life is about choices (even if they are difficult ones), and tracking down and debunking the inner stories that were driving my behavior, including my belief that I did not have a choice.

Conscious leaders are awake and aware enough to catch themselves using stories and to help others around them to see their own excuses dressed up as stories, even if those stories hold a great deal of truth. As we have already discussed, choices and ownership of choices are at the heart of conscious leadership, and the stories that we choose to either accept or put down will have a dramatic effect on our leadership and our impact.

"I Don't Know"

Another of the most beguiling stories is one that seems to be the most true, which is precisely why it can be so vexing and almost seductive. The best way to introduce this distracting story is through a recent example. I was having lunch with my friend Allan, who was struggling with what direction to take in his professional life. He had been working in the same industry and for the same company for many years, and he had finally found the courage to leave the comfort of what he knew to go in search of his life's next adventure, and perhaps even to connect with his personal passion and purpose. After a lengthy discussion about ideas and options, I asked Allan a simple question that led to the following exchange:

Jeff: What do you really want to do?

Allan: I don't know.

Jeff: Yes you do.

Allan: I really don't know.

Jeff: I think you know.

Allan: Screw you, Jeff! [Said with smirk on his face] I do know, but why am I so certain that I don't know?

Jeff: You already know inside, but you can't admit you know because then it's really difficult not to take action to pursue what you know.

This is the curse and the allure of the "I don't know" story.

I hear many people say that they "don't know." They don't know what to do, they don't know what job they want, they don't know what relationship they want, etc. In reality, I think many people do know, but they don't *want* to know. Once you know (and admit you know), then you have two options: 1. Take action in pursuit of what you know; or 2. Admit that you know and still choose not to take action to pursue what you know. Not surprisingly, for many people, it's easier to claim not to know.

When you admit what you know, you limit yourself to the two options listed above. Obviously, you must take action to achieve that which you desire. Unfortunately, taking action has risks associated with it. You might make mistakes. You might get off-course. You might come up short. You might even fail. While taking action in pursuit of your knowing is the only way to move toward your desired results, taking action has risks.

In apparent contrast, knowing but choosing not to take action *seems* to be the safer route. While choosing not to take action will ensure that you never achieve your desired outcomes or results, this course of inaction has fewer risks—or does it? You think you cannot make mistakes through inaction, but the choice of inaction itself is often the biggest mistake. You think you cannot get off-course by inaction, but inaction by definition keeps you off-course, and most people who are pondering these questions are already off-course. You think you cannot fail by choosing inaction, but the choice of inaction itself ensures that you will fail in the most important aspects of your life. Are you getting the point? Taking action in pursuit of your own knowing and choosing to ignore your knowing and failing to take action are **both** fraught with the same risks, but only action offers you a potential reward.

This dichotomy seems to argue strongly in favor of taking action, and it is true—taking action is the path to choose once you have acknowledged your own knowing. However, the foregoing highlights how seductive not knowing can be. By not knowing, you avoid facing the difficult choice between action and conscious inaction. Not knowing is seemingly the safest route. Not knowing (which is being unconscious) is the only way to stay in your comfort zone, and we love our comfort zones. Remaining unconscious is the best and only way to avoid experiencing your own state of being lost, the only way to avoid the internal disruption that exists when you are aware of a need for change, but you choose to stay as you are and where you are. The truths are real, and they illustrate how comforting and comfortable not knowing can be. This is the reason that "I don't know" can be such a debilitating state of mind and being.

The next time you find or hear yourself saying "I don't know," I hope you will reflect on what you have seen and experienced above. Challenge yourself and your own "I don't know," and also surround yourself with people willing to challenge your "I don't know's" in the same way. Finally, when you find that you are holding on tight to your own "I don't know," flip your perspective by asking yourself this one question: "What IF I *did* know?" This seemingly minor twist of the question has the power to open your eyes, your mind and your spirit to deeper understandings and truths. It can also be the pathway for you to get past your "I don't know" and to discover and unleash that which you already *do know*. I believe that you already know and that the only question is whether you are willing to embrace your knowing and then to take action on that knowing.

What is your big "I don't know?" What is the question you keep asking yourself for which your answer is always "I don't know?" Now is your time to break out of the "I don't know" and step into your conscious knowing. Take a few minutes and write down the top three "I don't know's" in your life:

_____

_____

_____

_____

Next, create a quiet time and space simply to sit with these seemingly unanswered questions. Do not try to figure out the answers, but instead allow the answers to come to you. If you feel stuck, then try out the question above: What if you *did* know? When you have the answers—most of which are probably already there—you will experience a state of knowing and self-empowerment that you have never experienced before. Armed with this knowing, you can then take purposeful action to turn what you know into what you desire. The only thing that might get in your way is addressed below.

That Nasty Four-Letter Word

Here it comes. I waited until this point in the book to address this topic because I know that it might offend some people. This four-letter word (F * * *) is one of the most avoided and taboo words in the English language, especially in the business world, and yet it is critical that we shine a light on it as part of the journey to conscious leadership. No one is talking about it, and no one wants to be the person to bring it to the table for consideration, but conscious leaders know it well, acknowledge it and lean into it so that it does not get in their way, either consciously or unconsciously. You guessed it … the word is

FEAR

This is the one word and experience that does more to block our way in business and in life than any other belief or story.

Yes, there are many other inside stories that we carry around about ourselves, but these stories all underlie and feed into the outcome effect of fear. For example, if you have stories in your head about not being good enough, then it will likely show up in your thoughts and actions as a fear of being alone. With every inside, self-limiting story, there is an associated fear. I am a simple person (life is easier that way), and if I am not doing something that I say is important or I am continuing to do something that I say I need to stop doing, then I immediately take a look at what I am afraid of. It really is that simple. Unless and until I am fully conscious about my choices and the drivers for those choices, fear will be driving the train in my life, including all of my thoughts, actions or non-actions.

There is an old adage about fear that it stands for False Expectations Appearing Real, because of the fact that the things we fear almost never actually happen; however, unlike some other writers, I am *not* going to tell you simply to get over it and just do what you need to do. That may work in the movies and for a small percentage of people, but telling someone that fear is silly or not a big deal has been shown not to be effective. Rather, you must identify your fear, understand your fear and then decide whether you will proceed despite your fear. For this reason, shining a light on your fear drivers and bringing them into your conscious thoughts for processing is one of the keys to becoming a conscious leader, both for you and in leading others toward an action-oriented existence.

My personal approach to fear has been to understand it and its underlying sources inside of me, to determine what I am truly afraid of, to acknowledge my fear and then to make a conscious decision about what is more important—honoring my fear (which I do when I fail to act because of the fear) or honoring myself and my objectives (which I do when I take action despite my fear to make my objectives a reality). Like all things, it is a choice—a choice that I want to make as consciously as possible. I also undertake a process to determine what is truly at risk in moving past my fears (personally or professionally, tangibly or intangibly), as well as to assess what is at risk if I stay where I already am. This is a powerful inquiry because I often find that what I fear (the place I might end up if I take a risk), is the place that I am already living, creating and sustaining. Once I have this realization, I can proceed with more confidence, knowing that even if I end up in the same place I already am, I at least took the shot at getting what I want.

Imagine that you are in a relationship that is not meeting your needs, but you are afraid that if you end the relationship (or even ask for what you want) you will end up alone and without someone in your life. While

> Rather, you must identify your fear, understand your fear and then decide whether you will proceed despite your fear.

being in a relationship may mean that you are not technically alone because there is someone physically in your life, this process of questions will likely help you to see that you are already effectively alone in the current relationship in all the ways that really matter to you. Therefore, what you thought was at risk is not really at risk at all, which makes it much easier to take action to change your current reality. This is a common process that I use with my friends and clients to help them see their risks differently, see more clearly where they already are, and better understand the costs of their own choices to date. The same strategy applies equally to business and personal challenges.

Many years ago, I saw a skit which included a piece on dealing with our fears. There was a person on stage playing the role of another person's fear. It was interesting to experience fear as a separate person or entity, and it has been helpful for me (and for my clients) to visualize and understand that fear is not a part of me. It is actually a message or voice inside my head that is separate from me so that I have the ability to put it aside, and I do not have to live with it or listen to it. Getting back to the skit, the person playing the role opposite his fear was asked where he wanted to place his fear in his life. At first he placed his fear physically in front of him, but then he said that he did not want his fear there because it blocked him from things, kept him from trying things and often got in the way of his desires, decisions and dreams.

Next he placed his fear behind him, but he explained that behind him was not a good position either because from behind him his fear could not protect him. You see, we allow our fear to exist to protect us, and some of those protections are good, valid and helpful. There are some risks that we should at least be aware of for physical safety reasons. He said that if his fear was behind him, he would go off without any filters or limitations, and that would not best serve him.

Finally, he put his fear beside him (he actually put his arm around his fear) so that the fear could whisper in his ear when it had concerns or hesitations. Still, it was not blocking his way or vision, and it was not lost behind him. In this way he could hear the fears and choose whether to honor them by stopping or moving forward despite the fears. I loved this visualization, and I have embraced it in my life. In fact, if you had a video camera in my office or car, you would sometimes see me seemingly talking to myself with my arm wrapped around an invisible person next to me. That is my fear, and I am thanking him for the input, but making a choice to proceed anyway.

Conscious leadership involves acknowledging your fears but making choices and acting on them despite those fears. Embracing your fears does not mean that you do everything or take every chance, but it does mean that you are intentional about your fears and hesitations and that you are purposeful in taking a hard and deep look at those fears and underlying drivers. In *The Tender Bar*, J.R. Moehinger discussed fear in a similar way:

> "You must do everything that frightens you. Everything. I'm not talking about risking your life, but everything else. Think about fear, decide right now how you are going to deal with fear, because fear is going to be the great issue of your life, I promise you. Fear will be the fuel for all your success, and the root cause of all your failures, and the underlying dilemma in every story you tell yourself about yourself. And the only chance you'll have against fear? Follow it. Steer by it. Don't think of fear as the villain. Think of fear as your guide, your pathfinder."

The Tender Bar at Page 133 (Hyperion 2006). Fear is not the issue. Your relationship *with* fear is what matters most.

Whether you use the above method for managing your fears (it certainly works for me) or some other approach, the critical element is to understand that fear itself is a story, a voice in your head that is neither true nor false, right nor wrong. This is why consciousness creates the opportunity for experiencing your fears in an entirely new and different way—a way in which you are back in control of your choices, your actions and your outcomes.

The biggest trouble with fear is that no one is talking about it. When it remains a dirty little secret we cannot change it, and leaders (unconscious ones) are often the least likely to acknowledge it based upon the false belief that acknowledging fear is a weakness. Some leaders not only fail to acknowledge it but claim that they never have any fears! I have a word for those leaders—liars. I have spoken to men and women who have experienced things and situations in their lives that I cannot even imagine, and they have all admitted that they experienced fear. Even combat veterans admit that they have fear, but their training and their commitment to their unit and the mission allows them to proceed *despite the fear*. I am not naively suggesting that you can banish fear from your life, but rather suggesting that you can change your relationship with fear, the way you experience fear and the control that fear has over your life and your outcomes. By modeling this new way of being in regards to fear and thereby debunking the old stories about fear, you will be leading the way for others to find their own way through, past and around their fears. Think about the positive outcomes you can create in your business, your relationships and in your own life as you shift away from your own fear stories and help others create their own shift in the same direction.

Stories Are Tricky

Without knowing it, we often repeat the patterns that we grew up with. Whether conscious or unconscious, we are always modeling something and nearly always communicating some message, intended or unintended. Only when we wake up, become more aware, and consciously choose to change can we change the stories that we are living and passing along to the most important people in our lives. Make no mistake about it—we *can* change ourselves and in turn change the messages that we communicate to everyone around us. It is never too late to change our stories and thus the stories of the people that matter to us the most.

As I have walked my own journey of self-discovery and awakening, I have been continually struck by how naturally I create and embrace stories as a way to keep me from my inner truth. Even when I think that I have made a key self-discovery, touched a deep wound, or peered into my darkest shadows, I often find that the supposed breakthrough is yet another story designed to keep me from my deepest insights and my truest healing. So prevalent are the stories and so adept am I at creating them that I have learned this story-debunking essential: I must question *everything* to determine if it is true (to the best of my human discernment) or if it is yet another story designed to keep me from my truth and my healing.

The thing to remember is that your awakening and healing is about identifying, debunking, and putting down the old message and stories. It is not about blaming, condemning, or

> Ultimately, we must face and "own" our inner stories and chase down the messages that are driving our mostly unconscious choices and thus our largely unconscious and wound-driven life.

judging the potential sources of those messages and stories. Whatever or whomever the source of the messages, they were not original stories, and we may have picked up unintended and unspoken messages without even knowing it. In taking ownership and responsibility for our own lives, the process of identifying and shedding old stories is focused on awareness, understanding that the stories are just stories (they are not necessarily true), and taking steps to put down the stories and messages that no longer serve us.

Ultimately, we must face and "own" our inner stories and chase down the messages that are driving our mostly unconscious choices and thus our largely unconscious and wound-driven life. Today, in adulthood, having friends that support me by challenging me and helping me to debunk my inner stories is a great blessing, and having friends that will challenge you and call you out on *your* old stories is an important part of a relationship circle that helps you live beyond your old messages and stories. It is also incredibly helpful and valuable to surround yourself with people who believe in you and see more in you than you may see in yourself. Conscious leaders surround themselves with people who will play the dual role of motivational supporter and inquisitive challenger. Conscious leaders will also play this vital role for their teams and the other relationships in their lives.

Yet even with this support, I must make the choice for myself to face my inner stories, and I must choose to tell myself the truth about my stories. In some cases, this path is scary—facing our past, the old messages, and the events that created those messages can be frightening. On the other side of these fears and perhaps some pain, though, are the answers and insights that will help us and allow us to step out of the old stories and into our authentic story. As someone who has made these first steps and begun an ever-deepening journey into my essential and authentic self, I can tell you that it is a life and game changer, and it is worth it. More important, YOU are worth it!

CHAPTER 13: SILENCING THE STORIES IN YOUR HEAD (THE DEBUNKING LEADER)

"The stories we tell ourselves about our lives do not define who we truly are."

Debbie Ford

We all have stories—the things that we believe to be true about ourselves, about relationships, about business and about life. We use them to explain and justify what we do (or do not do) in and with our lives. Similarly, these stories (once identified and debunked) will be the *key* to creating change within yourself, in your thinking, in your leadership and for every outcome in your life and business. These internal and often self-limiting stories are the linchpin for change that you create for yourself and ultimately for the change that you can support and encourage in others. This is the vital role of conscious leaders in our world.

As we discussed in the prior chapter, the stories do not always seem logical, but when we find the story drivers for our behavior, then they are very logical in hindsight. In other words, the stories and our story-driven choices do not seem to make much sense and may even seem crazy (i.e. "Why on earth would you do or say that?"). For example, why would people act in a way that would clearly be detrimental to their businesses, their careers, or their personal relationships? Obviously, most rational people would not knowingly do things that would likely end up hurting them in some way, yet unconsciously, rational people regularly do just that–do things, say things or fail to do things that have a direct and negative impact on them and their life. Crazy! Yet when we can understand the underlying or subconscious drivers of this self-harming or self-blocking behavior, it is like connecting the dots in a drawing—everything starts to make perfect sense given the underlying story or view that the person has of himself or herself. This chapter is designed to help you navigate through, around and past the stories that are blocking your way.

Gandhi said that "Men often become what they believe themselves to be. If I believe I cannot do something, it makes me incapable of doing it. But when I believe I can, then I acquire the ability to do it even if I didn't have it in the beginning." Similarly, Henry Ford said that "if you think you can or you think you can't, you're right." Indeed, our self-beliefs are the foundation of who we are, what we become and what we achieve. Furthermore, these self-beliefs can be identified, debunked and changed. That is the power of awareness that conscious leaders can leverage for their own personal transformation.

In 2005, after my failed business and after struggling unsuccessfully to dig out of the financial hole that I had created, I filed for personal bankruptcy. This was perhaps the most personally devastating event in my life, as evidenced by the immense shame that I carried around over it for several years. The shame was so deep that I kept this dirty little secret from virtually every person in my life, including people that were closest to me, people that I was involved with in romantic relationships, and close friends that were struggling with their own personal financial challenges and bankruptcy filings. Even if I could have offered some loving support to another person and friend, I chose to stay silent for many years because of the shame that I carried over this financial and personal failure. Amazingly, I had never felt any shame about poor the life choices leading up to it, yet this financial failure was something I hid from virtually everyone.

Even as I looked back at that time, I could not understand how I had gotten to that disastrous financial situation. Over the years, I had made a great deal of money working for a large law firm and building my own law firm. By any stretch of the imagination in our society, I was a highly compensated professional, yet I had no money to show for it, even before the failure of my coaching business. Where had it all gone? We then lived in a nice house, but not an extravagant house. We took a couple weeks of vacation every year, but nothing expensive or crazy. We did not own lots of "toys" (e.g., boats, motorcycles, expensive hobby items, jet skis, etc.). We did not have a summer home, and there were no addiction issues at play (e.g. gambling, drugs or alcohol). Where did all the money go? What I eventually realized was that in little ways I had let the money I made slip away without even being aware that it was happening.

> It is in the rear-view mirror that you see that what you have created usually fits perfectly with the story and stories that you believe about yourself.

As I began my personal journey of discovery, I realized the truth—that my lack of self-worth (I felt I was not lovable) had subconsciously led me to believe that I did not deserve to have money. As a result, I (and my wife) had made poor choices with our money, and we had spent most of what we made without even realizing that we were doing it. I was asleep and not even aware of how I was allowing the money I made to slip through my fingers, resulting in a state of having little and then no and then even negative money. Crazy? Illogical? Perhaps, but when we connect the dots of my self-belief system of unworthiness with the outcome of bankruptcy, it all becomes crystal clear and makes perfect sense. How much money does someone that is not worthy have? Answer: little or none. Thus, I had subconsciously created a reality that fit who I believed I was, and this designing of a reality did and does make perfect sense. It is in the rear-view mirror that you see that what you have created usually fits perfectly with the story and stories that you believe about yourself.

Getting In Your Own Way

While it may seem crazy to do things that hurt you, limit you or hold you back, there is a logic to it once you understand the underlying drivers (internal beliefs or stories) for the behavior. Here is a simple example. I was working with a client, an employee named Alice, whose anger, inappropriate communication and demeaning sarcasm was holding her back from further advancement. Most coaches would have tried to understand the behaviors in a business sense and offered different tactics to help curb or minimize the behavior. One of those strategies might have been to try to slow down her thinking and reactions so that she could think before she spoke or acted, but these strategies rarely work because in those moments when we have been triggered (for whatever reason), the triggering keeps us from slowing down and thinking unless we are hyper-vigilant and aware, which is a significant and challenging shift.

In addition, trying to motivate Alice to change by focusing on the negative impact it was having on her career was likely to prove unsuccessful. She obviously knew that this type of behavior and communication was hurting or limiting her advancement opportunities, but she continued doing it despite this knowledge. This "crazy" behavior (doing things that you know are bad for you or your career) is rampant in our culture, yet we fail to address it because we do not realize that it is based solely on stories.

After a brief conversation, Alice and I began talking about one specific type of behavior that she regularly engaged in—sarcasm. While Alice believed that some sarcasm was appropriate and acceptable if intended and *received* solely as being clever or more sophisticated humor, she admitted that there were times when she used sarcasm against other employees. Specifically, Alice would use sarcasm that she knew others would not understand or "get" in order to show that she was smarter than other people. When I asked Alice why she wanted to show herself to be smarter, after some soul searching, she shared that this type of sarcastic communication was intended to demonstrate her intelligence as greater than others' so that she would be respected. In Alice's mind, smart people are or should be respected, so her own internal stories told her that demonstrating herself smarter than others would result in her being respected.

Here is a simple formula to show how Alice *thought* (but without consciously thinking) her behavior would serve her:

Sarcasm = Smarter Than; Smarter Than = Respected

While the formula looks good, we all know that it quickly falls apart because the *actual* outcome of this type of communication (especially from the people being targeted with it—i.e. those people that Alice wanted to demonstrate that she was smarter than), was that Alice became **less respected**. Thus, Alice's behavior designed to make her more respected actually (and quite expectedly, though not to her) created the exact opposite outcome.

Why on earth, then, would Alice (who is obviously an intelligent person) engage in behavior that so clearly creates an undesirable outcome—less respect—in addition to significantly limiting her career advancement opportunities and perhaps even threatening her job? The logical and equally obvious answer can be found once we understand one of Alice's internal "stories." What kind of person would seek to be more respected as Alice did? Obviously, the answer is someone who does not feel respected or feels under-appreciated. While our first thought might be that this was Alice's perception based upon what others thought or said about her (that is the default thinking for many of us), the deeper truth is that the perception of lack of respect comes from within. This was how Alice saw *herself* and what she believed about herself. Awareness of this then leads to the next question.

What kind of people believe that they are not respected? Answer: People who do not fully respect themselves OR who do not believe that they are worthy of respect. Think about it: If you have a good self-image and see yourself in the metaphorical mirror as worthy, then it is difficult for other people's perceptions to take hold in your self-belief system.

There are generally two reasons that other people's perceptions of you are accepted by you as true:

1. You believe (even in a small way—enough for them to creep in) that their perceptions of you are true; and/or

2. Those perceptions come to you from people that you respect or who are in positions of apparent trust and authority (e.g. parents, siblings, family members, teachers, clergy, counselors, friends, etc.).

If we did not have some part of their perceptions already in our inner stories and belief systems, other people's perceptions would bounce off of us and never penetrate. Likewise, when perceptions come from people that we trust or who are in positions of authority, we open ourselves up enough for their perceptions to get inside of us. Once inside of us, those perceptions can quickly become our own inner stories and belief systems so that they are no longer the perceptions of others, but rather how we see ourselves and what we believe about ourselves.

This self-reality was the case with Alice, who eventually acknowledged to me that for most of her life she had held a belief about herself that she was different in ways that made her less worthy of respect. As a result, she had unknowingly and unconsciously developed the habit of using sarcasm in an attempt to get the respect that she did not fully embrace for herself. We can now connect the dots to see how Alice's use of sarcasm (a seemingly obvious example of detrimental conduct) is very logical. Because Alice believed that she was not worthy of respect, she engaged (again, unconsciously) in behavior designed to create the reality of not being respected that was consistent with her inner story that she was not worthy of respect.

Here it is in a simple formula:

Unconscious Thought: Sarcasm = Smarter Than; Smarter Than = Respected

---

Actual Outcome: Sarcasm = Less Respected

Inner Story/Belief: Unworthy of Respect

Actual Outcome (Less Respected) = Inner Belief (Not Respectable)

As crazy as this might sound, you have a deep desire to create a reality that fits with how you see the world and how you see yourself. As a result, you often unconsciously create a reality that is in alignment with what you believe about yourself. For Alice, this meant that she engaged in behavior that made her less respected, a perception fully consistent with how she saw herself. Alice's story is an example of what is often called self-sabotage, which almost always is occurring unconsciously.

While this may initially seem complicated, it is actually simple to apply once you understand two things: First, your fundamental nature is to create outcomes that align with your internal and core beliefs about yourself, about business and about life; second, you should always suspect the logical and look for the logical in the crazy. In other words, the things that seem to make obvious sense and that appear logical are often not what they appear to be and typically are masking some other, deeper truth. Likewise, when you see things, situations or behaviors that do not seem to make sense, look for the logic in the crazy. Using the Alice example, it does not seem logical that she would engage in behavior that most reasonable people would *know* would create an outcome inconsistent with her desires. Still, when we look for the logic in the crazy, we discover how Alice's internal beliefs were perfectly aligned with her behavior. Thus we see the logic in the crazy, and when you find the logic in the crazy, you are finally digging deep into the issues, obstacles and opportunities that will make the most difference in your leadership and your life.

Once we identified this self-sabotaging element and understood its source as her "story" of not being worthy of respect, Alice could look to change her behavior to create positive outcomes for her in several ways. First, she needed to become more self-aware of how her communication (sarcasm) was hurting her. Second, she could now take steps to put down her old story of being unworthy of respect and thereby also be able to defend herself against other people's perceptions. Additionally, once she took the foregoing steps, Alice would not have the need to use sarcasm to attempt to secure respect because her more authentic self story would become that she was worthy of respect. Therefore, Alice would not need to seek respect outside of herself, whether from the people that she worked with or anyone else. If you are really *with me*, then you probably also realize the other positive outcome for Alice: Once she faced and put down her old inner story (her old way of being), she could begin to interact with others, including her co-workers, from a place of self-respect. And what does self-respect attract? More respect.

> Thus we see the logic in the crazy, and when you find the logic in the crazy, you are finally digging deep into the issues, obstacles and opportunities that will make the most difference in your leadership and your life.

Self-Sabotage and Leadership

About a year ago, I was introduced to a business leader in Raleigh, North Carolina with many years of business and leadership experience. It was immediately clear that he had extensive business knowledge and wisdom and that he had studied many of the management and leadership philosophies and strategies of our time. Certainly, he was someone from whom I could learn a great deal about business and leadership. Over coffee, I began to share with him some of my personal journey as well as stories of business leaders that I have worked with as a coach or consultant.

During this part of the conversation, I shared several stories with him about people who had been stuck, off-course or lost in their professional career, all because of an inside story. When I shared these stories, he acted surprised and did not fully understand the concept. When I shared with him the concept of self-sabotage, he said that he had never heard of it and was intrigued by how it impacted people's performance in business and personal life. Initially, I was surprised that he had never heard of or been aware of self-sabotage, but then it hit me—there are many people (even seasoned and successful leaders) who are not aware of the ways that our inside stories impact and influence our outside outcomes. This new awareness for me was part of the motivation to write this book—to share with more people the realities of the beliefs and stories that get in our way and to assure you and others that you do not have to be defined by your past or your inside stories and voices. I also want you to know that you are not alone in living with these inside stories.

Conscious leadership is mostly the process of facing these inside stories and setting them aside so that you can live and lead as you were meant to, as well as mentor and guide others on their own personal journeys of clarity and consciousness.

Let us look at another self-sabotage example with even deeper implications. I had the pleasure to connect with a young woman (let's call her Lisa) who was struggling personally and professionally. She had been unemployed for a significant period of time, she was rapidly losing self confidence, she was feeling lost, and she was experiencing very negative emotions (and perhaps even depression). One thing is certain: what I just described is NOT the mental or emotional state to be in when you are seeking a new job. Not surprisingly, these self-defeating emotions and states of mind can become a bitter spiral that takes many people beyond unfortunate circumstances such as losing a job to serious emotional conditions, including depression and loss of hope. This is precisely what had happened to Lisa.

After I spoke to a group where Lisa was in attendance about how critical our emotional state of being is when looking for a job (e.g. how we see ourselves in the morning each day), Lisa approached me with tearful eyes and thanked me for opening her eyes to what was really going on with her. After a brief conversation, Lisa left, but she reached out to me to have a face-to-face conversation a couple of weeks later. Why did she wait a couple of weeks? Lisa questioned whether I would want to spend any time with her because her story had become "Why would someone like Jeff want to spend time with me?" Can you see how deeply Lisa was slipping into negative self-beliefs and stories?

The problem is that most people (and most coaches) would look at Lisa and see her issues mostly as a problem of lacking confidence *because of her loss of a job* and then try to build confidence and prepare Lisa to go get a job. In fact, this is precisely what Lisa thought was the situation and her need. When we got together and I asked her how she thought I could help her, Lisa said "I want to be confident like you." Lisa's desire for confidence seems logical and is probably what many people who are unemployed and looking for a job are thinking about and seeking: confidence.

Likewise, most people and coaches would believe that Lisa's problem (how she sees herself) could and would be fixed once she got a job—thinking that Lisa's lack of confidence was simply the result of her unemployment status and job search difficulties. In reality, as in the cases of so many other people, Lisa's self-perceptions existed long before she lost her job and long before she had struggled to find a new one. Lisa's low self-esteem (and even worse, as you will read below) had been with her for decades and, as do so many people, Lisa had faked it, settled for less, and gotten by for most of her life. When she lost her job, though, all of the faking it quickly fell apart, especially when she was unable to find another job quickly to fill up the inner void with being busy.

I spent several hours with Lisa that evening and poked, prodded (emotionally and mentally) with questions, seeking to find out what was most true for Lisa, especially in terms of how she saw herself. After a considerable amount of time and after Lisa acknowledged that she had been playing it safe her entire life, I finally asked Lisa this question: "What's holding you back from really going for it in your life, your career and your relationships?" Since I believe that fear is typically the thing that holds us back from taking action that we seem to desire, I also asked Lisa what she was afraid might happen if she were to really put her all into her life. Lisa said that she had never totally gone for it in her life because she might get it—she might actually be successful and have the job, relationships and life she always dreamed of having. Her answer, like so many situations involving inner stories and self-beliefs, seemed illogical (almost crazy), but as we saw above, our inner stories and self-beliefs are so powerful that they create thinking, beliefs, behaviors and actions that appear illogical but which are actually quite logical once we connect the dots with the self-limiting stories.

What? You are probably asking why on earth Lisa (or anyone else) would be afraid of getting the life or job of her dreams. Lisa's answer explained it all: "I've never believed that I deserved anything good in my life." She went on to say that since she does not think she is worthy of anything good, if she somehow got the life of her dreams, that would be totally inconsistent with her inside story of being unworthy and undeserving. Lisa had clearly and perfectly described the nature of self-sabotage: We create an outcome that fits with how we see ourselves because creating an outcome or a reality that is *inconsistent* with our inside story creates a conflict. We so deeply believe our self-limiting story that we are often incapable of creating a

> If you are leading a team or organization, be assured that many of your people (including some high performers) are struggling with their own inside stories, even if they are not yet aware of it.

reality that conflicts with that story. When we do somehow create a reality that is better than our self-limiting story, we unconsciously act (or fail to act) in ways that are designed to and typically do accomplish the loss of that incompatible reality. To clarify using this example, if Lisa believes that she is not worthy of a great job, of financial security, of a great relationship, etc., then she will either fail to take actions that would move her closer to these inconsistent realities or, if she achieves them, she will find a way to lose them.

It is this precise scenario, one that is played out in so many ways and in so many people, that keeps us from achieving our goals, objectives, and dreams. The complexity of it—especially when we are living mostly unconsciously, when we are caught up in it because our disempowering stories are masterful at tricking our minds—often makes it difficult for us to identify the real issue. In fact, the underlying issue itself (the self-limiting story) is designed to keep us from seeing what we need to see in order to change our perspective and our reality. If you are leading a team or organization, be assured that many of your people (including some high performers) are struggling with their own inside stories, even if they are not yet aware of it.

The Art of Story Debunking

Three things are often true when it comes to debunking, overcoming and putting down your self-defeating inner stories:

1. You must become more aware and conscious in order to navigate past and through your self-limiting stories;

2. Until you become more conscious and aware, you need an objective, outside perspective to help you see what you cannot see for yourself;

3. You typically have to be prepared to face your self-limiting stories and their sources in order to move past them, put them down and move on.

Make no mistake: the last of these three is often the biggest challenge. With the outsider's perspective of someone with gifts of intuition that is skilled in asking questions to explore the deepest truths, we can become more awake, conscious, and aware. We can also get right to the "edge" of our stories, but this edge may be more like a precipice overlooking darkness, a place where our fear rises up to protect us—or perhaps it is our own self-limiting story that is telling us to turn back.

In some cases, there is a part of us that does not want to know our inner truth or the source of our self-limiting stories. It may touch things that we truly have never been aware of, and we are all afraid of the unknown when it relates to ourselves. It may also touch things that we are aware of, but which are very painful and which we have consciously or unconsciously hidden and buried for years. It may open painful memories that we do not want to re-experience. It may cause us to question who we are or will be once we face and put down the old stories.

While it may seem odd, it is perfectly natural for us to become content (and to feel safe) with who we have become, especially after living that "story" for many years. Thus, the idea of changing into someone that we do not know can be terrifying and create even more blocks to change. It is the combined weight of all of these complexities and obstacles to change that explains why typical self-help concepts, affirmations, and attempts to believe in oneself come up short for so many people that are feeling lost, off-course or stuck. When you are working to evolve from an old way of being to a new way of being, tricks and tips are often insufficient to create the type of inside-out and fundamental shifts that are required to achieve significant and sustainable change—transformational change (whether it is a big "story" or a little "story").

Small Acorns to Big Stories Grow

The funny or strange thing about our inner stories is that they are often self-created, based upon experiences we have rather than explicit messages intended by someone. In fact, many times the messages that we pick up (by the way, if you pick them up, you have the power to put them down) were not directly spoken to us and often not even intended by the person from whom we *picked them up*.

Consider Mary's *story*. Mary's mother was the daughter of two alcoholics, which left Mary's mother to find her own way in life, including mostly having to take care of herself. Mary's mother's parents were not active or involved in her life because their lives were lost in alcohol. Not surprisingly, Mary's mother was determined to break the cycle of alcoholism in her family and to be there as a Mom for her daughter, Mary. To her great credit, Mary's mother was able to break the alcoholism cycle, and she honored her commitment to be there for her daughter (something that she never had as a child). Mary's mother was fully present and actively involved in Mary's life and did things with Mary and for Mary that she had missed out on as a child.

One way that Mary's mother honored her commitment was to do things with Mary, including taking her shopping and making sure that Mary had nice things and nice clothes and always looked nice. Make no mistake about it—Mary's mother was driven by genuine and heartfelt love for her daughter, and she genuinely wanted Mary to have everything that she had not had growing up. The good news is that Mary's mother was completely successful. She made sure that Mary always looked good and was well groomed. She spent time with Mary going shopping and buying Mary pretty clothes, dresses, and outfits, all in the name of a mother's love for her daughter.

Mary *received* this love and attention and felt, knew and trusted her mother's love (at least consciously). When all was said and done, though, Mary also picked up another message, a message that her mother surely never intended to communicate. What was this message that Mary heard? "*If I'm not perfect, I'm not loved.*" What did you say? How did Mary possibly "hear" this message from her mother's acts of love and attention? In fact, little girls (and little boys) often pick up messages that may never have been intended. Sadly, but not surprisingly, children can pick up a negative self-message from a single incident, a single conversation or even (as you will hear below for Barbara) from events that could not possibly logically support the message that the child picks up.

Yes, there are many people who have knowingly and even maliciously inflicted pain, hate or even evil onto children. Physical, mental, sexual, emotional, and psychological abuse are unfortunately a reality in our society. Many trusted people have violated that trust in illegal and immoral ways, causing deep and profound wounds in children. Certainly we would never doubt or question the negative self-image messages that these children of abuse carry with them for all or parts of their lives, stories leading to repeated cycles of the behavior and self-destructive or self-sabotaging ways of being that can last a lifetime. Still, these children have the opportunity to face their wounds, move through the pain, and re-connect with their brilliant and essential selves. The wounds are real, but the healing is just as real.

However, the same is equally true for the millions of people who are living their lives through the lenses of self-defeating or self-limiting stories and messages, the sources of which are less obvious than other more intentional and abusive behaviors. The lesson that I have learned through my journey of personal awareness, growth, and healing is that all wounds are just that—wounds that must be healed. None are better or worse than others. None are easier or more difficult to heal. None are more damaging or less damaging to a life. While the conduct that caused the wounds may have been more obviously destructive, unloving, or even evil, the negative impact of these self-limiting messages and internal stories can be devastating no matter what the cause, the source, or the motives.

For Mary, the outcome was not surprising—her self-belief that she was not lovable unless she was perfect led to significant eating disorders and depression. Without knowing it until she became aware enough to step out of the old story, Mary ended up living her life as a character (a tragic figure, in fact) in her own life "story." In this story, Mary had to strive continually for perfection in order to find the elusive love that she craved, yet it was an impossible journey. Since her confirmed inner story was that she was not lovable and since perfection does not exist, nothing she did was ever good enough to change the story that she was not lovable. Even if she appeared to the world as in healthy shape, Mary needed to be even skinnier to feel worthy of love, yet it was never enough. Mary could never be thin enough, pretty enough, or well-dressed enough. She had an insatiable appetite for personal and physical perfection that could never be satisfied, and likewise her unconscious thirst for love also could not be quenched. As a result, Mary's life was an endless circle of destructive behavior all based upon a story she picked up as a little girl, but Mary was not aware enough for much of her life to take action to debunk her inner story and put down this destructive message.

Lest you think that Mary's belief story only impacted her personally, it probably will not surprise you to find that Mary struggled in business with her need for perfection. Everything had to be perfect, which led to over-thinking, procrastination and the reluctance to take action. Mary was always trying to figure out the best way to do things in order to avoid the potential for a failure or even a small mistake. Even today, Mary must continually check in with herself to assess whether she is being appropriately diligent or instead is listening to her "I must be perfect" story.

Thankfully, Mary eventually woke up, became more aware, and committed to stopping these unhealthy habits in her life and her business. At last, Mary did face herself and her inner stories, and she began to debunk and unwind the story and messages (such as "I'm not lovable") that had been her subconscious drivers for so many years. As many strong women do, Mary (almost through sheer will) was able to shift her behaviors away from the destructive eating habits and depression that had been driving her choices and her life. Mary was able to move past these behaviors and ways of being so that she could live a physically healthy life predominantly free of the unhealthy *habits* that had been so prevalent in her life.

Likewise, many people are able to break old and unhealthy habits and move into a healthier way of being, physically, mentally, or emotionally. However, what so many people miss (and what

> Only then can you achieve true and transformational change in your life by ridding yourself of the story itself so that it does not impact or impede your path in any way.

Mary missed until years later) is that while the behaviors may change, the underlying self-limiting stories or messages often remain and continue to block our life path in innumerable ways unless and until we face our stories head on, unravel them, debunk them and see them for what they are—merely stories *that are not true*. Only then can you achieve true and transformational change in your life by ridding yourself of the story itself so that it does not impact or impede your path in any way.

As Mary became more conscious of her stories and passionately committed to changing her life, she was able to see the many and deep ways that her old stories continued to define her life, and Mary was finally able to move towards a depth of personal healing that allowed her to put down the stories for good. Primarily by being willing to uncover her inner story despite the painful process, Mary was able to see that the story was just a story, that her mother had always loved her, and that Mary herself had always been beautiful and lovable from the inside out.

No Matter How Crazy, Stories Are Just Stories

The funny thing about our inside stories is that while they may at first blush seem crazy (they do not make sense), once we connect the dots from the stories to the person's internal beliefs and behaviors, we see how consistent the beliefs and behaviors are with the stories. In other words, the beliefs and behaviors often line up perfectly with the internal stories, which is not surprising since the stories are typically the direct drivers of those beliefs and behaviors.

Barbara lost her father when he suddenly passed away when she was 18 months old. In Barbara's case, her father's death was unusual—he died in a plane crash. We might suspect that an 18-month-old would not have much awareness of that death, other than vague memories of her father, which is true for Barbara. Later, Barbara's mother remarried, and Barbara was blessed with a great step-dad who she grew up respecting and admiring. While death always creates some level of sadness, it is often less significant for young children because they are too young to remember the parent or their death. They may not even remember the parent at all, let alone their death or the emotions surrounding the death. This was true for Barbara (who had few specific memories), but the impact on her life was profound and negative, all because of a story that was created in Barbara's subconscious mind.

For reasons unknown to Barbara or to anyone else, the death of her father in a plane crash led to Barbara's creating this story: "My father would rather die in a plane crash than be my father." What? How could Barbara possibly manifest that story as a result of an accident (albeit a tragic one)? Nonetheless, this story was so real for Barbara that it led her to a lifetime of on-again, off-again eating disorders because she saw herself as unworthy or not good enough. That is the trouble with our inside stories—they can come out of nowhere and be so seemingly illogical that we ignore them or, even worse, we are not aware of them—and we cannot transcend and put away a story that we are not aware of. Only through conscious awareness can you begin to debunk your stories, put them down, and move past them.

Not only did this created story have a destructive impact in Barbara's personal life, but its remnants continue to show up in her professional life. With this undercurrent of unworthiness, Barbara sometimes hesitates to stand up for herself, to take action without permission, to make decisions or to take risks. Barbara must be vigilant to ignore the old story and the old voices that tell her to play it safe and to pursue acceptance. Your stories are <u>your stories</u>, and they impact <u>you</u>, whether it is in your business, career, relationships or personal life.

Consider, however, that these seemingly illogical stories might actually make perfect sense. Imagine 18-month-old Barbara trying to cope with the death of her father but not having the mental or emotional maturity to understand or comprehend any of what was going on. Because she lacked the tools to understand such a sudden and tragic death, we assume (another reason to beware assumptions) and perhaps even hope that Barbara will have no tangible understanding. In reality, Barbara is seeking (perhaps even unconsciously) a way for everything to make sense. For a young child, it may be difficult or impossible to believe that someone that you love (as well as you can understand love), that loves and cares for you and who is one of your primary care givers would be taken from you. It does not make sense to an 18-month-old little girl, but she has an innate desire to understand, so she creates a story that explains things—it must somehow be her fault because she does not have any other explanation to fill the gap.

This same way of coping also explains why children that are the victims of child abuse often resort to self-blame for the abuse—because they cannot fathom that a revered, respected, and loved family member would hurt them in that way. This common form of unconscious self-protection explains many examples of children blaming themselves for sad, painful, or negative experiences, because this *blaming story* makes more sense than anything else that they can formulate from the unthinkable, unfathomable, or unexpected. Because these blaming stories are created in the subconscious and often develop in young children, they are not aware of the existence of these stories; the children grow into young adulthood and then adulthood living (and believing based upon) the inside stories of their childhood. Barbara and many other men and women live their entire lives never being aware that their self-beliefs, which are often destructive or limiting, are driving the train of their lives.

Are you one of these people who lives according to stories that were created in you when you were a child? Only when you become aware of the stories (and often only when you also become aware of the source or genesis of the story) will you be able to face, debunk, and put down these inside stories that no longer serve you, your business or your life. Over time, Barbara did become aware of her false core story—that she was unworthy because her father would rather die in a plane crash than be her father—and, as a result, she was able to begin the process and the journey toward personal healing. While Barbara may or may not ever fully put down this story, her awareness (as an emotionally mature adult) has allowed her to make great strides towards living her life outside of her inside story. Because our inside stories are often unconscious (or have been "buried" as another act of self-protection), we often need other people to help us see them. We need friends, family, and coaches to question us, challenge us, and help us see that which we cannot see (and which we may have created) in order to find and overcome these blind spots. Conscious leaders surround themselves with people for this important role and also play this important role in the lives of others.

Real People, Real Stories

Every "story tale" that I have shared in this book is real—real people working through real obstacles to their personal or professional success. The good news (actually the tremendous news) is that each of these people was aware and courageous enough to be willing to participate in an awakening experience so that they could begin to understand the sources and impacts of their inside stories. We all have and live stories, and most of us are being negatively impacted by them to a much greater degree than we imagine. In fact, it is likely that our inside stories are the primary reason for everything that is off-course in our businesses, our relationships and our lives. A bold statement? Yes, and it comes from personal experience, thousands of other people's experiences and from paying attention to things in our world that are not working for no apparent reason. The truth is that there are reasons, and most of them are living inside of us.

The following is a very short list of stories that I have heard from people who woke up enough to decide that they were off-course and did not want to stay there:

- Story: In order to be loved, I have to be perfect.
  - Outcome: It's never good enough or finished. I'm constantly having to refine and perfect things so that I never actually start anything.
- Story: I am not as smart as my sister.
  - Outcome: I have a lack of confidence, and I'm always deferring to others to make decisions and tell me what to do.
- Story: I am not important.
  - Outcome: I'm always deferring to others and hesitant to make decisions or mistakes.
- Story: I am stupid (connected to a learning disability).

- Outcome: I can't do anything, and everyone is smarter than me, so who am I to think I can do anything important?
- Story: I have never been good enough.
  - Outcome: I continually fail to do the little things needed to achieve business success, thereby creating the self-fulfilling prophecy of not being good enough.
- Story: I am not lovable.
  - Outcome: I create obstacles to healthy relationships and create the reality of being alone.

My message to you and every person is this: *You are not alone*, and it is time for a bright light to shine on your many stories and the sources of those stories. In this way, you can take back control of your life and your outcomes and begin to live and achieve according to who you truly are rather than who you believed you were based upon some old stories in your head.

Despite the existence of these self-limiting stories inside of me and others, I am always encouraged by the following perspective from Marianne Williamson:

> Our deepest fear is not that we are inadequate. Our deepest fear is that we are powerful beyond measure. It is our light, not our darkness, that most frightens us. We ask ourselves, Who am I to be brilliant, gorgeous, talented, fabulous? Actually, who are you *not* to be? You are a child of God. Your playing small does not serve the world. There is nothing enlightened about shrinking so that other people won't feel insecure around you. We are

My message to you and every person is this: You are not alone, and it is time for a bright light to shine on your many stories and the sources of those stories.

all meant to shine, as children do. We were born to make manifest the glory of God that is within us. It's not just in some of us; it's in everyone. And as we let our own light shine, we unconsciously give other people permission to do the same. As we are liberated from our own fear, our presence automatically liberates others.

Marianne Williamson, in *A Return To Love: Reflections on the Principles of A Course in Miracles*. Indeed, the deepest fear for many of us is that we are "powerful beyond measure."

In preparing for a keynote speech a couple of months ago—on the topic of reclaiming your confidence—I stumbled across this quote:

"The voice in your head that says you can't do this is a liar." *Anonymous*

It is time to silence those lies and to take back your life, all as a conscious leader. I told the audience that day that confidence is not something that you build but something that you reclaim and re-access by peeling away the false stories that you have accumulated and accepted about yourself.

Conscious Leaders Face Their Shadows

If you are already on the road to being a conscious leader, then you may already know about the concept of "shadow." Perhaps you have even read about or studied shadow in some way. For those of you who already understand shadow, I apologize for this basic summary, but we could talk about shadow for hours or for an entire book. For purpose of this discussion, I want only to plant the seed about shadow so that you can begin to keep your own eyes and ears open for your shadow, as well as having others do the same for you.

Carl Jung once described your shadow as "the person you would rather not be." Debbie Ford (who sadly passed away in 2013) wrote several books on personal shadow, and she described shadow as follows:

Imagine there is a part of every human being that has the power to be our teacher, our trainer and our guide, leading us to strength, creativity, brilliance and happiness. Imagine this part of us is just waiting to be seen, to be heard and to be embraced. But it is not patient, and when left unexamined and ignored, *this part of us has the power to sabotage our life, destroying our relationships, killing our spirit and keeping us from fulfilling our dreams.* So what is this mysterious part of us, buried deep inside our consciousness? It is our human shadow. Our shadow, formed long ago, contains all the parts of ourselves that we have tried to hide or deny, the parts we believe are not acceptable to our family, friends and, most importantly, ourselves.

Debbie Ford (emphasis added). Indeed, your shadow is the parts of you that you hide, repress or deny (often subconsciously and without being aware of your behaviors or even the existence of this shadow). And the only way to deal with any shadow is by bringing it into the light.

Another way to describe your shadow is the stories your tell yourself about yourself—not good enough, not lovable, not worthy, not smart enough, not pretty enough, not, not, not. These are the stories that are in charge of your life unless and until you choose to bring them consciously into the light. Imagine your shadow as all the small but compelling voices in your head that whisper self-limiting statements or stories to you such as:

- Don't take a risk, you might fail—and then who will you be?
- Who do you think you are to think that you can achieve that?
- Don't get too full of yourself—you should play small.
- Make sure that you conform and do what everyone else does—otherwise you might be rejected.
- Don't get your hopes up or you'll be disappointed.

The core messages in all of these voices are the same—don't, can't, stop, not you, not now, be careful, who do you think you are, play small and safe, etc. If you have not already "got it," these are just stories and voices. They are not real and they are not true—unless you make them true by choosing to stay put, play small, play it safe, stop, live in fear, conform, be silent and give up.

I saw a bumper sticker that embodied the message we all need to hear in order to get past our voices and inside stories: "Don't believe everything you think." Sounds counter-intuitive, doesn't it? Don't I need to figure this out? The problem is that you cannot figure shadow and inside stories out using logical thought. Your head is where it all started and where those stories and voices have been living for most of your life. Your head is the source of these lies, and you cannot break out of them by going back to their source and the place where they live. Instead, you have to turn on your intuition and get past the simplistic thinking. When you ask yourself deep questions, you often have to go past the first, second and third level of answers, all of which will be answers from your shadow and from the very voices that started it all.

Unconscious people and leaders never ask the tough and scary inside questions—and if they do ask, they stop with the first or second level of answers, so thus ends the inquiry. They now have an "answer" that feels better and feels like a deeper truth, but it is usually still a superficial and story-driven answer. The deceptive nature of stories is another reason that you need people in your life who will help you see more than you can see, ask more than you can ask, and discover more than you can discover alone. Your shadow is a blind spot which you cannot see. When you turn your head to see it, it is not there because it is still in your blind spot. Because blind spots are often hidden and seek to remain hidden, having others to help you see them and bring them around into your line of sight will be immensely valuable to you.

In contrast, conscious leaders (while imperfect) crave the challenging and potentially scary questions. Conscious leaders understand that by facing their shadows on the inside, they can find clarity and alignment in their lives and uncork the true potential of those lives. Conscious leaders know that they have to go past the first several layers of questions and answers to self-discover their inside stories, voices and drivers. They also understand that they must beware of every voice and answer because it might just be that pesky shadow working to keep them stuck where they are. Your shadow does not want you to change and will work on you from the inside to keep you from exploring and finding your way into the light. Conscious leaders love questions, pursue challenges and thrive on shining a light on their shadows, even if it is hard and even if it is scary. In this way, conscious leaders are the consummate warriors—ready to face difficult challenges for their greater good and the greater good of the world.

What Is Your Core Story?

In the beginning of your life, there was a story and that story defined you, your life and your outcomes. For many years, that story served you and served you well. It kept you safe and it protected you in many positive and healthy ways. That story also got in your way and protected you in ways that were not then and still are not healthy. That story defined you and caused you to see yourself as "less than" or as how someone else saw you (or how you *should be*). Conscious leaders do not live in the world of what should be, how things are supposed to be or how they themselves are *supposed* to be. Conscious leaders live and thrive in a world of possibilities and what is meant to be—based upon who you truly are, why you are here and what you are meant to create as part of your personal journey.

If you have not yet discovered your core self-limiting story, then now is the time to begin. If you are already on the conscious journey inside yourself and working to uncover and put down those old stories, then congratulations and full speed ahead. The time is now—*your* time is now. Those old stories and beliefs are no longer serving you, and they are keeping you from stepping into all that you are capable of being and all that you are meant to be. Know that you are not alone with your stories. We all have stories, and there are many who are ready, willing and able to support you as you unwrap and put away your stories. Conscious leadership is the process of rewriting your stories and helping others to rewrite their stories, all for the greater good.

WHAT ARE YOU PREPARED TO DO?

"Wake up! If you knew for certain you had a terminal illness–
if you had little time left to live–you would waste precious little
of it! Well, I'm telling you ...you do have a terminal illness: It's
called birth. You don't have more than a few years left. No one
does! So be happy now, without reason–or you will never be
at all."

Dan Millman

Congratulations—you finished the book. If you are reading this final note, then you are no doubt awake and aware (or at least awakening). You are also hungry—hungry for more of and for yourself; hungry to create more; hungry to have an impact with people and in the world; hungry to lead yourself and others in a profoundly new way. In truth, it is not new–conscious living and leading has been a part of our world for thousands of years, but it has been a small and too silent minority of our world. Our culture and our society have fallen asleep and become content with good enough. We are a culture that celebrates the superficial external world and hides the significant things going on inside each of us.

We are off-course in our businesses, our relationships and our lives. In many ways, we are lost, and the first step for anyone who is lost is to admit to being lost. Only then can you make course and life corrections. If things are good enough, then there is no incentive to change, especially if that change is foreign and frightening. Conscious *livingship* is and will be a war—a battle for your spirit, for your light and for some of you, for your life. Conscious leaders therefore must be courageously vulnerable and willing to peel back their many layers to find the truth.

This is the role of a warrior—a conscious, awake and aware warrior—whose armor consists of vulnerability, authenticity, trust, courage, integrity, accountability, questions and love. This love is love for yourself but also particularly love for others, enough to be willing to ask the difficult questions, to challenge other people at the risk of rejection and to speak your truth even when it is not popular or widely understood.

Last year, my coach challenged me in a profound way. He reminded me of the people that I admire for their courage and commitment to changing things for the better, even in the face of fear, obstacles or even threats. These are iconic leaders who championed authentic changes in the world. An icon of this type of leadership is Nelson Mandela, a man who overcame seemingly insurmountable challenges to change the world in a big way. Nelson Mandela lived and breathed many of the same beliefs explained in this book, and he said: "There is no passion to be found playing small–in settling for a life that is less than the one you are capable of living." I admire men and women such as Nelson Mandela, Mother Teresa, Martin Luther King, Rosa Parks, Mahatma Gandhi, Margaret Mead, Steve Jobs, and Oprah Winfrey. They were mission-driven people who had vision and took risks to create transformational change.

What they all shared was that they cared enough to take the risk of being rejected in order to change things. Remember, Steve Jobs of Apple called these types of people the Crazy Ones. They did not do it all, but they led from the front—authentic, vulnerable, and passionate. My coach challenged me with this question: "What is the rejection rate for people that desire to create transformational change?" When he asked me this question, my body literally contorted, anticipating the next question. I told him that the first number that came to me was at least fifty percent–at least half of the people disagree with or oppose new and different ideas and thinking. He agreed, and all of the people I listed above faced these types of opposition and detractors. Some of them even faced death threats and ultimately assassinations. My "who am I" voice was coming online in a big way, a story as old as the story of Moses.

My coach asked me where I thought my rejection rate was at that time, and here is where my body had its truth response: "Five percent on my best day," I said. My coach's next statement to me is ingrained in my memory forever: "The only question is whether you have the courage to risk the rejection of the majority in order to share your authentic message and be the change you have envisioned for the world." This is MY question, and writing this book is part of my answer.

Yes, I am willing to be authentic and vulnerable. Yes, I am willing to risk rejection in order to share a message about a different way of living, loving and leading. Yes, I am prepared to do whatever it takes to make my dreams a reality and to live the life that I was put here to live—the life and path that God ordained for me. Yes, I am willing to expose myself and my ideas to the world, knowing that many people may not be ready. Shortly before I began writing this book, I had an extraordinary breakfast with a friend of mine, Stacy. We had an authentic and intimate conversation about life, stories, blocks, etc.—many of the topics in this book—and I felt blessed by the conversations. A few days later, I received a handwritten thank-you note from Stacy that touched my heart and inspired my spirit.

> I am in still in awe of our meeting. The more I live, the more I truly understand that nothing happens by chance. Jeff, your coach is right–these are my words, though, not his exactly: "The World is not ready for you. But they better get ready." Thank you for not being afraid to be bold and maintaining a gentle nature. You have no idea of how you impacted my life and the magnitude that your words are carrying for me right now.

Like my coach, Stacy spoke to me in the words of my deepest fear—the world is not ready for me—but she inspired me with these five words:

"But they better get ready." I framed her thank-you note and posted it in a prominent place for me to see as I wrote this book: a loving reminder to keep going even when it is scary or uncertain. Thank you, Stacy!

I have made my decision. I have to reaffirm it every day in my actions, but I have chosen to step into the role of a conscious leader in my life and in the lives of everyone that I work with, know or interact with. I have also already answered the question—"What are you prepared to do?"— with a resounding and actionized *Whatever It Takes*! This is who I am and how I am showing up in my life every day.

You now have a couple of choices to make for yourself and your life.

At the opening of this book, I invoked the metaphor from the movie *The Matrix* about the choice between the red pill and the blue pill. I chose the red pill, and it changed everything. You have the same question to answer—will you take the blue pill and keep living, thinking and doing as you have always done, OR will you take the red pill and choose to wake up, to change how you think and to question everything? Know this— if you choose the red pill, things *will* change for you, in your life and for you as a leader—Guaranteed. You will likely face new and different challenges in your business and in your life—challenges that will continue to sharpen you as a conscious leader, but still challenges. If your results in your business, your relationships and your life are all that you desire, then why are you reading this book? If, however, you are hungry for a change, then you can begin that journey now. Choose the red pill and commit to doing whatever it takes.

So I ask you, *what are you prepared to do*? If you read this book, then you have woken up. Whether you stay awake or go back to sleep is your

> You have the same question to answer—will you take the blue pill and keep living, thinking and doing as you have always done, OR will you take the red pill and choose to wake up, to change how you think and to question everything?

choice. It is decision time. Hold out your left hand and envision a blue pill in it. Hold out your right hand and envision a red pill in it. Close your eyes, listen to your heart and take one of the pills. Whatever your answer, I welcome you to the world of conscious choice and hopefully to your new role as a conscious leader. The world needs more conscious leaders. The world needs you. Your life, your relationships and your business also need a more conscious you. And your ***inside out*** journey of *livingship* continues NOW!

ABOUT THE AUTHOR

Emerson posited that "life is a journey, not a destination," and Jeff Nischwitz has indeed been on a journey, the journey of a lifetime. His most recent book, *Unmask: Let Go of Who You're "Supposed" to Be & Unleash Your True Leader*, is a road map for navigating your own personal journey as a leader in your business, career, relationships and life.

Speaker… Accelerator… Relationship Builder… Master Storyteller… Chief Inquisitor… Story Debunker… Inspirational Model for Change! This is how business leaders and people describe Jeff Nischwitz. Jeff is the Founder and Chief Story Debunker of The Nischwitz Group, a speaking, consulting and coaching company that transforms people and organizations—one story at a time! Jeff helps businesses accelerate revenue, develop effective leaders, nurture high-performing teams, and execute on their objectives.

Recently called the "Wayne Dyer of business," Jeff Nischwitz is a force of nature and is waking up business and association audiences across the country with his messages about conscious leadership, a new way of being (personally and professionally), and his courageous injection of authenticity, vulnerability and intimate relationships into the business world. Big in stature and bigger in heart, Jeff Nischwitz is leading people and organizations on a magical journey of self-awareness and discovery that is transforming organizations, leaders, teams, and people!

As a national keynote speaker and master facilitator, Jeff energizes audiences across the country and challenges people to take charge of their businesses and their lives. You'll laugh, you'll cry, you'll challenge your old ways, and you'll leave with the tools and different thinking you need to transform your business, your relationships, and your life. Jeff energizes and captivates audiences on a wide range of topics including:

conscious leadership, revenue acceleration, accountable high-performing teams, relationship building and business development, overcoming self-limiting beliefs, the power of questions and personal transformation. At the core, Jeff empowers audiences to debunk and overcome the stories that are blocking their way. Jeff's audiences experience disruptive thinking, challenging questions, vulnerable sharing, and inspired perspectives on the impact of stories in their businesses and their lives—an experience that has been called Getting Jeffed!

Jeff received a BS in Business Administration (summa cum laude) from Ohio Northern University (1981) and a JD (summa cum laude) from The Ohio State University (1984). Beginning as a successful lawyer, Jeff first modeled courageous change when he left the corporate law firm where he was a partner to take the leap into entrepreneurship by creating his own law firm. After building and growing that firm into a northeast Ohio success story (on the foundation of a clear why and a different way of a law firm adding value to its clients), Jeff did what few dare to even consider: *he left that which he knew and which was successful to go in search of his true calling.* For Jeff, getting by or merely succeeding without loving what he does was not acceptable.

Jeff is also the author of *Think Again! Innovative Approaches to the Business of Law* (American Bar Association 2007), which offers innovative and practical advice on building an exceptional law firm, including empowering your people, building successful teams, and adding value to pure legal services. Jeff shares his unique perspectives on building a great law business, including secrets of effective selling through existing relationships, how to take advantage of everyday opportunities, and consistent and reliable ways to get (and keep) new clients.

To contact Jeff Nischwitz, visit www.nischwitzgroup.com.

THE NISCHWITZ GROUP

(www.nischwitzgroup.com)

"You bring your life into your business and your business
will only be as good as your life."

Jeff Nischwitz

We are inspired by men and women like Nelson Mandela, Mother Teresa, Martin Luther King, Rosa Parks, Mahatma Gandhi, Margaret Mead, Steve Jobs and Oprah Winfrey. They were mission driven people with vision who took risks to create transformational change. We want to work with the same kinds of clients... visionaries, risk takers and conscious leaders. Are you one of these? In addition to igniting audiences and inspiring change, The Nischwitz Group works with organizations and people across five core areas.

1. **Unleashing Conscious Leaders**

   This is the outcome when people, leaders, and organizations are awake, aware, authentic, accountable and aligned. Beyond business talk and strategic think, connect to this transformational leadership model and a new way of leading and being that will accelerate personal and team effectiveness, engagement and execution.

2. **Unleashing Rainmakers**

   Professional rainmakers have two success essentials: a commitment to investing in relationships and the habits to build relationships and create opportunities. We help your team shift their perspectives, embrace relationship building habits, and identify and debunk the internal "stories" that get in the way. Experience the business acceleration that comes from the magic of relationships.

3. Unleashing Accountable Teams

Imagine if your team consistently made clear commitments. Imagine if your team consistently did what they said they would do. Imagine if your business had a culture of accountability and your team modeled self-accountability. No imagination necessary with our team engagement and acceleration programs, which will help your team go from merely doing to effective and purposeful execution.

4. Unleashing Lives

Are you feeling stuck? Are you ready to question everything? Our clients were, because much of what they thought and did was not working. This is your opportunity to take positive action to change your life, your business and your outcomes. Our transformational coaching programs will help you challenge your old stories and unleash your full potential!

5. Unleashing Audiences

Recently called the "Wayne Dyer of business," Jeff Nischwitz is a force of nature and is waking up audiences across the country with his messages about conscious leadership and his courageous injection of awareness, authenticity and vulnerability into the business world. Big in stature and bigger in heart, Jeff Nischwitz is leading audiences on a magical journey of self awareness and discovery that is transforming organizations, leaders, teams, and people! Jeff energizes and captivates audiences on a wide range of topics including Conscious Leadership … Relationship Building and Business Development … Accountable High Performing Teams … Navigating Change … Overcoming Self-Limiting Beliefs … and Personal Inspiration.

To learn more and unleash your business, team or life, contact us via www.nischwitzgroup.com.

CPSIA information can be obtained at www.ICGtesting.com
Printed in the USA
BVOW11s0220230615

404771BV00014B/13/P